"In *Embodying Integration*, Neff and McMin~~ their subtitle—*A Fresh Look at Christianity in the therapy room*~~~ their conversational writing style is enlivening and consistent with their stated values, yet their perspectives remain richly informed by psychological research, theological reflection, and clinical wisdom. The opening chapter on lament is worth the price of the book and takes us deep into their personal commitments to integrating spirituality, honesty, and compassion. At a time when many of us are weary of overly cognitive or idealistic discussions of 'integration,' this book can help us sense the rhythms of a more relational and fully embodied approach to both clinical practice and our lived theologies and psychologies."

Steven J. Sandage, Danielsen Professor of Psychology of Religion and Theology, Boston University

"I expected a great book from Neff and McMinn, but I didn't expect to be so moved, and challenged, and changed. This book wrestles with the ultimate questions of living, not just for my patients or students but for me. The authors share personal stories and experiences that literally put flesh on a totally new way of integrating faith and psychology. God is doing something new here."

Jennifer Ripley, Hughes Endowed Chair of Christian Thought in Mental Health Practice, Regent University

"*Embodying Integration* is, bar none, the most exciting innovation in integration since the pioneer days, fifty years ago. Instead of creating tightly reasoned relationships between psychology and theology, Megan Anna Neff and Mark R. McMinn have an extended daughter-father conversation. And that conversation transforms integration into a living, embodied, conversational quest for wisdom and connection—between psychotherapists and patients, among professionals, and between ourselves and God. This book will be the new standard textbook for integration courses."

Everett L. Worthington Jr., coauthor of *Forgiveness and Spirituality in Psychotherapy: A Relational Approach*

"Neff and McMinn offer a creative look at teaching the integration of psychology and Christian faith in a postmodern world. They begin with issues in theology and then explore their import for the practice of therapy. This approach will engage younger clinicians who often want to know *why* integration is important before learning *how* to practice it. *Embodying Integration* is both theological and psychotherapeutically sophisticated. It is practically helpful to therapists-in-training as well as the professors who teach them."

Brad D. Strawn, professor and chair of the integration of psychology and theology at Fuller Seminary's graduate program in clinical psychology

"Megan Anna Neff and Mark McMinn have opened up new possibilities for how we talk about integration and live it out in the twenty-first century. Their wonderfully written book has profound implications for psychologists and counselors as they sit with themselves and their patients. It is accessible, honest, wise, and heartfelt. I was drawn in and delighted by this conversation. You will be too."

William B. Whitney, associate professor of psychology, Azusa Pacific University

"The world of the integration of Christianity and psychology is ripe for a shift. Although they have served an important function in their time, classical texts on integration were largely predicated on models that were both theoretical and abstract. Furthermore, these models were assumed to transcend context, being equally applicable to individuals of varying dimensions of identity. Indeed, while our faith identity represents the starting point and central facet of who we are, it does not negate the many other facets that also reflect God's handiwork in creating us as uniquely—us. This is perhaps most evident when I teach integration in other parts of the world. I am realizing more and more that what I have learned about integration is not integration par excellence but rather *Western* psychology and *Western* theology, integrated in a *Western* way. And while this is still helpful, it does not represent all there is to say about integration. A new conversation needs to be started that offers a fresh look on the topic, taking local context seriously. *Embodying Integration*, written out of a posture of humility and life that has been lived, represents such a text, and I am happy to offer it my wholehearted endorsement."

David C. Wang, associate professor of psychology at the Rosemead School of Psychology, Biola University

"In this collaborative effort, Megan Anna Neff and Mark McMinn employ postmodernism as a vehicle through which to challenge some of the defining characteristics of the decades-old 'integration' movement, dually encouraging Christian practitioners to evolve and advocating for new possibilities for Christian clients in psychotherapy. At times prioritizing future above past, dynamic above static, process above content, mystery above certainty, concrete above abstract, being above doing, questioning above answering, journeying above arriving, and accepting above changing, the authors have shifted the conversation to highlight some of the often-overlooked psychological and spiritual needs of Christians in the twenty-first-century therapy room. In doing so, they are attempting to dialogue directly and authentically with our rapidly changing postmodern culture by grappling with the role that Christianity will play in compassionately responding to a suffering world. An important read!"

Joshua J. Knabb, director of the doctor of psychology (PsyD) program and associate professor of psychology, California Baptist University

"As Megan Anna and Mark state, this is a 'novel and somewhat messy approach to integration'—one that I thoroughly enjoyed reading and welcome to my classroom. I have long been a fan of Mark McMinn's writings and use them frequently in my teaching and writing. He taught me the field of integration from afar, for which I am grateful. In this volume, however, they go a step further. I've known for quite some time that we need to have deeper conversations about integration as it emerges in the counseling office. I've felt this from my students and have tried to accommodate. Mark and Megan Anna did not give the formula, but they modeled how it can be done with biblical and theological wisdom, psychological refinement, and academic depth. Thank you for taking us a big step further along in the integration journey."

Fred Gingrich, professor of counseling at Denver Seminary, coauthor of *Skills for Effective Counseling* and *Treating Trauma in Christian Counseling*

Embodying Integration

A Fresh Look at Christianity in the Therapy Room

MEGAN ANNA NEFF

and MARK R. McMINN

Academic

An imprint of InterVarsity Press
Downers Grove, Illinois

InterVarsity Press
P.O. Box 1400, Downers Grove, IL 60515-1426
ivpress.com
email@ivpress.com

InterVarsity Press® is the book-publishing division of InterVarsity Christian Fellowship/USA®, a movement of students and faculty active on campus at hundreds of universities, colleges, and schools of nursing in the United States of America, and a member movement of the International Fellowship of Evangelical Students. For information about local and regional activities, visit intervarsity.org.

Scripture quotations, unless otherwise noted, are from the New Revised Standard Version of the Bible, copyright 1989 by the Division of Christian Education of the National Council of the Churches of Christ in the USA. Used by permission. All rights reserved.

While any stories in this book are true, some names and identifying information may have been changed to protect the privacy of individuals.

Figures 1 and 2 are used courtesy of Luke Neff.

Cover design and image composite: Autumn Short
Interior design: Daniel van Loon
Images: ©David M. Shrader/iStock/Getty Images Plus

ISBN 978-0-8308-2867-8 (print)
ISBN 978-0-8308-3188-3 (digital)

Printed in the United States of America ♾

InterVarsity Press is committed to ecological stewardship and to the conservation of natural resources in all our operations. This book was printed using sustainably sourced paper.

Library of Congress Cataloging-in-Publication Data
A catalog record for this book is available from the Library of Congress.

P	25	24	23	22	21	20	19	18	17	16	15	14	13	12	11	10	9	8	7	6	5	4	3	2
Y	40	39	38	37	36	35	34	33	32	31	30	29	28	27	26	25	24	23	22	21

TO MY DAD

who taught me to hold complex questions

with patience and faithfulness.

Megan Anna

TO MY DAUGHTER

whose vision, resilience,

courage, and kindness inspire me.

Mark

Contents

Gratitudes

TOGETHER AS COAUTHORS WE ARE GRATEFUL for the ways this book emerged through conversations with many others. In the George Fox University Graduate School of Clinical Psychology, we have both found a community of support and encouragement. We are especially grateful to the students who read and interacted with early versions of this manuscript. Their lived experience with the text informed later revisions and their insights were helpful. Our department chair, Mary Peterson, has provided enduring support for each of us and for this project. She has been an unwavering conversation partner as we reimagine integration training for the twenty-first century. Lanaya Wade and Hans Stoltzfus served as discussion leaders and teaching team members in our early efforts to teach integration through conversation.

We are particularly grateful for Lisa McMinn, who read each word of our first draft, and helped make this project better with her insight as a sociologist, writer, and spiritual director. Our editor at IVP Academic, Jon Boyd, caught the vision for this work early in the process and helped us revise and clarify our focus throughout. Others working with the IVP Academic team, including peer reviewers and editors, have also been helpful in guiding us forward.

In addition to these collective gratitudes, each of our integrative journeys has been formed through relationships, conversations, and engagement with others. Given our focus on relationally oriented integration, we turn to a few words of gratitude for those who have been key influencers in our integration journeys.

I, Megan Anna, have been fortunate to have a multitude of mentors who have graced the dis-integrative spaces of my journey that have prepared me to be an integrator. Paul Robinson was an early formative mentor at Wheaton College from whom I caught a vision of Christianity that expanded beyond the limits of my cultural lens. Alvero Nieves and Lisa McMinn taught me to think about identity through a contextual and cultural lens. Daniel Treier ignited my love of theology and supported my voice when I entered his advanced theology courses as the sole female student.

My gratitude also extends to my African "mommy," Stella Kasirye, who embodies Christianity as she works alongside and empowers the church in Malawi toward transformative and holistic mission. Her fierce efforts in empowering women, loving the least of these, and caring for the poor and vulnerable have shaped my understanding of embodied faith. To the African Independent Church in northern Malawi, who graciously opened their community to me and my research on African indigenous churches, I am forever grateful. My experience with this church community transformed my understanding of church and faithful mission.

I experience persistent gratitude for Ellen Charry, Choon-Leong Seow, and John Flett, who shaped my theological thinking while at Princeton Theological Seminary. The mentorship of Mary Peterson, Nancy Thurston, and Winston Seegobin while studying clinical psychology at George Fox University has informed my identity as a teacher, mentor, and psychotherapist. The supervision of Jeri Turgesen and Bill Buhrow has shaped how I embody integration clinically. My thinking around emerging integration has been expanded through influential conversation partners—Brooke Kuhnhausen and Michael J. Vogel.

While I was not fortunate enough to meet Randy Sorenson, discovering his writing felt like finding oxygen. His work deeply changed and inspired me and became my access point to the integration conversation. Without his prophetic, imaginative, and humble voice I likely would not have persisted in my studies, research, and writing around integration. I am also grateful to my patients, who have been some of my most formative teachers.

Embodying integration naturally involves undergoing experiences and seasons of dis-integration. I am particularly grateful for those who have been present in both the seasons of integration and dis-integration, including the Friends of Freud (FoF) analytic reading and consultation group. And given our emphasis on embodied and experiential integration, it seems appropriate that one of the influential mentors along the way has been my personal therapist, who embodies and exemplifies what it means to offer an integrative presence while providing space for both dis-integrative and integrative work.

My deepest gratitude goes to my patient, supportive, and enduring husband, Luke Neff, who allowed me to be pulled into the "writing vortex" on many occasions throughout the course of this project. And my children, Grace and Mark, who help keep me grounded, anchored, and embodied.

I, Mark, have been graced with so many colleagues and students over the years who have helped me think better about integration, both at Wheaton College and George Fox University. It would be a mistake to try to name them because of all I would inadvertently leave off the list. And while I have never had an abundance of friends, those whom I have known as friends hold a special and deep place of gratitude in my heart. You know who you are, and I am grateful for all the ways you have helped me integrate psychology and Christianity in my personal and professional life.

My deepest gratitude belongs to Lisa, my life partner and spouse of forty-one years. We have a small sign, cast in bronze, on our dining room table that reads, "I am still learning." These words, attributed to Michelangelo, characterize who Lisa has always been. First a nurse and an at-home mom, then a sociologist and college professor, then a farmer and a seminary student, and now a spiritual director. She and I built a goat barn and a treehouse this past year, learning as we went, which is the way we try to live.

Introduction

REFLECTIONS ON CONTEMPORARY INTEGRATION

In the spring of 2017 the world felt afire with striking political shifts in the United States and the United Kingdom. Closer to home, our local Quaker church—a place where we both learned the beauty of worship, silence, and how social justice could be married to the fundamentals of Christian belief—was in the process of rupturing into two factions. During this tumultuous time, we began meeting biweekly for coffee and walks to discuss theology, church, and personal life. We don't think it was an accident that amidst the local and global confusion our conversations began to drift toward what anchors us, and how these anchoring points are the same in today's world as they were thirty years ago and how they are changing. As religion and evangelicalism are shifting and turning within a new landscape, what is the integration of psychology and theology going to look like? This book arises from those conversations between daughter and father, and with a hope that others might want to join us as we ponder integration in a changing world. We think it is both possible and timely to take a fresh look at integration, but it will require all of us—authors and readers—to break away from a few well-established traditions and assumptions. We believe the integration movement is at a tipping point, and this book explores the contours of what this might look like.

A Fresh Look at Integration

I (Megan Anna) remember sneaking peeks at inkblots as my father worked on creating scoring software for the Rorschach test. I remember two-way mirrored rooms and the enthusiasm of putting blocks and puzzles together while psychology students practiced their assessment skills. I also remember family prayers, riveting games of Bible trivia, family communion, and sitting restlessly on wooden pews at our evangelical Quaker church. Christianity and psychology were deeply infused and interwoven in the fabric of my childhood.

When I was eight my family moved from Oregon to Wheaton, Illinois, where my dad helped establish the PsyD program at Wheaton College—at the time the fourth clinical psychology doctoral program in the United States to explicitly integrate psychology and Christianity. Dad worked with pastors throughout much of my childhood, and he wrote journal articles and books about integration. At home I received the message that both my faith and mental health deeply mattered. And so when I suffered from depression in high school it was only natural that I would go to a therapist, and because Christianity formed a significant part of my identity, it was only natural to go to a therapist who was comfortable and competent to address my spiritual concerns. It didn't occur to me that some may perceive these two fields to be at odds.

Recognizing I have a unique vantage point, I also believe my experience marks a significant cultural shift. The integration movement of the last fifty years has been so successful in creating the landscape and frame for integration that many of us are now growing up taking the integration of Christianity and psychology for granted. Similarly, since the "relational turn" in philosophy and the social sciences, we've seen an increase in interdisciplinary dialog over the last twenty years (Shults, 2003; Sandage & Brown, 2018). While there are still subcultures that struggle with integration (from both scientific and Christian camps), the growing trend is toward increased awareness that psychology can be beneficial to the church and that spirituality has something to say about well-being.

From Abstraction to Praxis

Another important cultural shift is a move toward a more contextual frame of reference. My generation and the generation following grew up in a world influenced by postmodernity, resulting in a tendency to have increased comfort with holding multiple perspectives, and viewing knowledge through a contextual and relational frame.[1] This cultural shift combined with the work of the integration movement has led to an increased comfort with the intersection of religion and psychology. At the same time, the postmodern world is opening up more complex spaces. Nationally, the church is in the middle of a massive split over biblical interpretation, sexuality, and how faith is to be translated in our political choices and values. Increasingly people are looking for spiritual connection and meaning outside of institutionalized religion (Gallup, 2018; Pew Research Center, 2011).

This shift to a more contextual frame of reference is also opening up new conversations. We're now talking more about social and cultural location and multiple identities (e.g., how gender, race, culture, socioeconomic class, and religion intersect). Challenges, issues, and experiences that perhaps were not given the same attention in modernity are increasingly being given language in culture and being addressed in the therapy office. Individuals are exploring religion and spirituality and how these intersect with other aspects of their identity. It turns out these conversations are messy, complicated, and nuanced. Engaging in these emerging, contextually informed conversations is complex work.

As I sat with clients hosting these messy conversations, I had many questions about integration: What does integration look like when sitting with a trans adolescent who is struggling in their relationship with their religious parents and who is uncertain of their own beliefs about God and how they relate to God? What does integration look like while sitting with a mom whose daughter has suddenly died in an accident as she wonders if this was God's divine plan or truly an accident? What might I say (and what might I believe) about God and God's ability to act in the world? What does integration look like with my Wiccan patient[2] whose spiritual experience provides her hope, meaning, and grounding in a life otherwise marked with trauma

---

[1] The modern era is the historical-cultural period influenced by the seventeenth-century Renaissance and the eighteenth-century Enlightenment or "Age of Reason." Shifts in philosophy, the social sciences, and technology toward a more industrialized, rational, and linear approach to the world contributed to the emergence of "modernity" three to four hundred years ago. While many would say we are living in post-postmodern times, for sake of ease we will simplify and use the term *postmodern* throughout the book to encompass both postmodernity and post-postmodernity.
[2] Throughout the book we are using the word *patient* ("one who suffers") rather than the word *client* ("one who pays").

and chaos? And what do I make of the countertransference that these questions are kicking up for me?

These questions stirred a sense of urgency, urgency which I brought with me to my first integration class. Sadly, as I sat through the first, second, and third lecture, I was uncertain if there was space for my complex questions. It wasn't for lack of content—we were provided with a thorough and comprehensive overview of the integration movement, and we learned about models of integration and the philosophical justification for the integration of psychology and religion. Many of the traditional integration models and theories were built in the height of modernity, and therefore focused on abstracted theoretical models.

As my classmates and I pondered what we were learning, one question kept swirling around in our conversations: "Yes, but what does this look like in the therapy room?" While we were learning important content, it didn't speak to the complexity we were witnessing or the "boots on the ground" questions we had about the practical nature of the clinical work we were learning to do. The class was successfully teaching us integration (theories and models), but it wasn't training us to *be integrators.*

Hidden in this anecdote is the primary purpose of this book. In the classroom, my classmates and I were learning the *content* of integration, and then we were having *conversations* outside the classroom—conversations that reflected our deep *curiosity* about how integration actually fits into our lives. But what if all these could come together in the same place? What if integration content could somehow be embodied with our curiosity and the conversations we longed to have with one another? We are convinced this is not only possible but essential in twenty-first-century integration training. This requires a paradigm shift that moves us from teaching integration toward training integrators.[3]

Integration as Conversation

In the academy we most often teach content, and so it is natural to teach integration as content in our Christian institutions. In these courses, a professor

---

[3]In the fall of 2018, we did a nationwide program evaluation of integration training at explicitly Christian APA-accredited programs where similar themes emerged. Students reported a desire for increased applied, contextual, dialogical, relational, and embodied learning of integration.

typically outlines and articulates what has happened, and is happening, in the integration of psychology and Christianity. We are not criticizing this model; it has served the field well over many years. Integration scholarship over the last fifty years has provided critical and necessary groundwork, and has influenced the profession of psychology in meaningful ways. Religion and spirituality are now seen as important diversity markers in many clinical training programs; the American Psychological Association (APA) has a division (Division 36), two journals, and many books devoted to religion and spirituality; and increasingly therapists are creating space for religion and spirituality to enter the therapy room. Still, as I talked with my classmates I noticed two things. First, there was an assumed comfort with integration between psychology and religion. Second, the context in which integration is happening is becoming increasingly complex.

As the two of us continued to have conversations about the changing landscape of integration, we wondered what it might look like to bring the hallway conversations that happen after class into the classroom itself. What if these curious conversations among students in a graduate program could help prepare them for the tens of thousands of conversations they will have with patients over the course of their careers? What if integration was more a verb than a noun? Imagining these possibilities calls us to locate and embody integration in the person of the psychotherapist more than in the pages of a textbook or journal article. We began referring to this approach as "integration as conversation." By this we mean much more than a method of learning integration in the classroom. Conversation is also the product of integration—conversations with one another as we consider how to live well in a complex world, conversations between old ways of thinking and new ones, conversations between religion and science, and conversations we host in the therapy office. As we bring our messy, embodied lives into conversation with one another, we engage in integration.

We had the rare opportunity of using this book in teaching an integration class prior to its publication. This also allowed us to listen to students and make final revisions before sending it off to the publisher. Over the first few weeks, students struggled a bit to understand the metaphor of "integration as conversation." That changed the day I (Mark) did a simple math problem on the whiteboard.

Let's assume you become a full-time psychologist and see twenty-five patients a week, fifty weeks a year, over a career of thirty years. This means that you will have 37,500 professional clinical conversations over the course of a career. Many of these will be deeply meaningful to your patients, and to you, and some will be life changing. When we talk about integration as conversation, this is not just a metaphor or a teaching method for this class, but it is actually the way you will be integrators through your entire career. You will have conversations, and they will probe the depths of what it means to be human, what it means to be made by and loved by God, how to handle suffering and spiritual struggle, and how to experience and enjoy the good gifts life offers. You will be present to other human beings in the midst of their deepest questions about life and death, and you will likely do it over thirty-five thousand times in your career. Conversation is not just a teaching method, it is the product of being an integrator.

At the end of each class we had students write something they took away from the class. After my math problem, one student wrote: "Today I feel I finally understood what integration as conversation really means."

I sometimes imagine what is no doubt an idealized image of European graduate education. In this grand vision I see a professor or two and a handful of students sitting around an English pub discussing the nuances of their academic studies. In reality, this vision has some problems. It is culturally narrow because most of the world doesn't sit around having conversations in English pubs, and at least where I teach in the United States, neither faculty nor students have (or take) the time for this sort of conversation very often. Still, even with the profound limits of my particular vision, when it comes to integration the time seems right for more conversation. We hope reading this book is worthwhile and helpful, but imagine that the key to effective integration lies not in the specific content of this book but in how our words encourage you to sink further into conversation with yourself and others.

If Megan Anna is correct, and I believe she is, many students don't need apologetics any more when it comes to integrating psychology and Christianity. They don't want models and views that tend to simplify complexity into categories. They are looking for conversation that helps them dive into the complexity, to ponder the nuances and messiness of integration.

Asking Hard Questions

It would be nice if conversation were always lighthearted fun, perhaps while eating chips in the English pub, but it's important to remember that a conversational approach to integration brings us face-to-face with some of life's most difficult topics and questions. As simple formulations fall away, we are left staring at a new sort of complexity that can be disarming at first, but ultimately allows for hope and meaning to be formed amidst the greatest challenges we face in our uncertain times.

I (Megan Anna) know a thing or two about facing uncertainty. As I wrapped up my studies at Wheaton College and set off for Princeton Theological Seminary (PTS), I learned how encountering different theological views and new ways of looking at Scripture can induce anxiety. I also learned it can bring freedom and hope. Studying at PTS opened my eyes to the wide breadth of theologies coexisting with evangelicalism within the umbrella of orthodoxy. Since childhood I struggled with certain aspects of the traditional evangelical narrative and at times felt like I was trying to fit square pegs into circles. I lean toward an all-or-nothing thinking style, and so for me, running into pieces of the narrative that didn't fit felt like it might cause my entire faith paradigm to crumble. Studying theology widened my view of various ways of looking at theological concepts within orthodoxy. I learned from encountering a diversity of thought—both a vertical diversity of theology (how theology has shifted throughout the last three thousand years) and a horizontal diversity (how theology manifests across different cultures and within different branches of Christianity). Being exposed to alternative views of atonement, sanctification, suffering, and sin deepened my faith, allowing breathing room for questions and complexity. By creating space for uncertainty and questions my faith became sturdier; it became stronger, less threatened by new information and facts.

My time in seminary helped and challenged me in all sorts of ways, but perhaps the most enduring impact has been a Christian spirituality that fits well in a postmodern context. That may sound uncomfortable to some because it means engaging hard questions that challenge beliefs and assumptions about the world and how we live in it. But if a theological system is facing troubles in a cultural milieu, it seems we have two options. One is to forcefully move forward, insisting that the rest of the world has it wrong and our theology is correct. The other is to consider our finitude and cultural blinders, and the possibility that older theologies—or newer ones—may nudge us toward greater insight and wisdom regarding God, ourselves, one another, and the world in which we live. Maybe asking hard questions is exactly what we ought to be doing. If we can't ask hard questions, and start fumbling for some answers, then I wonder what the future holds for the integration movement that my father's generation worked so hard to establish.

Even as we extol the virtues of a conversational approach to integration, we should also acknowledge that conversation has its limits. An impressively thorough approach to integration would be to write a lengthy text that explores and explains in detail the complex relationship of various theologies and psychologies. Some have done this remarkably well. Reading a text like Eric Johnson's *Foundations for Soul Care* (2007) or *God and Soul Care* (2017) is like sitting at the feet of a master teacher who understands and explains well the nuances of Christianity and psychology. Our book does not replace the need for comprehensive integrative works such as these. But the conversational approach we take in this book is different, and at times will feel both frustrating and enlivening.

Conversation can be frustrating because it is never comprehensive. Even those lengthy conversations that last well into the night leave a person pondering, *What about this?* or *We haven't even talked about that other thing.* Conversation is limited in scope and depth. You will not finish this book and have the sense that we have covered any topic thoroughly. While we can never cover a topic fully in conversation, we can hope that it is enlivening enough that new conversations spiral off of earlier ones and that people are informed and transformed as a result. Our hope is that you will finish this book and want to talk more about it—with your faculty and students, colleagues and peers, friends and family members, and with us whenever we run into each other at professional conferences and meetings. Good conversations inspire curiosity, and curiosity inspires good conversations. We invite you into this upward spiral of curious conversation, knowing that none of us will fully answer the biggest questions of life by being together, but at least we will be together, listening to and learning from one another.

Conversation is storied and is more about exploring the margins than plumbing the depths. In conversation we consider our own experiences, listen to others' experiences, try on new ideas, and imagine possibilities. "What if this is the way it works?" "Have you ever considered this idea?" Exploring these questions requires a kind of humble vulnerability that can feel disarming but also brings new hope and meaning to topics that may have started to feel stale or even untenable.

Conversation is contextual. Each of us brings a story to the task of integration and those stories influence our ways of understanding God, ourselves, the world around us, and the work we do in counseling and psychotherapy. As authors, we also bring stories to this task, and at times throughout the book you will hear parts of our stories. In the spirit of conversation, it is our hope to give readers access to our personal, spiritual, intellectual, and relational journey as we navigate integration conversations.

Probing Beyond Evangelicalism

As Megan Anna has already suggested, I (Mark) have been deeply influenced by and committed to the integration of psychology and Christianity throughout my career. The epicenter of the integration movement has occurred in Christian doctoral programs in clinical psychology, and I have had the privilege of teaching at two of these institutions.

I remember my early years teaching at Wheaton College as being remarkable in various ways, one of which was the simple joy I experienced in walking through the Billy Graham Center each day as I entered the psychology department offices. Back then, when it seemed that Billy Graham represented the very center of evangelicalism, my identity as a Christian seemed remarkably easy. The focus of faith could be clearly on Jesus, and just as Graham met in the Oval Office with presidents of all varieties and faiths, it seemed clear that people of various political persuasions could and did identify as evangelical.

Things changed. Perhaps I changed, or perhaps evangelicalism did, or maybe it's both. But for whatever reason the evangelical identity seems more closely tied with a particular political ideology these days, and this connection seems unfortunate for both Republicans and Democrats because we all tend to lose our primary focus on Word-centered living ("Word" meaning both Jesus, as in John 1, and the grand narrative of Scripture). We easily resort to labels, such as conservative and liberal—which mostly mean we just don't understand one another well—and we're inclined to create God in our own image. Today's evangelicals have become identified with contemporary debates about climate or guns or taxation or rights to life and women's rights to choose. While these are all central questions, they are also distracting us from the center of the evangelical message that characterized Billy Graham's ministry and brought joy to my strolls through the Wheaton College campus back in the 1990s.

Near the end of the last century, Richard Foster (1998) published *Streams of Living Water*—a book I have frequently referred to as the most important book I have read in my adult life. Foster does a nice job identifying and describing the evangelical tradition, but then also presents other Christian "streams" of thought, including the contemplative tradition, the holiness tradition, the charismatic tradition, the social justice tradition, and the incarnational tradition. These six streams demonstrate a breadth of Christian traditions and of God's presence with humanity. I suppose we could quibble as to whether there are six streams, or eight, or twelve, or fifty, but that would miss the point. Foster points us toward the possibility of multiple ways of knowing and experiencing Christian faith, and this changed everything for me.

If the Christian faith is not limited to evangelical approaches, what if the integration of Christianity and psychology could also benefit from conversations that probe outside the edges of the evangelical tradition? By embracing more complexity and nuance in our faith, might we find a sort of integration that works in the complex postmodern world that Megan Anna and her peers were discussing in the hallways after that first doctoral integration class? Might there be fresh (and old) theological views that if incorporated into integration conversations might have profound implications for the work that psychologists and counselors do every day?

Considering Local Contexts More than Global Taxonomies

In the early years of integration, we were quite enamored with grand theoretical models that attempted to explore major portions of theology in relation to sizable chunks of psychology. We were incredibly ambitious to attempt this, but still successful to some extent. One of the most useful products of this sort of integration was offered by Carter and Narramore (1979) in a book that still is used in integration courses around the world. A more recent example is the *Five Views* book edited by Johnson (2010). Until very recently this has remained my preferred way to teach an introductory integration course. Students find it helpful to consider the various ways people can approach the two disciplines, ranging from biblical counselors who view most of psychology suspiciously to integrationists who want to look boldly at both psychology and theology and see how each might help inform and transform the other.

Over the years I have noticed that I spend less and less time on model building as I teach integration. Taxonomies that help make sense of these two immense fields were incredibly helpful to me when I was a young scholar and clinician, but today's young professional doesn't seem to be as helped by models as I once was. This likely reflects changes in how we go about learning and practicing what we learn.

Our world is changing, and with that our relationship to knowledge is shifting as we move more fully into a postmodern, context-as-frame reference point. I (Megan Anna) learned just how rapidly this shift is occurring through a recent teaching experience. Introducing the class to feminist therapy, I wanted to highlight the epistemological backdrop (i.e., feminist theory starts with an experiential approach to knowledge rather than beginning with abstract, universal, and theoretical knowledge). To illustrate what a drastically different approach this is, I asked the students at the beginning of the class: "How do you know? How do you come to knowledge?" I suspected that at an evangelical institution we would have about a 50/50 mix of top-down (starting with an explicit general concept and applying it downward to specific situations) and bottom-up (starting with concrete experiences and applying upward). I was shocked to find more of a 10/90 split. Most students talked about how we come to knowledge through experience: ours and others. A few talked about absolute truth, but by and large the students started with their context and experience. This anecdote illustrates a major shift away from approaches that have traditionally been conceptualized as "left brain" (linear, rational, objective thought) processes toward more "right brain" (experiential, contextual, relational, embodied, intuitive) processes (Schore, 2014). We are trading in binary constructs for continua, and abstract models and systems for contextual thinking. For education to be transformational it will need to meet the new learner in this contextual-experiential frame of reference.

One unfortunate characterization that can arise from this conversation around shifting knowledge is the idea that, "Millennials don't care about ideas;

they just want process and experience." I lament such characterizations. It's not that we don't like ideas; we just want them to be anchored in context. We are an urgent generation, coming of age in the aftermath of 9/11. With the rise of digital communication we are bombarded with global tragedy. So perhaps we have less patience for abstract ideas for the sake of ideas. We want them to be meaningful, to make sense for the context in which we live. When we see why an idea matters we engage, and we engage deeply—with passion, creativity, and vigor.

Ideas become more meaningful as they are anchored in context (Knowles, Holton, & Swanson, 2012; Blair, 1997). At the same time, it's important that in this shift of epistemology we don't lose the ideas and theoretical frames that help anchor us. I like the phrase *anchored ideas*, which involves exploring a construct (e.g., a theological assertion, such as being made in the image of God) while considering how it fits within one's context (e.g., what the implications are for my understanding of how God sees me, for how I relate to God, for how I relate to others, my clients, and myself).

Even as we are probing outside the boundaries of evangelicalism in this book, it seems important to note that leading evangelical scholars are also looking toward anchored ideas. For example, Vanhoozer and Treier (2015) put forward a model for evangelical theology that moves away from defining evangelical theology through static boundaries (clearly defined doctrinal limits) and toward a dynamic center grounded in the triune being of God. An evangelical theology that moves toward an anchored center engages big questions with curiosity and complexity, as we are attempting to do in this book.

Each chapter of this book takes a fairly deep dive into theological constructs, but we attempt to anchor these ideas within the context of lived experience. For this reason, you will find questions for conversations throughout each chapter, so that these ideas can be tied closely with the real lives of our readers and those they serve as counselors and psychotherapists.

Integration Conversation Starters

1. As you ponder your own age and cultural context, what assumptions and values might influence how you understand the integration of psychology and Christianity?

2. In regard to the integration conversations that will emerge from this book, what might you hope to learn from others of differing ages and cultural backgrounds?

Moving Toward Authentic, Hospitable, Generous Conversation

We are not arguing for free-flowing, aimless conversation in the classroom, but rather for conversation that is anchored in theological and psychological content and lived experience. You will see throughout the chapters in this book that we take on big theological questions. But rather than cinching down specific answers, we prefer to explore the content and then learn ways to be generous and hospitable in talking with others who may have diverse experiences and views. The task in the classroom begins to look like the task in the counseling office as we learn to listen well, respond in kindness, notice countertransference, and consider ways that multiple perspectives may help us all.

Prior to his untimely death, Christian psychologist Randall Sorenson famously noted that integration is "caught" more than "taught." After a series of studies using a complex methodology called "multidimensional scaling," Sorenson, Derflinger, Bufford, and McMinn (2004) concluded that students want "real access" (p. 364) to those teaching them integration. This is not just an academic exercise about teaching a series of propositional assertions regarding faith and science.

> Instead, students want access to someone who is modeling integration before them as a living, breathing, flesh-and-blood manifestation of integration-in-process. Students want broad and candid access to integrators so they can see how their mentors think, weigh choices, make clinical judgments, pursue courses of research, and, most importantly, how they interact with themselves and others, including God. (Sorenson et al., 2004, p. 364)

Sorenson's words, offered well over a decade prior to this book, prophetically named what I (Megan Anna) and my cohort were longing for in contemporary integration training. We were looking for real conversation with peers and professors who were willing to wade into the messiness of this topic.

Because we are promoting conversation as both a method for teaching integration and the actual product of integration, it seems important to ponder what we mean by "conversation," even as we acknowledge that true conversation is difficult in our day and age. As a nation we are currently more ideologically polarized than ever (Pew Research Center, 2014). Intensifying the polarization, we exist in filtered realities, from "red" and "blue" social media feeds to Google searches curated to our preferences, all eager to confirm our biases. After retiring from late-night television, David Letterman (2018) began having conversations on *My Guest Needs No Introduction* with people who, well, needed no introduction, such as former US president Barack Obama. During their conversation Obama referenced a small science experiment done during the Egypt uprising where a liberal, a conservative, and a moderate were instructed to google "Egypt." Depending on their political leanings very different results popped up. For those more liberal, stories of the uprising surfaced. For those more conservative, information about radical Islam and terrorism was shown. The moderates received information about travel destinations. While slightly humorous in the Letterman interview, this is also incredibly frightening. How do we bring our lives into conversation with one another when we live in such different contexts? Dare we even say we live in different realities?[4]

At the same time that we are digitally living divided, our churches also divide (Emerson & Smith, 2001). At the surface there is typically an issue at stake—usually one that has sociopolitical implications—but these issues tend to also have important theological roots (epistemology, hermeneutics, authority, and so on). With so much division, how do we learn to bring our lives into contact with one another in meaningful ways? How might we be in relationship with one another in ways that make us all better?

We are drawn to the work of Krista Tippett, particularly in her passion for bringing people's lives together in meaningful ways through the use of conversations. Tippett, a seminary-trained and renowned journalist, has spent her life bringing people into conversation. In her podcast, *On Being*, she brings contemporary voices into conversation. Following a recent heated political event that once again revealed incredible polarization in public response, Tippett tweeted:

> Heartsick at the "right" & the "left." Politics has become the thinnest of veneers over human brokenness. The vast majority of us don't want to live this way. It is left to each of us, where we live, to start having the conversations we want to be hearing & grow this culture up. (2018a)

This tweet sparked a heated discussion around the nature of true conversation when dealing with difficult concerns. For Tippett, conversation becomes a medium for us to discover how to occupy space with one another

---

[4]As an experiment you can go to http://graphics.wsj.com/blue-feed-red-feed/ where you can look at "liberal" and "conservative" Facebook feeds side by side on a given issue.

differently. It's much more than words; by bringing ourselves into conversation we are learning to live together differently. And this is the start of social change.

> It is not just about words passing between mouths and ears. It's about shared life. . . . Listening is about bringing our lives into conversation.
>
> That's what I mean when I say conversation. I mean something much bigger than talk. We also can all think to the most important conversations we've had in our lives, the hardest, the ones that were turning points—they have a lot of silence in them; they have trust in them, which often has had to be earned before that conversation was possible. When I'm talking about creating a better conversation, I'm thinking about the entire complex of what goes into that. (Tippett, 2018b)

Conversation starts with building the trust and safety—a container which can hold the conversation. In order to cultivate transformative conversations, first there is work to be done to create spaces characterized by trust, courage, and authenticity.

> Right now we have work to do to create the spaces and the trust to even have the kinds of conversations I'm talking about. The work is bigger. A conversation begins before any words are spoken. The tone is set. What is possible is framed. So that's what I think of, also, when I think of conversation. I think of the fact that conversation done well strengthens relationship, and we certainly need relationship. (Tippett, 2018b)

Forming Wisdom More than Resolving Issues

Our culture is drawn to issue-based conversations, which involve debating issues with competing certainties in the hopes of finding a resolution or perhaps even a "winner." The hope of issue-based conversations is to find common ground so we can move on with our lives. An alternative perspective is to have conversations that get beneath the issues, what we might call "wisdom conversations." This is to have searching conversations where we come to understand one another more deeply and then move on with our lives all the wiser. These conversations are not about who is right or wrong or about getting to a tolerable compromise. Rather, these conversations seek understanding of what it means to live in human community with those who hold varying ideas. As Tippett reflects, "There is value in learning to speak together honestly and relate to each other with dignity, without rushing to common ground that would leave all the hard questions hanging" (Tippett, 2016, p. 31).

Wisdom conversations unapologetically bring our specific experiences into conversation. We are storied people, so when we converse at an experiential level we're getting underneath the issues to explore the impact on the human person and the implications the issues have for humanity. A second characteristic of wisdom conversations is that they tend to contain genuine, searching questions. Good conversations involve good questions (Tippett, 2018b).

Conversations form and strengthen relationships while providing the opportunity for growth and transformation. Our hope for this book is to help promote wisdom conversations where we generate a spirit of curiosity and provide space to ask searching questions. Whether reading this in the context of a classroom, as a professional in the field, or as an interested lay reader, our hope is that you will join us in these conversations.

Looking at problems from disparate perspectives is hardwired into the work of psychologists and counselors. When working with a woman whose son is in the cold grip of addiction, and whose interpretation of Jesus' statement to forgive seventy-seven times (Mt 18:22) manifests as behavior that psychologists would label "enabling," what is our role in this? When a patient presents Scripture and the meaning they have attached to it is clearly wrong given the cultural context of the text and of today, is it ever appropriate in therapy to correct a person's hermeneutics? These are the sorts of questions Christian counselors and psychologists grapple with every day, and in the process, we learn to look at situations through multiple perspectives. Perhaps it is not surprising that scientists who study wisdom have found that psychologists tend to score higher than others on various measures of wisdom (Baltes, Staudinger, Maercker, & Smith, 1995).

Within the Hebrew Scriptures there are two kinds of wisdom.[5] Proverbs and Psalms are known as *conventional wisdom*. Such wisdom draws on traditional

---

[5]We will use the term "Hebrew Scriptures" to refer to the Old Testament.

views of the day, tends to be straightforward, and makes common sense. There are also some predominant themes, such as if you're a good person, goodness will come to you.

We might consider conventional wisdom a primer on how to find and live the good life, and as such it has been an enormous resource to people over many centuries. But sometimes the general principles of living the good life seem to falter in the vicissitudes and unpredictability of life. Cancer diagnoses, losses, and broken relationships enter our worlds, turning everything upside down. Thankfully, the Hebrew Scriptures address this also. Books such as Job and Ecclesiastes offer insight into a second form of wisdom called *critical wisdom*. Critical wisdom walks alongside us, engaging nuanced and complex thoughts and questions when life doesn't make sense. In the messy context of therapy, in an increasingly complex world, we need both conventional and critical wisdom. The approach we take in this book is primarily focused on developing critical wisdom, which increases as we learn to look at a thing from multiple perspectives (McMinn, 2017).

Critical wisdom is nurtured as people step outside of the common and often dominant manner of thinking in order to engage alternative views from the margins. When we create space for voices from the margins (i.e., the margins of history, the margins of culture and society), it helps us to get out of the way in order to look at the thing more clearly and completely. Even if we don't get it right, we will get it better by stepping out and having a more comprehensive view.

It is no coincidence that the birthplace of my (Megan Anna's) love of the church occurred while in conversation with Malawian pastors and leaders (see sidebar). As I listened to their wisdom, strength, and passion as they mobilized the church as a transforming agent for society, and as I saw their vision of the kingdom of heaven being lived out, my passion was ignited. While at the time I didn't have language for it, I have since come to understand that this was the process of engaging critical wisdom as I encountered voices and views from the margins of my own experience. The narratives I had known about God, and therefore about myself, were expanding. Expanding our worldviews and our narratives is a natural byproduct of humbly being in conversation with those who are familiar with an alternative story. This is the process by which critical wisdom develops.

AFRICAN RELIGIONS AND EVERYDAY LIFE

My (Megan Anna's) love of theology began early. One needn't look further than my Christmas wish list to determine I was not quite a normal teenager. It was with delight and enthusiasm that my fourteen-year-old self tore through Santa Claus wrapping paper to discover matching, shiny Old and New Testament commentaries. I spent nights pouring over these and making notes. While my love of theology began early, I struggled more with the church.

My love of theology *and* the church took a significant shift when I found myself at the age of twenty-one living in Malawi. I was interning with World Relief Malawi working alongside Malawians and other Africans (Ghanaians and Ugandans) who were mobilizing the church to action—helping to equip churches to combat poverty, hunger, and HIV/AIDs through community gardens, education, building projects, and child-development programs. The works these churches engaged in were not separate tasks from the work of spiritual formation; rather, they were one and the same—social and spiritual concerns fold into an integrated whole. Partly because of the holistic way in which Malawians tend to see the world, one cannot separate these tasks: everything is intrinsically spiritual and sacred. Kenyan priest and philosopher John Mbiti

(1990) writes about the inseparability of religion for the African, suggesting, "Wherever the African is" so is their religion: it's with them in the fields, the market, the funeral ceremony, or in the classroom (p. 2). Religion transcends and infuses every ordinary moment with the sacred. The worldview (often referred to as the "primal imagination" by African theologians such as Kwame Bediako [1994]) is much more similar to the writers of the Hebrew Scriptures than my post-Enlightenment brain could comprehend. Each Monday, we began our time at World Relief with a Bible study. I treasured this time of gleaning wisdom from my coworkers as they read Scripture through their African lenses. They frequently used allegory in their interpretations and found meaningful and creative connections from the life of David, Abraham, or Joseph to their everyday life. They used a hermeneutic of wisdom when reading Scripture. They created space for layered meanings of the text and due to the holistic view of humans and the cosmos they naturally integrated religious values and ideals with the mundane and profound tasks of daily living. They were doing more than simply excavating facts and history, they were creatively interpreting and applying Scripture. During these morning Bible studies, Scripture felt enlivened. I then saw this enlivened reading of Scripture lived out in churches who were caring for the poor, taking care of orphans, widows, and the dying in their community. These communities were worshiping together, doing life together, suffering together, and serving together.

In addition to being incredibly inspiring, it also happens that this is the new (and old) face of Christianity.[a] The center of Christianity is no longer in the West or the "Global North," as 61% of all Chris-

tians now live in the Global South (Gingrich and Smith, 2014). This shift in Christianity signals the importance of including theologies and voices from different cultures in the integration conversation. Particularly as these voices are arising from a cultural landscape that naturally integrates religion with everyday life, they have something profound to teach Christian counselors and psychologists in the Global North interested in the work of integration.

---

[a] While this is the "new" face of Christianity, it is also the old face. The early church was heavily influenced by Africa as many of the early church fathers were African, such as St. Augustine (Kalu, 2005).

This book is an exercise in engaging critical wisdom to converse about some of the essential theological concepts of our day and to explore the psychological significance of holding a nuanced view of these concepts. Something powerful happens when we step outside of the traditional and known way of looking at a thing. We can begin to see a thing from a different perspective, and gain wisdom. The goal is not to correct wrong belief or to prove an alternative view as the right belief. Rather, this is an innovative, conversational integration, offered by a woman who was raised in a postmodern time and her father who was not. Our hope is that by considering various perspectives on Scripture and theology we may come to a more comprehensive, fresh, and enlivening reading of the text, which invariably has implications for the way we have conversations in the counseling office. If this sounds like a messy task, then you have it right. But counseling is messy, too, and so is wisdom. It's time that integration be a bit messier than it has been.

What to Expect

Why do we need another book about integration? Because we have a new generation of integrators, and they are asking tough questions that need to be asked. We hope you will find the questions and conversations that follow

> ### *Integration Conversation Starters*
>
> 1. We have just outlined seven distinctive ways we will be exploring integration in this book: (a) shifting from abstraction to praxis, (b) integration as conversation, (c) asking hard questions, (d) probing beyond evangelicalism, (e) considering local contexts more than global taxonomies, (f) moving toward authentic, hospitable, generous conversation, and (g) forming wisdom more than resolving issues. What about this approach energizes you and makes you look forward to the pages ahead?
> 2. What concerns do you have about this approach to integration?
> 3. What changes would you like to see in your own integration journey by the time you reach the end of the book?

useful in your work as students, Christian counselors, and psychotherapists. Join us in some challenging and important dialog.

With the paradigm shift that is occurring among today's learners, traditional ways of learning systematic philosophy and thought are giving way to more contextual learning. As such, we are not providing a systematic exploration of Christian history, theology, or biblical studies, and we won't be making grand unifying assertions of how all theology and all psychology can fit together. Rather, we hope to enter into several of the most challenging quandaries and complexities of Christian counseling and psychotherapy and to embody a conversational and contextual way of doing integration in the process. Sandage and Brown (2018) recently proposed a model of relational integration in which they discuss the importance of interpersonal and interdisciplinary dynamics of integration that are contextually informed. Our attempt is to engage the model put forward by Sandage and Brown as we sit with theological and psychological concepts and explore them in the context of twenty-first-century counseling and psychotherapy. Of course, there are multiple contexts to consider, ranging from the particular sociocultural backgrounds pertaining to the theological and biblical concepts we explore to the contemporary multicultural milieu that is an essential part of contemporary counseling and psychotherapy.

LOCATING OURSELVES

We have discussed moving from abstract theory toward conversations pertaining to the person of the integrator. Still, it may be helpful to locate ourselves theoretically. Strawn, Bland, and Flores (2018) identify three waves of integration as apologetics, model building, and empirical validation, while acknowledging whispers of an emerging fourth wave. This fourth wave emphasizes clinical application and experiential learning, and is characterized by increased inclusion of diverse voices (theologically, culturally) as well as greater inclusion of case conceptualization. This frame understands integration as an emerging process flowing from the relational and social contexts of people's lives. As Sandage and Brown (2018) reflect, "A relational perspective helpfully attends to the reality that the processes of relational integration of psychology and theology unfold within diverse social contexts and personal experiences" (pp. 10-11).

This emerging wave of integration emphasizes relational spirituality, relational integration, and integration as crosscultural dialog (Augustyn, Hall, Wang, & Hill, 2017; Bailey et al., 2016; Hoffman, 2011; Sandage & Brown, 2018). It is both interpersonal and intrapersonal, deeply process oriented, and emerges out of particular sociocultural contexts. A conversational approach fits within this emerging fourth wave of integration well because conversation tends to be contextual, postmodern, and fluid in nature.

There will likely never be a shortage of theoretical models, such as those developed early in the integration movement. We honor and appreciate these models, while also agreeing with Sandage and Brown (2018) when they suggest that integration too often becomes about

integrating disciplines or abstract bodies of knowledge. . . . Yet it is obvious that disciplines are not "doing integration." For that matter, books and journal articles are not the actors in the work of integration. Rather, it is real people who attempt (or avoid) collaborative integration as part of relational and cultural systems. (p. 9)

Randy Sorenson (1996) observed something similar over twenty years ago:

Integration must occur in persons, and to omit or ignore this element is to doom our endeavors. . . . Integration is personal in the sense that it occurs through contact with persons-in-relation, including both other creatures and God. . . . It also means that our communities and our theories are related. Who we are to each other, how we treat each other—as faculty, students, and staff; as supervisors, therapists, and patients; as pastors, parishioners, and elders—has direct bearing on the quality of the integrative models we can imagine and sustain. (p. 208)

In order to locate ourselves within the broader world of integration approaches, it seems fair to name certain premises we hold—premises that have certainly influenced us in writing this book.

1. Integration happens between people. More specifically, integration happens in conversation. We host these conversations in our therapy offices, with people from other disciplines, between faculty and students, and so on.

2. Integration is lived out in real lives, embodied in the person of the psychotherapist, which means it is more desirable to train integrators than to attempt mastering, articulating, or communicating a discipline known as "integration."

3. Integration is embedded in social and cultural contexts and therefore will have some variance to it.

4. All truth is God's truth. This is not to say that everything is true, but rather every true thing comes from God. Christianity and psychology both belong in the conversation, and each can help transform our understanding of the other.

5. Ideas are important. Ideas explored in interaction with particular contexts are particularly meaningful.

This is a book about conversations, and as such we have attempted to organize it by considering the types of big questions and conversations that show up in counseling and psychotherapy offices. Part one is about facing difficulty, which is familiar territory for every person who sits in the office, whether counselor or patient. How can we talk about this in a way that respects theology, psychology, and the person across from us in the room? We attempt to do so by looking at the topics of lament (chapter one) and enjoyment (chapter two).

In Part two we ponder God, especially how God understands humanity and how humans understand God. In a sense, people are always pondering God, whether they believe in God or not, which is why it is deemed dangerous in almost any extended family unit to have conversations about religion. But dangerous topics can also promote wisdom, so we venture in with chapters on imaging God (chapter three) and narratives of the cross (chapter four). Our hope is that we can hold space for difference as we strive toward genuine conversation about ultimate meaning.

In Part three we consider God in the world. You will likely notice throughout the book that we emphasize being present, living in the moment, as we do clinical work. But this hints at some greater presence, difficult to capture with doctrines or theories or certainties of any sort. Here in the mystery we find God present and active in our world and in human lives. We open space for this conversation with chapters on the mission of God (chapter five) and God being with us (chapter six).

You will notice some conversational strategies throughout the book. You have already been introduced to our Integration Conversation Starters, and these will continue throughout the pages that follow. Additionally, you'll find a few Intrapersonal Conversation Starters throughout to encourage continued self-reflection. We also provide suggestions for further reading and reflection at the end of each chapter. Also, the two of us will be conversing with one another at times in this book even as we invite you, our readers, into the conversation as well.

Given our novel and somewhat messy approach to integration, and our desire to explore the margins that may have been overlooked in traditional integration literature, you will likely feel some discomfort at times. Even our choice of which Bible translation to use may engender some controversy in a time when we have so many choices to consider. We have opted for the New Revised Standard Version unless otherwise noted. But even more, we will all be pushed to consider some different theological imaginations about who and how God is; how God views our beautiful, broken world; and who we are in relation to God. These are challenges we face in writing the book, both as we probe the margins of evangelicalism and as we remember that evangelicalism is still an important part of the conversation. Indeed, if you do not feel uncomfortable with some of this book then we have probably not accomplished our task well. As authors, we choose to lean into the discomfort caused by some of the most difficult questions people are asking these days, and we invite you to do the same.

Tips for handling discomfort:

1. Welcome curiosity: Reactions to different ideas, materials, and people provide us helpful insights into our inner workings and ways of seeing

the world. Hermeneutics is the branch of knowledge that deals with how we interpret and understand things. We interpret texts, people, and situations. Our minds are always busy interpreting. If you notice a reaction while reading, good! What is this reaction telling you about your interpretive lens? About your values, core beliefs, and assumptions? What can you learn about yourself from this reaction you're having?

2. Practice perspective taking: Perspective taking (taking on another person's point of view) is a critical skill for therapists. When you find yourself struggling with a new idea, this is a great opportunity to practice. Try this "perspective taking" exercise: hold a new view in mind for two to three minutes, looking for what may be beneficial about this view. Then release the view and let it settle how it may. You may find yourself seeing things differently than before, or not, but either way you have practiced the skill of considering something from a new perspective.

PART ONE

Facing Difficulty

Psychiatrist M. Scott Peck opened one of the bestselling nonfiction books of all time with the now-famous words, "Life is difficult" (Peck, 1978, p. 15). With these three words, he summarized the first conversation that begins almost every counseling and psychotherapy relationship. People come to us in pain, experiencing struggle and hardship and dis-ease of every sort. They come to us for healing and help.

This is our work, perhaps even our calling, as counselors. Because we meet people in pain, we start almost every conversation this way as we create safe spaces where our patients explore life's difficulties. And in some way that still mystifies us (despite thousands of efficacy studies over many years)—something about allowing space for others' difficulties is indeed healing and helpful.

Even as we offer space and healing to others, we quietly notice that we ourselves also find life to be difficult. Years of training bring us into the offices where we live out our calling, but training doesn't fully prepare us to understand the deepest aches of living and dying, to make sense of our years on earth and matters of ultimate meaning.

So here is where we begin our integration conversation, in the mire of life's pain and deepest questions. Here, where the questions are bigger than the answers, where we lean into uncertainties and doubts, where meaning seems elusive, we find some surprises about God.

1

Lament

HOW DO WE MAKE SENSE OF THE DEEP ACHES IN LIFE?

IT WAS A BEAUTIFUL JUNE DAY. We were just leaving the wet, dreary Oregon winter behind and all around me (Megan Anna) the world was thrusting forward with new life. Excited for my first appointment with this new pregnancy and just five days before my daughter's second birthday, there was much to be celebrating. The life blossoming within mirrored the bustling of life flourishing around me. Just three months prior I'd experienced my first miscarriage. This pregnancy felt different, I was nine weeks along and all signs pointed to new life (i.e., lots of nausea, sickness, and fatigue). The beginning of my appointment began with enthusiasm and warmth—excited to reconnect with my nurse midwife, Vicky. The mood in the room shifted when she began the ultrasound.

While I remember my daughter, Grace, grape-sized and enthusiastically bouncing around, this grape-sized baby was not moving. *Perhaps this is a very mellow baby.* Grace being a wild and lively toddler who infrequently slept, yes, I could do a mellow baby. Vicky sunk into silence and began looking more intensively at the ultrasound screen. After a few minutes she explained that this was not the size of baby we would expect to see at nine weeks, and that more concerning she wasn't picking up a heartbeat. There could be a few possibilities: perhaps dating was off and it was too small to yet pick up a heartbeat, or perhaps the baby stopped growing and developing toward life. We needed an ultrasound with higher resolution to confirm. They scheduled me an afternoon ultrasound at the hospital. I knew it in my bones, I saw it in Vicky's face, but the formal ultrasound was policy.

Between my OB visit and hospital ultrasound I returned to my car on the fifth floor of the parking garage. Sitting in the passenger seat in the darkness, I called my husband and told him we were having another miscarriage. Mostly, I held it together; I hold things together under stress. But after hanging up the phone, in the safety of the dark parking garage, I allowed myself space for not holding it together. I contacted the terror, dread, anger, and pain. Warm tears ran down my cheeks as I lashed out in anger. The words I muttered with clenched fists: "Why? Why again? No, not again." I'm not sure who those words were directed to: perhaps God, the universe, perhaps my body which I felt was betraying me. I spoke angry, tearful words of lament. In that moment they needed out, they needed to be voiced.

At one level, some may wonder if this is a story about grief or lament; it can be confusing to differentiate the two. Lament is relational. It's taking our grief and pain and expressing it to one who will listen. It's one thing to feel a sorrow, and quite another to express it boldly. By clenching my fists and crying out to God, I expressed the ache in my soul and trusted my grief to the possibility that someone might be listening. In this, lament is grief, directed at God, with a particular shape or form (Brueggemann, 1995).

So what is lament? It first involves suffering. But suffering itself is not enough. Second, lament also requires crying out, giving voice to the ache deep in our bones. We plead for someone to hear our pain. Third, lament expresses resistance for the way things are, and calls for the other to be moved in sorrow and act to make things better. Perhaps paradoxically, the final part of lament is experiencing some confidence and trust in the person receiving our words. In the wake of his blood cancer diagnosis, J. Todd Billings (2015) writes: "As strange as it sounds, prayers of lament in a biblical pattern are actually a form of praise to God and an expression of trust in his promises" (p. 43). Similarly, M. Elizabeth Lewis Hall (2016) writes, "biblical lament contains an unexpected element that differs radically from 'sorrow, regret, or unhappiness'; it contains sometimes exuberant praise to God" (p. 221). And so, lament contains deep sorrow and suffering as well as its expression and cries for change, but it also holds the possibility of connection and even grateful reflection toward the other who receives our expressions of pain.

Medical settings are often places of lament. Anyone who has spent time in an oncology unit knows the deep questions and longings that stir in the human soul, and they have witnessed the cries of anguish that emerge from those questions and longings. Kathleen O'Connor (2002) begins her fine book on Lamentations by recounting sitting with her husband in a hospital oncology room, noting the quiet wisdom of the nurses and staff. She writes:

> They accepted fear and rage, along with the physical and spiritual manifestations of disease. They spoke with their patients as human beings, learned about their families, their lives, and treated them as agents in their own care. Together they enacted the theological insight at the core of this book that I call "a theology of witnessing." (p. xiii)

These are poignant words showing how lament brings suffering into a relational space where others bear witness to the weight of the world. And so it is also in the psychotherapy office, whether situated in a medical setting or somewhere else. We are called to be those who bear witness to suffering, pain, struggle, despair, and anger. And if we are to be these witnesses, we desperately need a theology of witnessing.

As counselors and psychotherapists, we might lean toward understanding lament as an individual phenomenon, but it can also be a collective activity. I (Mark) recently listened to a profound sermon by an African American telling his story of living in a country where black male bodies are distrusted and maligned. During the sermon the speaker mentioned "black lament"— words that pierced my heart. In the Quaker tradition we sit in silence for a time—usually between five and fifteen minutes—after a sermon, and it seemed clear to me that day that we were a congregation sitting together in lament. As a predominantly white group, we probably could never fully understand black lament, but we could at least sit before God and cry out for justice and shalom.

In our work as psychotherapists, we encounter both individual and collective lament. Our patients bring their individual pain, but they also bring ways of being wounded in an unjust and difficult world. Many of us are comfortable with grief work, and while lament and grief work certainly overlap they are also distinct from one another. Biblical theologian Clifton Black (2005) suggests that while grief has traditionally been understood by psychotherapists as progressing through stages, lament is not something we move out of, as all of life and joy is intertwined with death this side of Eden. Lament leads us deeper into the "inmost heart of God" (p. 53). When it comes to lament and grief, Christianity has much to offer the world of counseling, and arguably the whole Western world.

LAMENT AND FORMFUL GRIEF

Walter Brueggemann (1995), a biblical scholar who has written extensively on lament, notes how Elizabeth Kübler-Ross's work on the stages of grief has helped make grief formful. He suggests that lament is similarly formful. In other words, there are particular community standards that make lament bearable and somewhat predictable, and may even make it meaningful. Form helps contain the messy process occurring in the aftermath of loss.

Drawing on the structure of the Psalms, Brueggemann suggests that formful lament consists of an address to God, complaint, confession of trust, petition, words of assurance, and a vow to praise. This formful lament helps "define the experience of suffering" (Capps, 2005, p. 71). It also seems reasonable to argue the inverse—that if lament is given no place, no voice, in our places of worship and psychotherapy offices, then it lacks form, and the experience of suffering becomes undefined and amorphous, easily obscuring whatever hope and meaning could otherwise be found.

A Recipe for Disaster

It seems that for modern, Western Christians we are stuck between a rock and a hard place when it comes to expressing our grievances. Consider that the church has largely lost the prayers and avenues of lament that traditionally played a rich part in our tradition (Billman & Migliore, 1999). There are exceptions, such as the black church and feminist theologies, where lament has been done relatively well, but for the most part we have overlooked lament in our communities of worship. Hall (2016) notes that only about 4% of hymns in contemporary hymnals reflect the sort of lament that is present in 40% of Psalms—the Hebrew hymnal. If the "rock" is the lament-limited church, the "hard place" is increased exposure to crises and conflicts for which lament is the appropriate response. Perhaps the absence of lament has given way to expressions of anger expressed through disembodied forms (e.g., network media, social media, and so on). A fragmented lament finds life in new forms, as poet Rainer Maria Rilke writes: "Killing is one of the forms of our wandering mourning" (May, 1983, p. 125). Because we are not a culture that knows how to lament, we often let our mourning wander into destructive places. Complaint is one such place insofar as it divorces our grievances from a real relationship with God and becomes more grumbling about God than crying out to God (Hughes, 1993).

Christians who are psychologists and counselors often struggle to know how much of their personal faith to disclose to their patients. This is a complex and nuanced matter that goes well beyond the scope of this book, but one advantage of disclosing something about our faith to patients should be mentioned here. If our Christian patients know we share their faith, then bringing up spiritual struggles allows for the possibility of lament rather than complaint. That is, pain and struggle and confusion and anguish can be voiced in a context where belief is still a firm foundation and where hope lingers, however faintly, on the horizon.

Not having a culture of lament, or collective public spaces for lament, leaves us in a precarious situation of learning how to lament privately, or not learning at all. Given these modern-day tensions, it makes sense that conversing with ancient texts and non-Western cultures is essential to cultivating a framework for lament. Conversation with the Hebrew Scriptures can be especially helpful in providing language and a landscape for engaging lament.

How We Look at a Thing

Perhaps the complexity of the church's history to lament can be illustrated by how we interpret Jeremiah 31:15-17. Here, the imagery is of Rachel lamenting the loss of her children to the Babylonian exile:

> A voice is heard in Ramah,
>   lamentation and bitter weeping.
> Rachel is weeping for her children;
>   she refuses to be comforted for her children,
>   because they are no more.
> Thus says the Lord:
> Keep your voice from weeping,
>   and your eyes from tears;
> for there is a reward for your work,
>   says the Lord:
>   they shall come back from the land of the enemy;

there is hope for your future,
> says the LORD:
your children shall come back to their own country.

Where do your eyes land as you read this passage? In many of our Christian traditions we have tended to jump to the end, to the comfort of God's promise that Rachel's children will come back. And, in fact, after seventy years of Babylonian captivity the children of Rachel returned to their land. Read this way, the passage has a happy ending; and it also illustrates our Christian tendency to shy away from the complexity of lament. In contrast, the Jewish tradition and black theology have tended to place emphasis on Rachel refusing to be comforted as an appropriate response to having her children ripped from her breast. They have leaned into the lament tradition as a meaningful source of strength and hope amidst suffering (Billman & Migliore, 2007).

Those of us who are Christians may struggle staying present to suffering. We see the resurrection more than the crucifixion, the forgiving more than the estrangement. If we look for lament in the Bible at all, we're more likely to see the lament psalms, where we typically find a hopeful ending, than the book of Lamentations, where it is difficult to see hope at all. But still, those of us called to being counselors and psychotherapists are also called to be the ones who bear witness to the suffering of the world.

I (Mark) have spent my career as a cognitive-behavioral psychotherapist. For most of these years I have employed second-wave approaches where we evaluate and attempt to modify our patients' dysfunctional thoughts and maladaptive assumptions. More recently, I have been attracted to third-wave approaches to cognitive-behavioral therapy (CBT). One of the primary differences between second- and third-wave approaches mirrors the Christian and Jewish responses to Rachel's weeping described above. In second-wave approaches we tend to empathize with people's pain but then move them on to places of hope and possibility. So yes, unfortunate things have happened, but there are also good things in life that deserve our attention. These positive ways of viewing a thing are considered adaptive and healthy, whereas negative thoughts are considered dysfunctional and unhealthy. In contrast, third-wave approaches assume that suffering will be part of life. Rather than dismissing suffering or trying to replace it with more positive appraisals, we help our patients remain present to the suffering, to observe and notice how they experience and respond to their pain, to see how they may have developed avoidance strategies that help them escape their pain but often at great personal cost. We sit with our patients, bearing witness to the pain of the world.

Marla came for help with her depression and within the first few sessions landed on her profound feelings of being unwanted as a child. She described busy parents who seemed uninvested in and unconcerned about her well-being, including stories of being lost in a mall, spending many hours alone as a child, and being left with relatives while her parents vacationed. A second-wave approach might involve helping Marla reevaluate her childhood experiences and conclusion. Yes, her parents were busy, and some incidents could be interpreted to mean a lack of love or devotion on their part, but many other childhood experiences indicated her parents were present and loving toward her. They provided for her needs, attended her school events, and cared patiently for her during times of illness. By changing her interpretation of these childhood experiences, Marla might find her depression eases and she begins to feel more loved and secure in the world.

Notice how this approach has utility but leaves little room for lament. In contrast, a third-wave CBT approach moves right into Marla's pain. What was it like for her that day in second grade when she got lost in the mall? What emotions surged over her then, and how have those emotions continued to visit her throughout the years since? What did she conclude about the world back then, and how have those conclusions persisted? Are there ways she avoids the ongoing risk of being lost again, perhaps by staying out of vulnerable places in her current relationships? And how might those strategies to avoid pain actually be contributing to her current sense of isolation and depression? These third-wave instincts to move into suffering are messy and complicated, but ultimately provide a space for Marla to confront and lament her pain and uncertainty and to see how they may be contributing to her current problems.

There is a temptation in the face of immense suffering to wrap it up neatly and put a tidy bow on it. The temptation may be to bypass the pain and anguish of the years Rachel spent weeping, wondering about and crying for her children who were in exile, by jumping to the happy ending. It's striking that groups of people who have experienced significant suffering and powerlessness gravitate toward the complexity of Scripture and lament, toward the faithfulness of Rachel's refusal to be consoled. It seems the words we emphasize in the Bible may have a lot to do with our lived experiences.

Billman and Migliore (2007) note several striking examples of daring lament: Jeremiah accuses God of not holding up to God's character and promises (Jer 15:18), while Job is audacious enough to put God on trial (Job 23:3-4). The psalmist petitions God to "Wake up!" and to act rather than passively look upon the suffering of God's people (Ps 35:23). Lament also shows up in the New Testament: Jesus begging at Gethsemane to let the cup pass (Lk 22:42), Paul persistently begging God to remove the thorn from his side (2 Cor 12:8).

Lament is bold, powerful, and oftentimes disturbing in its intensity and passion. It allows distress, anger, and feelings of abandonment to flow freely. The writers of lament cry out to God, boldly questioning God and complaining of God's distance. But even here there is a surprising intimacy, a revealing of pain that only happens in the closest of relationships, or at least in those yearning for close relationship. Reading lament in the Hebrew Scriptures often feels like we are looking in on a passionate lovers' quarrel with God (Billman & Migliore, 2007).

This passionate, intense anger found in the lament passages is largely absent from most of our churches. Brueggemann (1986) reflects that the absence of our lament sends a powerful message that those who suffer should only speak praise. In essence they are rendered voiceless (Hall, 2016). So how did we travel from these bold, passionate passages of lament to where we are today, which seems to be a place of avoiding lament? And what bearing does it have on our work as counselors and psychotherapists?

Integration Conversation Starters

1. If you are a psychotherapist or counselor, how have you noticed yourself trying to tidy up the struggles and complaints your patients bring? What sort of fears do you confront in yourself as you consider resisting this impulse to tidy up your patients' anger and complaints?

2. What forces in the modern-day church keep us from lamenting in the ways we see in the Hebrew Scriptures?

3. In what relationships do you feel the freedom to express your deepest sorrows and complaints? Can you imagine having that sort of intimacy and freedom with God?

Jeremiah

Often deemed the weeping prophet, Jeremiah knew suffering. Jeremiah, who experienced his call as a curse (Jer 20:14-18), spent much of his life entrapped between his relationship with Yahweh and Israel. Jeremiah lived and prophesied during the time of the Babylonian invasions and deportations—a time Israel was in havoc. Israel was surrounded by large threats—the Neo-Babylonian Empire had recently become a powerhouse alongside Egypt. With these conflicting powers Israel was divided as to how to respond: some promoted alliance with Egypt while others, including Jeremiah, were pro-Babylonian. Further, the Babylonian invasions led to massive destruction: buildings were destroyed, families broken up, and not surprisingly this led to economic and social devastation (O'Connor, 2002). Amidst this season of upheaval and chaos, the looming question was how to make sense of God.

Jeremiah's role was to warn people. He received haunting visions of the violence and destruction to come. However, when he spoke these warnings he was persecuted. At the temple there were "optimistic prophets" who proclaimed a dramatically different message of hope and prosperity (Jer 14:13). Naturally, the king tended to listen to the optimistic prophets (confirmation bias was a thing even back then) and disregard Jeremiah as a false prophet who ought to be persecuted (Holladay, 1990). In addition to warning people, prophets would often intercede with God on behalf of their people. When the people did not listen to Jeremiah's message, God stripped Jeremiah of this privilege (Jer 7:16-20; 14:11). God declares that if Jeremiah attempts to plead for the people, God will refuse to hear (Jer 7:16). Jeremiah saw the devastation that was coming and yet was powerless to plead to God on his people's behalf.

At the same time, his people were not interested in hearing him either. When Jeremiah spoke the words God put on his lips, he was persecuted. But when he attempted to keep these words inside, they were "a burning fire shut up in my bones" (Jer 20:9). Jeremiah is in a cosmic double bind: if he speaks the words of God he becomes a laughingstock and persecuted. If he does not speak the words of God they burn like fire within him. Jeremiah's bones ached: he saw the pain of what was to come and yet was in a position of utter powerlessness.

As if this were not enough suffering, as a living metaphor of God's nullified covenant with Israel and as a sign of the barrenness that is about to hit Israel,

THEODICIES

As in Jeremiah's time, we are still trying to make sense of God. If God is all-loving and all-powerful, then why do so many bad things happen in the world? This has sometimes been called the "problem of evil," and many theologians and philosophers have attempted to offer solutions. Some have concluded that the problem is too great, and that God must not exist at all. Others have worked to hold onto belief in God while still making sense of suffering in the world. These efforts are known as theodicies.

There are many theodicies, and we highlight just three here. None of the theodicies answer all the questions and quandaries emerging from the problem of evil. Some people find it useful to combine theodicies because many of them can coexist. But still, even with multiple theodicies, questions remain.

FREE WILL THEODICY

God is committed to allow humans freedom, even if it means permitting evil (Plantinga, 1989). Anything less would be to create automatons that knowingly or unknowingly follow divine scripts through life. With freedom comes selfish choices, and with selfish choices pain is spread through the fallen world. A recent variant on this theodicy is open theism, which suggests that God is influenced by human events and may not have a prescribed blueprint for how the future unfolds (Sanders, 2007).

GROWTH

Creation is still in process. As unpleasant as pain may feel, it is also what prompts human morality to develop and grow over time. This is not to say that a particular individual is made better by pain—indeed, this often seems not to be the case. But even here we see the human capacity for empathy and love grow as we choose compassionate ways of being with others in their pain (Hick, 2010).

SUFFERING GOD

God is profoundly present in the hardships of life, evidenced in both the Hebrew Scriptures and the New Testament. In the Christian faith, the incarnation demonstrates that God will spare no cost to enter into the mire of human experience and suffer alongside us.

Jonathan Sacks (2011), a rabbi and a philosopher, makes an interesting distinction between left-brain (analytical) and right-brain (experiential) explanations of suffering, though he nuances this more carefully than many who write about the two hemispheres of the brain. The logical, philosophical (left-brain) approach begins with the logical question of how the world should be if God is all-powerful and all-loving, leading to various philosophical questions and quandaries. The free will and growth theodicies seem mostly to emerge out of this tradition. The experiential, meaning-making (right-brain) approach begins with the world as it is. The question then is not how to resolve the logical tensions, but how we can find meaning in a world where suffering exists. The suffering God theodicy, which exemplifies this approach, suggests that God enters into our suffering rather than rescuing us from it.

My (Megan Anna's) senior year of high school, my best friend David was diagnosed with a brain tumor. It was a wretched and painful year walking with David as the cancer slowly overtook his body. During David's progressive sickness he talked about his powerful experience of Christ walking with him. I too felt a palpable and profound sense of Christ's presence amidst the agony of losing David. The week he died I felt the presence of God as I fought to find sleep, as I struggled to get through the words of his eulogy. As I watched his casket slowly lowered into the ground, I felt the weeping presence of God beside me.

If God walks beside me in the hardest places of life, then I feel inspired to walk with others in the midst of their pain as well. This doesn't solve any logic problems about how a powerful and loving God can allow evil in the world, but it does give meaning to the difficult journeys we walk. As Martin Buber writes, "The world is not comprehensible but it is embraceable" (Buber, 1957, p. 27).

God calls Jeremiah to a life of isolation and celibacy (Jer 16:1-9) (Holladay, 1990). Jeremiah is called to social isolation—no longer allowed to attend funerals and weddings, the epicenter of social life (Jer 16:5-9). To call Jeremiah to a life of celibacy was to call for Jeremiah's social extinction. In the Hebrew Scripture people tended to envision themselves as living on through their children and grandchildren. Keep in mind that while celibacy is a theme Paul grapples with in the New Testament, there are no parallels within Hebrew Scripture to celibacy (Holladay, 1990). Given Jeremiah's isolation and sense of powerlessness, it is no surprise he experienced his relationship with God as deeply painful and problematic.

What is an appropriate response to such suffering and powerlessness? Even as Jeremiah is being faithful to God, and ostracized by his community as a result, it seems that God is also pushing Jeremiah away and not listening. Not surprisingly, Jeremiah experiences anger and engages in verbal wrestling with God. He simply can't make sense of such a God who would allow massive destruction, and not even allow pleas on behalf of the people about to be destroyed. Jeremiah's accusation against God and protest *to* God is fantastically bold:

O LORD, you have enticed me,
　　and I was enticed;
you have overpowered me,
　　and you have prevailed.
I have become a laughingstock all day long;
　　everyone mocks me.
For whenever I speak, I must cry out,
　　I must shout, "Violence and destruction!"
For the word of the LORD has become for me
　　a reproach and derision all day long.
If I say, "I will not mention him,
　　or speak any more in his name,"
then within me there is something like a burning fire
　　shut up in my bones;
I am weary with holding it in,
　　and I cannot. (Jer 20:7-9)

Within this passage Jeremiah accuses God of deceiving him. Jeremiah is making a relational accusation: "You have enticed, deceived, and overpowered me, Lord!" These accusations made within the context of an intimate relationship draw on past relational experiences to form his protest (Jer 1:4-19; 12:3; 15:17-20). Jeremiah recalls God's past promises to be with and deliver him (Jer 1:19; 15:20-21). By recalling God's promises, Jeremiah is calling forth the character of God, petitioning God on behalf of God's own character and promises. It's as if Jeremiah is asking, "God, will you be faithful to hold up your end of the bargain?"

Jeremiah's lament is the wrestling through of an inescapable paradox, but this wrestling ultimately births a greater hope and even a celebration of God's presence (Jer 20:11). Jeremiah finds hope on the other side of complexity, but getting there is a messy process. Jeremiah provides a model for how to wrestle with God faithfully amidst crises, he gives voice to those of us who have wondered if we dare to question God. As Christian counselors and psychotherapists, we likely encounter many of these "but God, why?" moments. As people who sit with the absurdity of suffering, knowing how to faithfully protest and wrestle with God can help us foster resilience in this work and in our faith. We need a theology that can hold the suffering that we hold. Jeremiah can serve as an exemplar for those of us who are seeking faith in what can often feel like a suffering and senseless world.

Implications for Counseling and Psychotherapy

Jeremiah does not find cheap hope; it is in entering into and wrestling with the messiness of lament that he finds hope. Hope lives within the complexity of lament. Hope and lament are intimately intertwined, "without lament, hope is stillborn" (Billman & Migliore, 1999, p. 16). Given the importance of hope in our work as counselors and psychotherapists, it seems important to consider the pathways of lament that may lead to hope. As it turns out, this has profound implications for how we do our work.

AUTHOR DIALOG: LAMENT AND GRACE

Megan Anna: Dad, you've been in this profession thirty-five years. What have you noticed in regard to cultural or social shifts around lament—does it feel like people are lamenting or grieving differently than they were thirty-five years ago? How has your personal experience of lament shifted throughout your career?

Mark: Honestly, I can't recall much conversation about lament at all from those early years of my career. We were all fighting so hard just to get psychologists open to considering religion and spirituality that I don't think we looked at much nuance regarding how people experienced faith. As you say in the introduction, this is no longer the time to develop apologetics for integration, so we can start to look more carefully at how people experience faith. Recently, I've been influenced by Dr. Julie Exline at Case Western Reserve University and her work on spiritual struggle, and also by Dr. Elizabeth Lewis Hall at Biola University and her work on lament. Both of these scholars bring a refreshing honesty to the study of how people experience God.

And oh my, you also asked about my personal experience. It's so much easier for me to talk about research! My most enduring theological interest throughout my life—both personally and professionally— has been the topic of grace. I think grace is where I have personally struggled the most because my default is to try to earn acceptance from God and others rather than thinking of acceptance as a gift freely given. In my heart, lament and grace are deeply intertwined. Lament requires a sort of confidence that God loves me and accepts me even if I am angry—that God will not abandon me even if I am irrational or emotional. Intellectually, I believe the theology and psychology of lament that we are describing in this chapter, but it is still difficult to let that sink down in the emotional core of who I am and how I understand myself in relation to God.

The question I am inclined to ask in return is whether you have found any connections between grace and lament in your theological studies. But maybe that's not the right question. Perhaps the better question is if you find any connection between these two in your heart.

Megan Anna: Such a good question. I wouldn't have thought to put grace and lament into a dialectical relationship like that. I'm glad you thought of it. Yes, of course, one needs safety before one can be free enough to feel their rage. Perhaps we are cut from the same cloth in that I, too, lean toward working for God's approval. It is hard to be angry at someone who you are frantically trying to win over. And so, of course, how can one be free enough to lament without also holding

the experience of grace? This conversation makes me think of something Francis Weller said in an interview about grief and gratitude:

> The work of the mature person is to carry grief in one hand and gratitude in the other and to be stretched large by them. How much sorrow can I hold? That's how much gratitude I can give. If I carry only grief, I'll bend toward cynicism and despair. If I have only gratitude, I'll become saccharine and won't develop much compassion for other people's suffering. Grief keeps the heart fluid and soft, which helps make compassion possible. (McKee, 2015)

It makes sense to me that the experience of God's grace makes lament possible, and I also like what Weller is saying—grief makes the heart softer, making compassion possible. I wonder if lament softens the heart, making us more open to experiencing God's gracious presence. And I say presence because isn't that precisely what grace is—the gift of encountering God's *being* in our lives. And how can we possibly thrash and beat our arms against this being, refusing to be prematurely consoled, unless we have first encountered and experienced the gracious being before us?

Creating space for both hope and lament. The first and most basic implication is that we must learn to create spaces for lament while simultaneously holding the possibility of hope. As clinicians, we may tend to tell an oscillating story about hope and lament more than a fully integrated story. By an oscillating story, we mean that it is easy to view lament and hope as opposing forces that alternate in human consciousness: either we hope or lament today, and tomorrow it may be different. But what if we ponder a fully integrated story instead—one that holds hope and lament together dialectically as we move through each season of life?

Philosopher and poet David Whyte (2015) hints at this integrated view in his insightful words about heartbreak:

> Heartbreak is unpreventable; the natural outcome of caring for people and things over which we have no control. . . . Heartbreak begins the moment we are asked to let go but cannot, in other words, it colors and inhabits and magnifies each and every day; heartbreak is not a visitation, but a path that human beings follow through even the most average life. Heartbreak is our indication of sincerity: in a love relationship, in a work, in trying to learn a musical instrument, in the attempt to shape a better more generous self. Heartbreak is the beautifully helpless side of love and affection and is just as much an essence and emblem of care. . . . Heartbreak has its own way of inhabiting time and its own beautiful and trying patience in coming and going.
>
> Heartbreak is inescapable; yet we use the word as if it only occurs when things have gone wrong: an unrequited love, a shattered dream, a child lost before their time. Heartbreak . . . is something we hope we can avoid; something to guard against, a chasm to be carefully looked for and then walked around; the hope is to find a way to place our feet where the elemental forces of life will keep us in the manner to which we want to be accustomed and which will also keep us from the losses that all other human beings have experienced without exception since the beginning of conscious time. But heartbreak may be the very essence of being human, of being on the journey from here to there, and of coming to care deeply for what we find along the way. (pp. 101-2)

If we are to be witness bearers to the suffering of the souls in our counseling offices, then we need to hold the possibility that hope and lament are not so much oscillations in the alternating currents of life, but rather the simultaneous realities of human existence. One is not to be avoided while the other pursued; both bring meaning to the other.

In our first visit, Leanne told me (Megan Anna) about her lifelong desire
to be a mom and her sense that God had instilled this passion and purpose
on her life. She had a growing sense of confusion about why God would
create her with this purpose when God was not coming through for her
wishes for a child. Leanne and her husband had been trying to conceive for
five years. Leanne had medical complications that made conception difficult,
and during our work together her medical complications led to a hysterectomy.
After grieving this loss, Leanne turned her eye toward adoption with passion
and joy. Much like the last five years had been filled with the infertility roller-
coaster of hope and lament, the adoption process proved to be a similar
pathway. They would learn about an adoption agency, become excited, and
then discover discouraging news dashing their hopes and causing them to
cycle back to grief. A person of deep faith, she felt troubled and perplexed
by the frequent comments of those in her faith community: "Just have hope,
God has a plan." The cycling between loss and hope caused her to question
God's plan and involvement in this process.

Leanne found complexity in her experiences of lament and hope, and that
led to the sense that she had to choose between the two at any given moment
of life. She wondered if her lament was a sort of armor for her, protecting her
from hoping and being disappointed yet again. At the same time, her partner
found it hard when she lamented because it felt like Leanne had given up
hope. And when Leanne allowed herself to hope she felt guilty for enjoying
life in the meantime—as if she had an obligation to be focused on the sadness.

Further complicating Leanne's relationship to sorrow, she was having a
difficult time expressing her lament publicly. At church she felt pressure to
be unrelentingly positive. Spiritually, she felt scared to invite God into the
pain—what if she did and God let her down. In a desire to protect her relationship to God, she was keeping God at bay from her pain.

Our work together involved me bearing witness to both her lament and
her hope, at the same time. In the process we encountered some meaningful
questions together: How do we make space for both hope and lament? How
do we hold these together? How are we faithful to our own complex emotions
when this is difficult for one's partner? As she progressed in treatment, Leanne
moved toward a more integrated view where both hope and lament could
coexist in the same moment.

The Bible is made up of a kaleidoscope of voices. These voices in the Bible are engaged in a conversation, at times a heated one. While there is a temptation to listen more closely to one voice over another, these voices of the Bible take on greater meaning and texture when held together. Hope and lament, which may appear antithetical—as they did for Leanne—are intertwined and mingled together. Both become more realized when held together.

Most biblical expressions of lament come from an unflinching frame of hope: it is a hope that God will hear and respond, that God is with us even when such a thing seems impossible, and that God will continue to persist in relationship with us amidst our suffering, pain, agony, and anger. We so often define hope as things getting better, but biblical expressions of hope are rooted in God's being—which is with and for us. Black (2005) writes, "Yet the spine of lament is hope: not the vacuous optimism that 'things will get better,' which in the short run is usually a lie, but the deep and irrepressible conviction, in the teeth of present evidence, that God has not severed the umbilical cord" (p. 54). Despite his anguishing circumstances, Jeremiah's confidence that God had not "severed the umbilical cord" propelled him to put forward a fiery protest before God. In contrast, Leanne was initially terrified of putting forward her anguish before God, unsure she could handle the strain on her faith if met with God's silence.

When we shy away from lament with our patients, might we inadvertently be reinforcing their ideas that God cannot handle such a thing? How might it look different to lean into lament, fully assured that God is prepared to hear and hold our anguish without fleeing or retaliating? At the same time, if we disallow, disembody, or neglect the formfulness of lament, we may inadvertently be encouraging a tepid sort of hope that presumes relationship with God to be so fragile that concerns are disallowed, and quarrels not possible. Locating and holding hope in a God who is not severed from us—who is present with us amidst the pain, and yet who may not intervene despite our concerns—is no simple task. What does it require?

First, this fully integrated view of hope and lament must be modeled by the psychotherapist or counselor. To what extent can we ourselves sit in the room with anguish and still hold hope? And in hopeful conversations, can we still remember and hold the complex places of loss and sorrow? There is an honesty in lament—in naming the brokenness and pain—that makes the naming of gratitude, praise, and thanksgiving all the more meaningful. In this way the rhythm of psychotherapy is much like the rhythm of prayer.

> Without the prayer of lament the other important elements of prayer—praise, thanksgiving, confession, intercession—atrophy and ring hollow. How can praise be free and joyful if the realities of broken human life are not named and lamented. How can heartfelt thanks be given for healing if the wounds are denied? (Billman & Migliore, 1999, p. 19)

Second, we need to look beyond spiritual defenses that might keep our patients from experiencing the fullness of life in God. By "spiritual defenses" we mean ways that religion or spirituality may be used to shield us from the brunt of our own emotions and lived experiences. These can keep us from fully knowing ourselves, and thus from bringing our whole selves to God. Imagine the following therapy dialog and where you might go next in the conversation:

Patient: I really don't mind this because I know God is bigger than any troubles I may face in life. God has always been my greatest source of hope and will continue to be even with this diagnosis.

Therapist: That's a beautiful expression of faith and hope in God. I'm wondering what the other moments look like for you.

Patient: I'm not sure what you mean.

Therapist: Well, you say you don't really mind this because God is bigger than your troubles, but I'm just wondering what it looks like when those words are more difficult to hold onto—maybe in the middle of the night as you ponder what it means to be diagnosed with Stage IV cancer, or when you see the sorrow in your children's eyes. What's it like in those moments when you *do* mind this?

Patient: God has always taken care of me.

Therapist: [sits silently as patient looks pensive]

Patient: I suppose I do feel afraid sometimes.

Therapist: I wonder if we could look at those feelings too.

In this example the therapist doesn't deny the patient's source of faith in God but pushes past what initially appears to be quite a protective understanding of hope toward a more complex and integrated perspective where lament and hope can intermingle.

Third, it can sometimes help for the therapist to intentionally create a formfulness to lament (see sidebar "Lament and Formful Grief"). This doesn't require us to have particular stages or worksheets for lament—it's not that formful! But it does call us to reflect on the nature of lament as we see our patients entering into it. For example, as a patient begins to express anger and uncertainty toward God, the therapist can gently point out the relational form of lament that is seen through the Scriptures.

> **Therapist:** Even in your tears and anger I hear the hope that someone may be there to hear you. Wherever God is, however abandoned you feel, you are crying out as if somewhere, somehow, God may be listening.

This sort of observation puts form back into lament and helps prevent it from devolving into free-floating bitterness. Notice this is not the same as positive thinking, and it is certainly not minimizing the emotions experienced by the patient. Instead, this places the grief, sorrow, and anger back into the relational form of lament.

Holding lament and hope together is the substance of living deeply. In knowing the loss of grief for friends and family who have died, we hold onto their memories with a bit more gratitude, joy, and thankfulness. In knowing the deep joy of loves that have fallen, the loss is all the greater. Pain is ever present with delight, and hope runs through them both.

Integration Conversation Starters

1. During times of turmoil, when do you most naturally lean toward hope or lament? What work might you need to do to hold the two together?

2. How do you make sense of holding onto hope in God while still knowing that God may not respond to your cries of protest as you would desire?

3. What forms do you put in place to keep lament from devolving into free-floating bitterness? Based on the strategies you personally use, what implications do you see for counseling and psychotherapy?

Embracing the full spectrum of emotion in psychotherapy. The first funeral I attended in Malawi was a bit jarring. I had attended a handful of funerals in the United States, which were marked with quiet tears, a quietness that felt respectful of those most intimately impacted by the loss. There were exchanges of compassionate words, and the occasional exchange of well-meaning plat-itudes. There is awkwardness in grief—a not knowing what to say.

This was not so in Malawi. When we arrived, I heard wailing as the biblical imagery of "gnashing of teeth" came to mind. A group of women paraded in wailing, hovered together, holding one another. Later in the afternoon I sat on a mat in the grassy field with a group of women as we prepared food for the group who had gathered. Throughout the food preparation there were moments of laughter and tears—deep laughter and deep grief displayed through women's bodies and vocal patterns. There was connection. Malawians are embodied people, willing to encounter the whole spectrum of emotions with their minds and hearts and bodies and voices.[1]

I was reminded of my Malawian friends when reading Brené Brown (2010): "There's no such thing as selective emotional numbing. There is a full spectrum of human emotions and when we numb the dark, we numb the light" (pp. 72-73). I experienced deep joy while living in Malawi, and I have come to wonder if part of this was because I experienced a wider spectrum of emotion—both ends of the continuum were opened up, suffering and pain as well as joy and gratitude.[2] I was touching lightness and darkness more fully.

Then I returned to my home in the United States—a country where pain medication is prescribed more than anywhere in the world (Humphreys, 2018), whose antidepressant use is skyrocketing along with drug and alcohol addiction. I'm grateful for the medications available in our country, and see their value, but I wonder if we have become vulnerable to seeing pain as optional in life. Might that, in turn, make us vulnerable to the sort of emo-tional numbing that Brené Brown is describing? If we take what Brown says to heart, our lives cannot be partitioned and selectively numbed. When we numb ourselves from the depths of the pain, we also numb ourselves from the height of joy and pleasure.

---

[1]This experience in Malawi resonates with philosophical and social scientific literature that has looked at mourning rituals in communities across the African continent. For example, Gladys Ijeoma Akunna (2015) explores the therapeutic aspects of embodied and holistic mourning ritu-als and rites among the Igbo communities in Nigeria, and Baloyi and Makobe-Rabothata (2014) consider cultural implications of an African conception of death.

[2]I juxtapose my cultural experience in the United States with Malawi as this is a meaningful refer-ence point for me. And it's important to note we don't have to go outside of the United States to see similar juxtapositions. For example, as in black lament mentioned above, those coming from "high context" cultures are more connected to embodied experiences than those who come from "low context" cultures, such as most white cultures (Hua, 2013). This will likely manifest itself in how one navigates grief and emotional expression.

This cultural temptation toward numbing and avoiding pain surely spills over into the church. It is manifest in the passages we choose to highlight in the Bible. This poses an intriguing question: do we selectively numb the emotions of the Bible in order to make it more palatable? If we struggle personally with some of the more complex emotions of anger, pain, lament, and protest, might we also tend to pull away from the biblical voices that wrestle with these emotions? Billman and Migliore (1999) suggest it may be the church's hesitancy to go to the complex portions of the Bible that contributes to today's growing biblical illiteracy. Parsing the Bible so that it fails to address suffering and lament is experienced as superficial and disconnected from people's lives.

If we have unwittingly engaged in collectively numbing complex emotions by neglecting part of the biblical witness, then what might be the implications for Christian counselors and psychotherapists? Might our patients fear there is no room to discuss anger, jealousy, lust, and despair? How do we create space for people to talk about difficult emotions?

In a society that struggles to create space for grief and lament, and where our silence suggests to grievers that they "should be over it by now," how do we recall the voice of the psalmist who asks: "How long, O LORD? Will you forget me forever? How long will you hide your face from me?" (Ps 13:1). Will we remember the anguish of a people mourning the destruction of their temple and their city, accusing God in their anger?

> He is a bear lying in wait for me,
> a lion in hiding;
> he led me off my way and tore me to pieces;
> he has made me desolate;
> he bent his bow and set me
> as a mark for his arrow.
>
> He shot into my vitals
> the arrows of his quiver;
> I have become the laughingstock of all my people,
> the object of their taunt-songs all day long.
> He has filled me with bitterness,
> he has sated me with wormwood.
>
> He has made my teeth grind on gravel,
> and made me cower in ashes;

my soul is bereft of peace;
    I have forgotten what happiness is;
so I say, "Gone is my glory,
    and all that I had hoped for from the LORD." (Lam 3:10-18)

Even in citing this provocative passage in Lamentations, we find ourselves eager to look ahead to the following verses: "But this I call to mind, and therefore I have hope: The steadfast love of the LORD never ceases, his mercies never come to an end; they are new every morning; great is your faithfulness" (Lam 3:21-23). Why are we so eager to press forward to the happy places that make up our praise choruses when the entire context is one of anguish and despair?

A fascinating website, topverses.com, which ranks all Bible verses based on how often they are used, shows the most popular verse in the book of Lamentations is 3:22 ("The steadfast love of the LORD never ceases"). How interesting that we note and cite this verse when the entirety of Lamentations 3 is, well, a lamentation. "He has driven and brought me into darkness without any light" (3:2). "He has made my flesh and my skin waste away, and broken my bones" (3:4). "He has besieged and enveloped me with bitterness and tribulation" (3:5). "He has walled me about so that I cannot escape" (3:7). "He is a bear lying in wait for me" (3:10). "He has shot into my vitals the arrows of his quiver" (3:13). "He has made my teeth grind on gravel" (3:16). "You have wrapped yourself with anger and pursued us, killing without pity" (3:43). "You have made us filth and rubbish" (3:45). We cite the hopeful interlude in the middle of the chapter most often, but the context is one of torment and misery. And so also it can be difficult to create space for our patients' distress and alienation to find voice and to see it as part of the sacred work we do as Christian therapists.

Liz, bright and serious, tended to speak in long-winded paragraphs with rapid speech and immediacy. I recall one session where she began with even more urgency than usual. She had recently started yet another new medication. Over the last year the pain from her endometriosis had made her world shrink: dropping out of school, reducing work hours, and experiencing strained relationships. She had already undergone two unsuccessful treatments in attempts to keep her pain at bay. A month into this medication she was experiencing less pain and beginning to imagine a future that didn't entail being bedridden for hours every day. However, having experienced much disappointment before, she was terrified of trusting this glimpse of hope. She worried, "What if God is tricking me?" This comment was discreetly embedded within a litany of other words.

When there was a pause, I inquired about God's trickery: "Do you feel like God has been tricking you?"

Liz replied with an enthusiastic yes. She noted how God had given her glimpses of relief before only for the pain to return twofold. Plus, she had experienced a number of other losses in her life, making it difficult to believe in a God who cares about her. She slowly had slinked away from her faith community and gave words to a faith that no longer held any practical significance in her life.

Liz had tried on the Christian answers to her grief: "God won't give you more than you can handle." Those answers rang hollow to her, and so I bore witness to her deep questions without offering any easy theological solutions. We explored Liz's protest and refusal to be consoled. Could this have even been a holy protest to her suffering? If Rachel's work, as Hebrew scholar Carolyn Sharp (2014) suggests, was to "keep watch in her terrible grief, insisting on fierce dissent from any and all platitudes designed to erase her loss" (para. 6), then perhaps Liz's anger was a holy endeavor following in the line of Rachel.

Resistance is part of lament—resisting the world the way it is—but when was the last time any of us sang a chorus about resistance at church? Resistance is rarely encouraged in the church. We are much more likely to emphasize compliance. Liz encountered resistance in her soul but felt she would need to muster a quiet compliance in order to return to church. We wonder what this assumption—that one should attend church only after one is done resisting—does for the individuals who might otherwise be part of a faith community and what it does for the community itself.

> The true believer, especially in the practice of prayer, is expected to exhibit compliance rather than resistance. . . . The exclusion of the lament screens out people who find the services shallow or harmful. . . . A clear consequence of banishing the many moods of the psalms of lament—among them, anguish, remorse, fury, protest, even hatred—is that we lose an essential resource in confronting the very emotions that terrify us, in a context where we might receive some help in admitting them, understanding them, and coping with them. (Billman & Migliore, 1999, p. 14)

Amidst a society, and sometimes a church, that collectively numbs out difficult emotions, Christian therapists can model a different way. We can bear witness to the complexity of the world, creating spaces that offer another way of interacting with anger and pain. We can provide a context to faithfully explore painful emotions. We model this as we help our patients find language to explore their angst and their voices of resistance and protest.

When Liz asked, "Is God tricking me?" she was attempting to voice her distress and alienation. She lacked a theological frame to make this an acceptable question, and so she retreated from the church. But what if we can bear witness to the people like Liz who pour out their emotions in our offices? What if it was okay for Liz to direct her distress *to* God rather than directing it sideways with a flurry of other words?

Integration Conversation Starters

1. In what ways do you agree and disagree with Brené Brown's idea that we cannot "selectively numb" emotion?
2. Drawing from the psalms, Christian prayer can be viewed as an invitation to full-spectrum living, including all our complex emotions. What forms of prayer have been most useful in bringing you to a full awareness of emotion?
3. We have just argued that resistance as a part of lament might help foster a deeper and richer faith. How might this voice of resistance spiral downward toward bitterness or loss of faith when a community cannot be found to bear witness? Conversely, how might resistance enhance faith for those who can find a community that accepts lament? Where does counseling fit into this conversation?

Embracing whole selves in psychotherapy. Having just discussed the importance of embracing a full array of emotions in psychotherapy, it should also be said that bodies matter. Clearly, our physical health affects our emotional well-being, and vice versa. Having a severe toothache, or being sleep deprived, or having persistent back spasms will almost certainly affect emotions such as joy, sadness, and hope. Conversely, emotional wellness affects physical health. One recent study shows that anxiety and depression predict medical illness as well as or better than obesity and smoking (Niles & O'Donovan, 2019).

I (Mark) recall seeing Eileen early in my career for emotional support, because after fourteen abdominal surgeries the physicians simply could not find a reason for her ongoing pain. We worked together for a year, and she found substantial relief in the process of psychotherapy. Unfortunately, my training rotation was ending and when I left Eileen opted not to see the person I referred her to. When I contacted her several months later for follow-up purposes, I learned that she had just gone through another surgery.

Lament as a spiritual practice is not limited to emotional pain or to physical pain, but is often a complex interaction of the two. We are embodied souls, or ensouled bodies if you prefer, and so when it comes to lament it is important to explore the intersections where physical and emotional pain meet. We are not suggesting that counselors should act like physicians. Of course, it is important to refer whenever new or troubling physical symptoms are disclosed in psychotherapy, but even then, we can remain present to lament emerging from physical suffering.

Christians face the persistent problem of Gnosticism that has plagued us since the early days of the church—a belief that spiritual knowledge matters the most and the physical reality of our existence quite a lot less. But it need not be this way, as Christianity itself is premised on God becoming human and living among us (Jn 1:14). By taking on materiality, God demonstrated its goodness and value. Our bodies matter, and so do the pains we experience in our bodies.

Theologian Kelly Kapic (2017) reflects on how physical suffering and pain influences our experience of God, observing how a person struggling with migraines or chronic pain may experience worship services (e.g., loud music or lights may trigger migraines). Our bodies, including our experiences of pain and suffering, impact our relationship to God and to our communities of faith. Pain causes us to ask God hard questions, and these questions are not only acceptable but are even healthy. Kapic observes, "Heartfelt cries and existential questions operate at the core of healthy theology, and suppressing them is more hurtful than a confession of ignorance" (p. 10). And later he writes, "Lament is a legitimate, even necessary, form of fellowship with God when we are in a place of pain" (p. 29).

Kapic's words serve as a good reminder to counselors and psychotherapists to view the complexity and multidimensionality of persons as we consider the place of lament in our work. Our patients will bring a complex array of sufferings, some of them physical and some emotional, and all of them worthy of our attention and care.

QUERIES FOR PATIENTS

Consider asking your patients questions such as:

1. You're describing an intense sadness. Can we stay here a moment? What if this feeling could just show up right here in the room with us? How would I see the sadness, or where might it show up in your body?

    This is helpful for patients who prefer to tell a cognitive story without exploring much emotion or bodily sensation. Help patients make the connection between their words, feelings, and somatic sensations so they can enter fully into the present moment.

2. As you deal with this diagnosis, and all the pain, how does this affect your heart? What sort of feelings are you wrestling with most these days?

    This is helpful for patients who tend to focus on physical problems and sensations, but not as much on emotions. Making connections between the two can be important for full-bodied lament.

Attachment and lament. Perhaps it's shared genes, but it seems one of the reasons we are both drawn to teaching is because of the mutually transforming work that occurs between professor and student. Mentoring students, watching them stretch, transform, flourish, and in return go into the world to help others flourish is exciting and meaningful work. As the George Fox University doctoral program shifted toward a conversational approach to integration, I (Megan Anna) began hosting book groups. I sensed students craving relational spaces to explore hard questions. Over the years I have hosted conversations exploring the intersection of grief, Christian theology, and psychotherapy.

As students explore hard questions that come up in the face of grief, a number of them have similar reactions: "I thought I was the only one asking these questions. I didn't know it was okay to ask them." Many students experience a collective sigh of relief upon realizing they aren't the only ones, and even deeper sighs of relief to finally have a safe space to explore these questions. Within this relational space we explore some very difficult questions. One topic that leads to enlivened conversation has to do with the intersection of attachment style and grief, exploring how attachment to God may contribute to our ability to ask hard questions, and our ability to engage honestly with our pain and anger. We explore how expressing anger can actually be indicative of a secure attachment: we have hope that God can withstand our anger. Our comfort to sit with lament may be related to how much we believe God can hold our anger and continue to be in relationship with us.[3] Seeing the sparkle of wonder flashing across students' eyes as they contemplate that perhaps God can hold their anger is a transcendent moment.

On YouTube one can find a powerful video enacting Ed Tronick's "Still Face Experiment" (University of Massachusetts, 2009). For a minute we see the mother beautifully attuned to her daughter as she mirrors back the baby's emotions and facial cues. Then, following Tronick's instructions, for two minutes the mom sits expressionless—still faced. The baby quickly notices this disconnection. Painfully, we witness the daughter attempt to engage mom, and when these attempts fail she quickly transitions into protest. The daughter furiously attempts to draw mom back into her world, to make contact, to engage mom as before. Then you begin to see fear and anxiety come across the baby as there is a loss of safety and hope in the face of her mom's stillness. Reflecting on this experiment, Gilligan and Snider (2017) write:

> In this brief two-minute window, we recognize how trust depends not on the goodness of the mother per se or the absence of disconnection, but on the discovery by mother and baby that *they can find one another again* after what in the course of daily living are the inevitable experiences of losing touch. (p. 174, emphasis ours)

When we engage in protest amidst our suffering, perhaps this is akin to the baby who is protesting in attempt to reestablish connection. Amidst suffering and moments of losing touch with God, perhaps we are asking: "God, are you still faced?" Protest is a reaching out to God, a reaching to find God's face amidst disorganizing suffering and pain.

---

[3]Melissa Kelly's (2010) book *Grief* offers a chapter on attachment style to God and grief.

WHAT IS ATTACHMENT THEORY?

Attachment theory grew out of developmental psychology and explores attachment behavior and the emotional ties binding humans together (Simpson & Beckes, 2018). John Bowlby, one of the early pioneers of attachment theory, believed motivation to be linked to an innate desire for emotional attachment (Bowlby, 2008). Attachment bonds early in life are intimately linked to feelings of security and safety (Worden, 2009). According to attachment theory, an individual's experiences with their attachment figure will impact much more than relationships; it influences their experience of "felt security" (Bretherton, 1985, p. 6). Our attachment system influences not only how we approach relationships but also how we self-soothe and find "felt security" during times of stress.

Mary Ainsworth's Strange Situation study (Ainsworth, Blehar, Waters, & Wall, 2015) highlighted different patterns of attachment. She observed how twelve- to eighteen-month-old children responded to undergoing a series of separations and reunions with their primary caregivers. Ainsworth noted that children who exhibited a secure attachment tended to utilize their caregiver as a secure base, meaning that while they were upset when separated they were easily soothed upon their return and could continue exploring their world. Ainsworth also noted another cluster of behaviors characteristic of children with anxious-resistant attachment styles. These children, rather than being soothed by the return of the caregiver would continue to be distressed and display behaviors of resentment and anger toward their caregiver. Finally, a third group deemed anxious-avoidant showed fewer signs of overt distress, but often had an elevated heart rate and would be distant and emotionally detached upon reunion with their caregiver. These children preferred to find methods for self-soothing in contrast to looking to their caregivers for comfort (Bretherton, 1985).

Attachment influences how we soothe negative emotion by affecting our beliefs about what sort of support is available. Those who have consistently experienced safety and comfort in others will likely turn toward another when distressed. Those who experienced less available support tend to prefer self-reliant strategies to control and reduce negative emotions. Those who experienced uncertainty about the comfort and availability of their caregivers may cope by hyperfocusing on significant relationships and anxiously ruminating about reasons why their attachment figure will abandon them (Simpson & Beckes, 2018). This, in turn, has implications for the nature and quality of our relationships throughout life.

Protest is a component of lament. The Gospel of Mark tells the story of the Syrophoenician woman—a Gentile who approaches Jesus bowing at his feet and requesting that he heal her daughter. Jesus' response was a bit cold: "Let the children be fed first, for it is not fair to take the children's food and throw it to the dogs" (Mk 7:27). Shockingly, Jesus uses a religious slur, "little dogs," in his encounter with this woman (Tolbert, 2003). Jesus denies this woman while insulting her religion, essentially responding to her pain with a still face. But the woman has faith and is persistent enough to protest as she undercuts Jesus argument, responding: "Sir, even the dogs under the table eat the children's crumbs" (Mk 7:28). Perhaps it's audacity, perhaps desperation, or perhaps she had enough faith to petition Jesus and trust that he would be impacted, that his face would be moved to respond to her protest.

Similarly, Rachel refused premature consolation and persisted in protesting to God. In the classic Ainsworth Strange Situation study, infants who were securely attached to their mothers protested when removed from their mothers and placed in an unfamiliar environment (Ainsworth et al., 2015). So too, our divine protest can be an indication of our attachment and the trust we experience with God. Protest is birthed in the hope that we believe God to hear and be impacted by us.

Bella learned anger to be a negative emotion during her childhood years, in part because she never witnessed it from her parents and in part by belonging to a performance-based faith community where anger was deemed to be unrighteous. She felt pressure to earn her parent's love through correct and compliant behavior. Perhaps remarkably, as an adult she maintained her relationship with God and continued to draw on God as a source of strength despite her early painful religious experiences.

Six months into our work together, Bella experienced a sexual assault. She felt confused and sad but didn't know how to be angry. She especially didn't know how to be angry with God. At first, she pushed this to the side by taking the anger on herself by believing God must be punishing her, that she did something to deserve this assault. The danger with believing God works in this cause-and-effect sort of way is that someone has to take on the badness: either God (for causing/allowing it) or oneself for doing something to deserve it. Bella was taking on the badness and internalizing it. She was unable to believe that God could hold her anger and continue to be in relation with her, much as Bella's mother was unable to hold Bella's negative emotions and continue to extend maternal love toward her. As Bella internalized this negative message she sunk deeper into a depression. I didn't directly challenge Bella's beliefs, which would have been too disorienting, but instead I gently probed to see if there was space to bring other voices alongside her theology. One session I brought the following words from Nicholas Wolterstorff (1987), written after his son died in a climbing accident:

> For a long time I knew that God is not the impassive, unresponsive, unchanging being portrayed by the classical theologians. I knew of the pathos of God. I knew of God's response of delight and of his response of displeasure. But strangely, his suffering I never saw before. God is not only the God of the sufferers but the God who suffers. The pain and fallenness of humanity have entered into his heart. Through the prism of my tears I have seen a suffering God. It is said of God that no one can behold his face and live. I always thought this meant that no one could see his splendor and live. A friend said perhaps it meant that no one could see his sorrow and live. Or perhaps his sorrow is splendor. And great mystery: to redeem our brokenness and lovelessness the God who suffers with us did not strike some mighty blow of power but sent his beloved son to suffer like us, through his suffering to redeem us from suffering and evil. Instead of explaining our suffering God shares it. (pp. 81-82)

Together we wondered if there was space in her life for a God who perhaps was suffering with her in this pain. This opened up a space where Bella was able to articulate a deep longing to be held by God and momentary glimpses in her life when she had experienced this maternal sense of God holding her. Not by deconstructing her theology, but by adding to it, we were able to explore a different aspect of Bella's attachment to God, a part of God who was able to be in the trenches with her, not over her orchestrating the drama, ensuring her misery. Together we explored her acute pain, acknowledged in the presence of a loving God. She allowed me to bear witness to her pain, and in some way this helped point her toward a God who will hold her most complex emotions and experiences.

Integration Conversation Starters

1. When you think about protesting to God or expressing your anger toward God, what comes to mind? In what ways does the idea of protesting comfort or alarm you?

2. After reviewing the Still Face video on YouTube (www.youtube.com/watch ?v=apzXGEbZht0), ponder moments in therapy when you may have inadvertently been like the still-faced parent. What does it look like to recover from these moments in therapy and repair the relationship with your patient? How does the recovery remind you of God's relationship with humanity?

3. Considering the relational nature of lament, how does the Christian psychotherapist represent God to patients in the therapy office, especially in the moments of deep anguish and despair? How might a psychotherapist misstep in these moments and fail to represent God well?

Moving away from and moving into human experience. As a part of the conversation book groups, mentioned above, I often open our time together with a poem. This often leads to the creation of shared metaphor and imagery we return to throughout the conversation. Recently, I brought in a poem by Nayyirah Waheed (2013)—a work that poignantly explores how people will constrict or expand when hearing another's story.

This poem became integral to our conversations together; we began exploring what it means to expand in the face of another's story, and what it looks like when we contract. We explored our own tendencies to either expand or contract in the face of grief.

One of the themes we have been exploring in this chapter is the vulnerability within Christian history toward constricting in the face of pain and grief. Christian history is scattered with such stories. We suspect this is partly due to the vulnerability to elevate the spiritual above the material (dualism). And yet, the Christian faith has always been about the eternal Word being made flesh. That is, Christianity—properly conceived—has always held to the dynamic interaction of materiality and spirituality so that the two cannot be neatly separated.

Even the great pioneers of the faith struggled with the tendency to be dualistic at times. For example, Augustine believed grief ought to be reserved for things pertaining to our relationship to God and saw sorrow over earthly attachments as weakness. Thus, Augustine reserved lament for his sins and held reservations about experiencing sorrow for the other losses life invariably brings. Interestingly, Augustine's conversion to Christianity—chronicled so beautifully in *Confessions*—actually made it more difficult for him to express sorrow (Augustine, trans. 1986). Prior to his conversion he freely grieved and mourned the loss of a close friend (expanding to fully experience and embrace the pain). After his conversion, when his mother died he intentionally constricted, holding back tears and berating himself for weeping, which he managed to isolate to just "part of an hour" (Billman & Migliore, 1999, p. 48). Believing that a Christian's grief ought to be restrained, Augustine lamented that emotions could grab hold of him in such a moment. He saw grief as a false attachment to something earthly, calling him to exert more reason to better control his emotions and affections.

Since Augustine, many theologians and church leaders have followed a similar pattern of thought: the image of God imparted in us is manifest most fully through human reason, and the role of human reason is to keep the body and emotions in check so that we can move toward greater sanctification and holiness. We move further from our experience of this world in order to move closer to the heavens. Holiness is found in constricting in the face of earthly pain.

When I brought in Nayyirah Waheed's poem to my conversation group, we talked about grief and meaning: how our meaning-making system (i.e., our religious or philosophical frame that helps us make meaning of the world) holds grief and at times is shifted by grief. At times, loss fits nicely into our system and we can integrate it in. For example, when an elderly person dies after a full and well-lived life, this can easily fit into many of our meaning-making systems. While this doesn't take the sting of loss away, it gives us a system from which to experience and hold the loss. Other times, the loss cannot be integrated (examples of losses that may be difficult to integrate include the loss of a child, a sudden divorce, and so on). The loss comes skyrocketing down, shattering our meaning-making system in the process. We're left with loss and without a narrative to hold it.

Melissa Kelly (2010), a pastoral counselor, discusses how one response to the loss of a meaning-making system is for a person's narrative to shrivel, to become frozen. People can become frozen in their shriveled narrative for a lifetime. The sterile, medicalized term we have given to such frozenness: complex grief. Complex grief—this feels like a frozen label. Perhaps we in the medical community, too, fall prey to frozen, shriveled narratives.

Expansion brings healing. The work of the therapist is to help narratives expand—to foster narratives that can take in new life and new meaning,

MOVING AWAY IN THE COUNSELING OFFICE

Lest we be too hard on Augustine, I (Mark) should note that I have faced a lifelong struggle moving away from human experience in the counseling office. It's as if I'm a psychotherapy gnostic. I know enough to look for emotion in my patients' faces, and to encourage free expression of feelings, but when the emotion shows up in the room, I have a tendency to turn and run from it.

Some years ago, I was asked to film a therapy session for the American Psychological Association's psychotherapy series. The focus of this particular series was on spirituality, and my session was to illustrate Christian counseling. By God's providence, I ended up working with a delightful patient named Celeste, who had enormous capacity to handle stress and manage multiple responsibilities. But with all the responsibility she took on, she sometimes felt overwhelmed and exhausted. Near the end of our session Celeste and I went through a brief prayer-based meditation exercise, and when we

opened our eyes I noticed tears streaming down her face. Every experienced psychotherapist knows this is a critical moment because the tears indicate that we have truly moved into an important emotional space for the patient. What did I do at that critical juncture? I escaped into a cognitive observation by saying, "Now we only did this exercise for a few moments, but I imagine if you did this at home it might have an even more powerful effect for you." Never mind that this was wrong —the power of doing the prayer exercise together made it powerful—it also distracted from this essential moment in our session.

Fortunately, I have gotten better over the years noticing when I distance from my patients' emotions. I caught myself quickly with Celeste, so the next thing out of my mouth was, "Talk about the tears. Where do the tears come from?" And with this, we were able to move back into that sacred space of human sorrow that she was experiencing in the moment.

expanding enough to take in all of what it means to be alive. As we discussed these ideas, the metaphor of thawing emerged. When we attempt to move with people too quickly this can cause breakage—their stories are icicles. Cultivating meaning starts with thawing. You don't try to shift an icicle or it breaks, fragmenting into pieces. First, you must thaw. Expanding around the icicle, cradling it; this is thawing. Therapy involves thawing, and yet it is difficult to host a thawing space when constricted. This work requires expanding in the face of grief. And perhaps, this is precisely what lament is: expansion in the face of suffering.

Intrapersonal Conversation Starters

1. Can you think of a time that someone expanded in the face of your story? What was that like for you? What about a time you shared something vulnerable and the person contracted? What was that like?
2. What does your relationship to grief look like? Do you find yourself more likely to expand or constrict in the face of grief? Do you respond differently to different kinds of grief/losses?

Depression and lament. Freud famously suggested that depression is anger turned inward toward the self. This assertion has been the topic of much scientific research over the years, with about half the studies supporting Freud's conclusion, a quarter contradicting it, and a quarter being inconclusive (Abi-Habib & Luyten, 2013). One of the challenges in testing Freud's idea is that depression itself is a complex array of different experiences that are not contained in a single diagnosis. Whereas a particular virus might cause a predictable set of symptoms—sore throat, congestion, fatigue—depression is multifaceted, arises from multiple causes, and cannot be easily described with particular symptoms.

Recent work in Belgium suggests that the dependent nature of depression—that is, the unhealthy yearning to be taken care of coupled with excessive fears of abandonment—is indeed related to the tendency to turn anger inward toward the self (Abi-Habib & Luyten, 2013). In this sense, anger is turned in toward an isolated, fearful place where the self can feel easily abandoned, alone in the cosmos. It's no wonder feelings of depression are related to this sort of loneliness. At its worst, depression feels like a lonely void where no one can understand, and no one is present to hear. And so, the anger turns inward to fester in isolation and despair, and the depressive cycle churns on.

In contrast, lament assumes someone else—someone bigger and more powerful—is present to listen to our grievances. We are not alone in the universe, but an ever-attending God is with us, present to our experiences. Those with close friends or partners will recognize that one privilege (and cost?) of intimacy is being present to the other in good days and bad. Lovers have quarrels, which in one sense is a great privilege because there is a lover present to quarrel with. We tend not to bring our deepest anguish to more casual friends—keeping the polite distance that is socially acceptable—but to those who know our hearts the best, we cry out our complaints, whether they are rational or not, whether our partner can fix or heal anything or not. Lament implies that God is close, that we have God's ear, that God cares for and about us.

In their book on pastoral care, Mitchell and Anderson (1983) write about the mysterious nature of loss and how it often causes us to hold scolding attitudes toward God.

> Raging at God is a part of the Hebrew tradition. The Psalms of lament are filled with anger at God for God's absence and seeming disregard for the plight of God's people. Anger, especially as a part of grief, is not contrary to faith or faithfulness. (p. 79)

Similarly, Jeremiah did not engage in self-pitying monologues, but in passionate and active dialogs with God. If depression involves turning away from others and turning inward, how much better it is to hold the hope of a listening other and to speak courageous words of lament. "It is not voicing pain in a vacuum that is healing, but voicing pain in concert with others" (Billman & Migliore, 1999, p. 78).

Notice also that lament, like a lovers' quarrel, implies the possibility of forward movement (Snow, McMinn, Bufford, & Brendlinger, 2011). If depression is turning anger to an inner void of aloneness, then lament goes the other direction—speaking out the anger, directing it toward God with the hope that balance and perspective and hope will somehow be regained.

But what do we make of anger toward God that exists without the hope of forward movement? Two decades of research demonstrate that longstanding anger toward God is associated with all sorts of physical and emotional problems, including depression, anxiety, stress, and relationship difficulties (Exline & Martin, 2005; Strelan, Acton, & Patrick, 2009; Wood et al., 2010).

Among those who are highly devoted to their religious faith, an interesting paradox emerges. They are more likely than others to see anger and protest at God as morally wrong and unacceptable, but at the same time they feel greater freedom to protest to God, especially if they experience secure attachment with God (Exline, Kaplan, & Grubbs, 2012). Those of us who are devoted to faith may find this a familiar place: we are initially hesitant to protest to God because we don't see much precedent these days for crying out to God. We may believe it to be morally wrong, or we may wonder if our relationship with God is secure enough to hold our anger. But if we believe God is on our side then we may be more likely to express our pain forthrightly. If we can push past the initial obstacles to lament, our cries spring forth with the hope that voicing a concern in the context of intimate relationship brings healing that can never be found in the silent void of unexpressed anger and grievances.

What does all this mean for how we think about treating depression from a Christian worldview? Several tentative conclusions seem important to consider, though much more theological and social scientific work needs to be done on the topic. First, some depressions tend to be marked by an increased longing for connection and desire to be cared for by others. These depressions are also characterized by a tendency to turn anger inward toward the self. Taken together, this yearning for connection coupled with an inward facing anger may cause a deep sense of isolation and despair—a profound existential aloneness. Second, when people of faith experience this sort of depression, they may feel quite abandoned by God in their aloneness. In that lonely place of festering anger, they may experience all sorts of physical and mental health concerns. Third, therapeutic missteps are easy in this situation. Traditional psychotherapy training, with its poverty of considering religious and spiritual issues (Vogel, McMinn, Peterson, & Gathercoal, 2013), may encourage us to ignore the spiritual dimensions of anger in these patients. Or even worse, some psychotherapists may be inclined to encourage their patients to further distance themselves from God by questioning their religious beliefs. Even those who are trained in Christian counseling might inadvertently discourage their patients from their feelings of anger and abandonment, as if such expressions are contrary to a life of faith. Fourth, one way forward is to gently help patients give voice to their anguish and feelings of abandonment, to express these openly to God, to expand rather than constrict, to allow a lovers' quarrel so that healing can ensue. This is the way of the Hebrew Scriptures as people experienced deep suffering and anguish, and ultimately found renewed hope in God by walking in the way of lament.

Integration Conversation Starters

1. Can you personally identify with the tendency to pull inward and silence your anger toward God? What would it look like to engage in a lovers' quarrel rather than isolating your feelings in your own interior world?

2. Sometimes counselors encourage patients to move away from their faith or their faith communities in times of deep question and doubt. Can you imagine ways this might actually worsen the problem?

Grief and lament. I (Megan Anna) met Pamela shortly after her daughter, Rose, died tragically during a traumatic birth. Pamela was struggling with flashbacks and trauma symptoms associated with the birth and losing Rose. Pamela described her experience of being in the hospital room holding Rose's body, her own body still out of sorts from the traumatic birth—sleepy eyed and tearful—when a social worker came in and handed her a handout on the stages of grief. Keep in mind that these are Pamela's memories. It's most likely that the social worker did more than this within this terribly awkward and painful situation, but the handout left Pamela feeling like it was an encounter marked by objectification, as if she were a patient needing a fix more than a suffering soul in need of a companion.

Inside of suffering and grief there is often a strong pull to constrict and to distance oneself from the one grieving. Death makes us uncomfortable as it brings awareness of our own mortality and existential terror to the surface. Death, dying, grief—these are mysterious things that no matter how hard we try we cannot control. And the mind likes to be in control. One way the mind tries to exert control is to hide the bereaving in our culture, to distance from the grieving.

Elisabeth Kübler-Ross (1969) did remarkable work in making the process of death and dying less mysterious by articulating discrete stages of grief in her work with terminally ill patients. Her work to help name the emotions and experiences around grief has been profoundly empowering for many. These stages of grief are now understood to be quite fluid rather than a step-by-step process for dealing with loss (Worden, 2009). When they are used well, they can be anchoring points for people to help gather their thoughts and name their experiences amidst the turmoil of loss. Unfortunately, at times the stages of grief have been used in a distancing manner, a way of trying to move people through and out of their grief as quickly as possible or to pin down an objective. In Pamela's situation, these stages had been delivered as an impersonal handout.

I (Mark) worked on a medical psychology floor years ago where the medical doctors often called the psychology staff to help out with the emotional dimensions of medical care. Sometimes we received referrals from physicians concerned that a patient was "in denial" after being diagnosed with a terminal illness. Denial is the first stage in Kübler-Ross's model, so our first task was often to educate the physician about the form grief often takes. But even more, these calls pointed toward a patient in crisis—one who had just been told that life is slipping away—who needed a compassionate presence more than an explanation of the pathology or an estimate of how many weeks or months of life might still remain. Those of us on the medical psychology staff would go sit with these patients in their grief, and allow them to explore and express their varying emotions, questions, and doubts. We helped give form to their grief by sitting with them in their denial or whatever else they might be experiencing in the darkest moments of life.

Notice two things in what we are writing about grief. First, it benefits from formfulness. One of Kübler-Ross's great gifts to the helping profession was offering a structure for how grief happens. To this, we would add that lament is about facilitating formful, transformative encounters within grief. We have mentioned the sidebar "Lament and Formful Grief" several times throughout this chapter because it mentions the importance of bringing formfulness into both lament and grief. By offering form we offer restoration and rehabilitation to those who suffer. In this chapter we have suggested a form to move from grief to lament where 1) suffering is experienced, 2) we cry out in our pain, 3) we resist the way things are, and 4) we experience some hope that our cries will be heard, and even grateful reflection that this is likely the case. This is not intended as a prescriptive form for lament, but as one structure that opens people up to the possibility of true encounter with God with all its potential for transformation.

Second, no amount of formfulness can ever replace the importance of a person-to-person encounter. Grief is not something we simply "get over." If we overemphasize form, we unwittingly contribute to the illusion that grief is more a passing trial than something we must learn to live with. Lament may be helpful in this regard because it assumes a relational dimension to suffering. Lament occurs when one person cries out to another. In this, it is not so much a process that starts and stops, but a conversation with God that we may return to at any point. As Black (2005) poignantly writes: "An impatient, death-denying society demands that sufferers 'get over it.' . . . In this life are things for which there's no getting over; such belong to the land of lament" (p. 55). This imagery that Black puts forth reminds us that form is not enough; we long for relational formfulness where a stable companion is willing to receive our words at every point along the journey. The attachments formed in this sort of journey never cease; they transform.

I (Mark) recall a transformative encounter with a fourteen-year-old girl dying of brain cancer. My job was to do an interview and conduct a neuro-psychology screener to assess her current level of cognitive functioning. In the process of preparing for the evaluation I spoke with this girl's parents and the physician overseeing her treatment and was simply overwhelmed with the angst and pathos they all experienced. I recall both a profound empathy and a feeling of uselessness going into this evaluation, wondering what words I could possibly offer to a dying girl. Working in a university hospital setting, I had heard many stories of ill-timed and painful words carelessly offered, and I imagined how readily I might slip into a similar place as I fumbled for words in the face of unspeakable tragedy.

When I walked into the room to sit with this young patient, I was carrying my own angst into the room with me, even as I longed to be present to hers. My soul settled quickly as two things became clear within the first five minutes of our interview. First, this girl loved her life and was sad to be letting it go. Second, she had made peace with dying, even more so than her parents, attending physician, or me. She had walked the journey of grief and loss with those who loved her and would be willing to give up their own lives if it would have saved hers, but the death was to be hers to bear. In awakening to the reality of death she demonstrated something that strangely resembled joy. It was an enlivening buoyancy, a profound awareness that she was dying but probably not today. Thirty-five years later this remains one of the most memorable encounters of my professional life, not so much because she had completed the stages of grief that Kübler-Ross suggested but because we shared a person-to-person encounter that was meaningful to both of us. Grief cannot be contained in a handout—it needs a relationship to bear witness to what is happening.

Integration Conversation Starters

1. Attachment language may be a helpful way of discussing one's relationship to grief counseling. For example, a counselor who relates anxiously to grief may feel pressure to hurry up and "fix" the patient, sprinting through interventions and creating a treatment plan to work quickly through the stages of grief. A counselor who avoidantly relates to grief may be quick to provide a patient with a handout but not engage emotionally. A counselor who securely relates to grief might sit still with the patient, allowing the feelings that are present to be there without a need to fix or run away. Realizing that your relationship to grief is not reflective of your overall attachment style, which mode of relating to grief do you feel pulled toward? What experiences do you notice when sitting with people in pain? When do you want to run, fix, be?

2. In reading through the lament psalms (Psalms 44, 60, 74, 79, 80, 85, 90), where do you notice the formfulness of lament? Where do you notice the relational encounters of lament?

Disembodied healing. Art critic Robert Hughes (1993) explores the complex relationship that America has with complaint, observing that "complaint gives you power—even when it's only the power of emotional bribery" (p. 9). In exploring our culture of complaint, Hughes ties this in to what he sees as a larger tendency of American culture toward experiencing a "fetish" with victimhood (p. 11).

It feels odd to be drawing from Hughes in a book about psychotherapy, as he was not a fan of our work. He criticizes psychologists as perpetuating America's culture of victimhood, accusing us of encouraging folks to overly focus on finding the "inner child" when we ought to be focusing on finding the "inner adult" (p. 8). As someone influenced by the psychoanalytic tradition, who believes exploring my inner child may indeed help me find my inner adult, I (Megan Anna) cringe at the binary created by Hughes. My natural reaction is to be defensive when reading his work. But this book is about conversation, so I'm leaning into his words to see if perhaps there are some truths in his social critique that are valuable to consider in our work as counselors and psychotherapists.

Embedded in Hughes's critique is his reflection of the tendency for Americans to be living increasingly fragmented and disembodied lives. Our obsession with complaint and victimhood is simply one symptom of this. Might it be that disembodied, fragmented living leads to disembodied grieving and healing? Perhaps synthetic grieving contributes to synthetic living.

Later in the book (chapter four), you will meet Beth, a woman who tragically lost her daughter at twenty-six weeks pregnant. She had the option to "stuff her grief" in a corner and not address it while also seeing that doing so would mean cutting off a part of herself. She could continue with her busy, hectic, disembodied lifestyle, or she could stop and listen for a moment. Beth was brave. She chose lament. She remained alive to her grief, embodied it, and carried it with her every day, and in the process she allowed it to mold, influence, and change her.

Could it be that even some forms of hope that we encounter in the counseling office are disembodied, tepid forms of hope contrived to help avoid feeling pain, disappointment, and grief? Stark (2019) refers to this as a "relentless hope," serving as a defense against the difficult work of grieving. In contrast, fearless grieving allows us to more deeply engage life. As we grieve what is not, what we wanted, and what we have lost, we have a mysterious and paradoxical opportunity to engage more fully in the present reality of life. And so it is with lament. Placed in a context of relationship, expressing the deepest anguish and sufferings of life can help us embrace life itself more fully.

Integration Conversation Starters

1. What is the cost of not grieving? What is the cost of grieving? Which cost are you willing to live with? How does that impact your work as a counselor or psychotherapist?

2. Where do you see "synthetic" or "disembodied" living; what are some of the contributing factors in your cultural context? As Christian psychotherapists and counselors, how can we speak to this culture and invite people into living embodied, whole lives?

Further Reading

Billings, J. T. (2015). *Rejoicing in lament: Wrestling with incurable cancer & life in Christ.* Grand Rapids: Brazos Press.

Hall, M. E. L. (2016). Suffering in God's presence: The role of lament in transformation. *Journal of Spiritual Formation & Soul Care, 9,* 219-32.

Kapic, K. M. (2017). *Embodied hope: A theological meditation on pain and suffering.* Downers Grove, IL: InterVarsity Press.

McKee, Tim. (2015, October). The geography of sorrow: Francis Weller on navigating our losses. *The Sun Magazine.* Retrieved from http://www.thesunmagazine.org/issues /478/the-geography-of-sorrow

Wolterstorff, N. (1987). *Lament for a son.* Grand Rapids: Eerdmans.

Further Listening/Watching

McInerny, N. (2019, April). *Nora McInerny: We don't move on from grief we move forward with it* [Video file]. Retrieved from http://www.ted.com/talks/nora_mcinerny_we_don _t_move_on_from_grief_we_move_forward_with_it?

Rosa, E. (Producer). (2019, May 20). "Defiant hope: Kelly Kapic on lament, finitude, community, and the cross" [Audio podcast]. *The Table Podcast.* Retrieved from http://cct .biola.edu/defiant-hope-kelly-kapic-lament-finitude-community-cross/

Rosa, E. (Producer). (2018, December 10). "Rejoicing in lament: J. Todd Billings on life with Christ and terminal cancer" [Audio podcast]. *The Table Podcast.* Retrieved from http://cct.biola.edu/rejoicing-lament-j-todd-billings-life-christ-terminal-cancer/

Tippett, K. (Host). (2018, December 18). "Walter Brueggemann—'The Prophetic Imagination'" [Audio podcast]. *On Being.* Retrieved from http://onbeing.org/programs/walter -brueggemann-the-prophetic-imagination-dec2018/

2

Uncertainty, Meaning, and Enjoyment

DOES ANYTHING MAKE SENSE WHEN THE WORLD IS SUCH A MESS?

I (MEGAN ANNA) BEGAN WORKING with Kennedy to address anxiety and depression shortly after she delivered her son. Kennedy described her partner, Alexandro, as loving, supportive, and one of the few relationships in her life where she experienced being seen, known, and loved. She discussed her anxiety about Alexandro being a "dreamer" (he immigrated to the United States in childhood, with his parents and without documentation, and prior to 2007). Under the Deferred Action for Childhood Arrivals (DACA) bill, his ability to stay in the country and have access to streamlined citizenship was safe. Though there had been a number of individuals deported in the communities surrounding us, Kennedy clung to Alexandro's DACA status as her beacon of hope.

One Monday morning I greeted Kennedy in the waiting room, noticing she appeared more visibly sad than previous weeks; she walked a little slower, eyes downcast. When we sat down she informed me of the news that DACA had been revoked that very day. After silently berating myself for not being on top of the news, I was able to catch back up to the moment and sit with her in the face of terror—this fear of the unknown in a climate of uncertainty. One of the questions Kennedy and I sat with that day looked something like this: How are we to be, how are we to live in the face of uncertainty and chaos?

Lately it feels like I sit with my patients in this question quite a lot. An elderly patient attended a 150-year-old church, an anchor of our community, that just endured a grueling and painful church split after a two-year process over disagreement about how to address human sexuality and Christian ethics. She and her children have different views on this, so the tidal wave that ripped through the church body is now tearing through her family. She is uncertain what the future of her family will look like. Then there is the young Buddhist journalist I see who engages life's existential questions. As the grip of her mortality takes hold she slips into panic attacks and a tendency to dissociate. Uncertain of the afterlife, she finds herself spinning in the uncertainty of it all, leaving her feeling that life is meaningless. She asks poignant and difficult questions: How do I live, how do I interact with my children, my partner, my work when life feels utterly meaningless?

I (Mark) recall sitting with a pastor whose wife had suddenly left him after reconnecting with a former boyfriend at a high school reunion. We sat together week after week pondering questions that seemed far too big for answers. One particular session lingers in my mind where we simply ran out of questions. We sat in silence for ten minutes or so, my patient in tears and me fighting back mine. In moments such as these, words often seem cheap and inadequate, so we simply sat together in uncertainty and confusion. Those ten minutes were the turning point in our work together—not because we solved anything, but because we were simply able to be together, to be aligned in a world that sometimes seems so misaligned.

We start this chapter with clinical examples, but the uncertainty and destabilization of the world settles on us as therapists just as surely as it settles on our patients. This is the world where millions of Jews were exterminated in death camps less than a century ago, where we now have bombs that can decimate the world, where terrorists fly planes into skyscrapers, where disillusioned young males show up with automatic weapons in public schools and movie theaters, and where information about all of these tragic realities is now instantly available on the phones in our pockets and the watches on our wrists. All of us—patients and therapists and everyone else—live as uncertain souls in a destabilized world.

This is not unique to our time or our smartphones. Humans across all times and cultures have asked questions around meaning and uncertainty.

Not surprisingly, these questions enter the therapeutic space. I (Megan Anna) recently heard psychoanalyst Marilyn Charles assert: "We aren't taking seriously that we are living in a destabilized world."[1] Global destabilization is with us in the therapy room. What are our guideposts and anchoring points amidst the destabilization and chaos? Theologically, what is our grounding during times of chaos? Psychologically, when public events are touching and impacting the personal lives of our patients, how do we navigate this—and how does our theology inform how we navigate this?

Questions such as these make us thankful that Ecclesiastes did in fact make it into the biblical canon. At a time when destabilization is causing many to question their faith, isn't it interesting that the sacred text of our faith includes a book about destabilization and disillusionment?

Ecclesiastes

Ecclesiastes has been described in all sorts of provocative and dark ways, ranging from being the strangest book of the Bible to being an obituary of humanity to having the smell of a tomb (Brown, 2011). So why is this strange obituary of a book that smells of death my favorite book in the Bible? Because this is where I (Megan Anna) can go in the biblical canon to find someone that gives me language amidst existential crises. And more so, the author of Ecclesiastes has an idea or two about how to live well amidst crises.

I experienced my own destabilization while at Wheaton College as I was beginning to rethink cornerstone beliefs of my evangelical faith. I channeled my existential anxiety into study and prayer. Ecclesiastes was soothing balm to my unnerved self. I've always been a sort of "messy" Christian, raising obnoxious questions in my attempt to better understand a thing. I loved the Gospels and portions of the Hebrew Scriptures, and struggled more with Paul's structured, systematic discourse, which felt a little too neat and tidy for my experience of the world. I wasn't sure there was a version of Christianity that I fit into. But while pouring over Ecclesiastes I began to see a version of faith, present in Scripture, that resonates with my questions. Ecclesiastes taught me how to live well and faithfully amidst the uncertainty of my many questions. Ecclesiastes spoke to my experience of being a paradoxical, complex human living in a messy world.

---

[1] Marilyn Charles, informal lecture, (November, 2017), George Fox University, Newberg, OR.

Ecclesiastes hovers at the margins of the biblical canon. No other book in the Bible has had its authority called into question as frequently. Even from the beginning, folks felt uncertain about its inclusion in the canon. Early rabbis attempted to remove it from circulation, arguing it was internally inconsistent and heretical. Finally, in 90 CE the book gained approval at the gathering of rabbis at Jamnia, but even after this decision questions about its fit continued to be raised for the next several centuries (Brown, 2011). In modern time Ecclesiastes remains at the margins with preachers, theologians, and readers, who are often uncertain of what to do with this mysterious and dark text.

Perhaps the reason preachers tend to avoid Ecclesiastes is that folks struggle to make sense of the apparent contradictions within the text. Much debate has centered around the author, Qoheleth. Was he a depressed workaholic, a cynic, an angry skeptic, or was he a preacher of joy, optimistically naive? How does Qoheleth say in one moment, "Everything is meaningless" (Eccles 1:1 NIV), and yet in the next breath say, "Eat and drink and be glad" (Eccles 8:15 NIV)? Is this our first biblical example of someone struggling with bipolar disorder? Some theologians explain the apparent contradictions in Ecclesiastes not by locating them within Qoheleth but rather by suggesting that he is observing contradictions in his world. He is raising the contradictions not to solve them but to bear witness to them (Fox, 1999).

This intermingling of joy and disillusionment is made more meaningful when understood within Qoheleth's sociohistorical context. Consider this an informed consent: the next few pages will be for those interested in theologically taking a deep dive with me (i.e., exercising your left brain through "anchored ideas" as discussed in the introduction).

The Problem of Hebel

Psychologists often speak of the biopsychosocial-spiritual model in conceptualizing patients. Put simply, we are contextual beings impacted by our backdrop. Similarly, the writing of Qoheleth was significantly influenced by his context. While there is certainly much debate around when Ecclesiastes was written, recent scholarship has converged on a postexilic dating. Based on distinctive linguistic features along with key phrases, idioms, and references to certain economic and social factors, many scholars place the

WHO IS QOHELETH?

You may notice that we are writing about the author of Ecclesiastes as Qoheleth. *Ecclesiastes* is the Greek translation of the Hebrew word *Qohelet,* which comes from the word *qahal* ("to assemble, gather"). *Qoheleth* is the book's supposed author and is understood as some sort of officer or "gatherer" of an assembly (Longman, 1998). Many have assumed the book to be written by Solomon because the author identifies himself as the son of David in the first sentence of the book. But the name Solomon is never mentioned in the book, and in one place the author refers to surpassing all who were before him in Jerusalem (Eccles 2:9). That would be a strange phrase for Solomon to write because his only predecessor as king would have been David, his father (Limburg, 2006). It may feel uncomfortable to consider authorship other than King Solomon; however, fictional autobiography was a common literary practice throughout the ancient Near East (Longman, 1998; Snell, 2008).

Scholars continue to debate the date of Ecclesiastes, though many agree that the distinctive linguistic features in Ecclesiastes preclude it from being written prior to the Babylonian exile (Longman, 1998; Seow, 1997). Part of the beauty of Scripture is that the various texts reflect God's character, the human personalities of the authors, and the literary styles and motifs of the day, such as linking Ecclesiastes to the wisdom of Solomon by the author identifying as the son of David (Limburg, 2006). The reason we bring authorship into this conversation at all is because the sociopolitical context (and therefore the dating) of this text matters a great deal in understanding the theology of Qoheleth. These are not simply the musings of a king late in life who spent his days living in extravagant luxury and his nights with one of a thousand wives or concubines, but rather the critical insights of a culture of wisdom gathered through centuries of Hebrew history.

writing of Ecclesiastes within the Persian rule (Achaemenid Empire) of Palestine around 450 to 225 BCE. This would have been after the seventy-year captivity in Babylon, after Cyrus the Great conquered Babylon, giving the Jews permission to return to Palestine (Brown, 2011; Limburg, 2006; Longman, 1998; Seow, 1997).

The Hebrew people were transitioning to their homeland: rebuilding homes and temples. This was done in the backdrop of global uncertainty and rapid political and economic changes. Perhaps the most significant shift had to do with the transition to currency as the standard means of trade.

Some readers may recall the fear and anxiety that occurred at the turn of the century due to the Y2K fear. Given our transition to a digital world with digital calendars and dates, problems arose with how we were going to enter into the next century. Thankfully, there were smart people who foresaw the potential pitfalls and prevented crises from occurring. But what if they hadn't? What might have happened if bank accounts, personal devices, and military software had all fallen off of the rails? It would have been a mess (hence people stocking up on food and water as if a disaster were about to strike)! Qoheleth's audience was living in a similar mess as the transition to a standardized economy was creating uncertainty, chaos, and unpredictability (Seow, 1997). As we know from psychology, the mind likes predictability, it likes taking the guesswork out of our daily lives. This is why habits form such a bedrock of our existence. Psychologist William James (1887) referred to habits as the "enormous fly-wheel of society" (p. 447). When we create habits, we automatically follow a preapproved pathway of actions and steps. Habits are a sort of shortcut for the brain, their predictability and reliability are soothing to the mind.[2] The mind craves predictability; this is part of what is so distressing when experiencing uncertainty. Qoheleth's world was an unpredictable world.

The infusion of money led to an economy that experienced both volatility and vitality. The market was volatile, which meant one could easily lose everything. But on the flip side, those who made lucky investments could become insanely rich overnight. The world Qoheleth spoke into was utterly turned upside down by the monetary revolution. While there was much to fear, there was also the allure of prosperity. It was the combination of being lured in by the fantasy of wealth paired with the likelihood of experiencing economic (and social) devastation that led Seow (2001) to describe this world as one marked with "openings and pitfalls" (p. 242). People were drawn into a fantasy only to find themselves falling into destruction, exacerbating people's existential angst.

On top of the monetary revolution the Persian empire also placed an oppressive tax system on the people. The taxation led to an overwhelming

---

[2]For more on habits and the mind, check out *The Power of Habit* by Charles Duhigg (2014).

burden on the common folks. People were borrowing money simply to pay their taxes. And they were borrowing money in an economy where interest rates were unpredictable and could skyrocket without notice, putting people at risk of defaulting on their loans. With no such thing as bankruptcy, to default on a loan meant foreclosure, detention, or even enslavement (Seow, 1997; Seow, 2001).

The dread and anxiety were further intensified because things that used to provide a sense of security and control were breaking down. Social roles no longer offered the security and peace of mind they once did. Even kings could fall into the pitfalls and meet utter destruction! Qoheleth laments this as he writes, "Folly is set in many high places, and the rich sit in a low place. I have seen slaves on horseback, and princes walking on foot like slaves" (Eccles 10:6-7). In this unpredictable world people struggled to feel secure and safe.

In addition to the social upheaval, keep in mind that the Hebrew people had recently returned to their Promised Land where God had delivered their ancestors, and with a religious conviction that righteousness buffered one from disaster. The wisdom tradition supported by Psalms and Proverbs suggests that God honors the righteous and punishes the wicked, thereby offering a sense of security and safety. Yet in Qoheleth's world it appears not to matter if one is righteous or wicked; all are at risk of falling into destruction. One can imagine Qoheleth simply shaking his head in disbelief as he writes: "There are righteous people who are treated according to the conduct of the wicked, and there are wicked people who are treated according to the conduct of the righteous" (Eccles 8:14). The very fabric of their theological code—the wisdom tradition that had brought a sense of comfort and safety—was breaking down.

With the old paradigm fraying (God will bless and protect the righteous, e.g., Ps 5:12), people were left feeling exposed and vulnerable. The more vulnerable people felt, the more they grasped for a sense of control, frantically attempting to cobble together a sense of security amidst an insecure and destabilized world. This fear drove people to engage in all sorts of behaviors in their attempt to find security: hoarding (Eccles 5:13), laboring endlessly out of anxiety or obsessive habit (2:18-23; 4:7-8), preoccupation with money (5:10-11), and envy (4:4) (Seow, 2001). Do any of these sound familiar?

Qoheleth reflects on one man so immobilized by fear that he hoards his money only to lose it all through misfortune. Qoheleth observes those "who have hoarded their riches and then lost them all in a bad investment or a stock market crash" (as paraphrased by Limberg, 2006, p. 76). But in this case the crash may have simply been a bank that went under (Seow, 2001). Even in trying to do the responsible thing he lost everything! Similar to what happens in modern-day casinos, the more people risked the more they labored away and hoarded in an attempt to find equilibrium and security. Ironically, the more people worked to offset their anxiety the more anxious they became. The more wealth the more anxiety, as they had more to lose. In fact, it was the anxiety related to losing their wealth that cost these individuals sleep (Eccles 5:12). And even when one did make it to the top, there was no sense of security that they could count on staying there (10:5-7).

One can see that human behavior is not all that different twenty-six hundred years later: obsessive and compulsive work habits, keeping up with the Joneses, compulsive monitoring of 401(k) plans. The human mind detests uncertainty, and left to its own devices will create illusions of certainty and control and obsessively chase after these.

Amidst this destabilization, the old way of seeing the world and understanding their relationship to God and one another was no longer working. This was a new context, and old belief structures no longer fit. They needed a new way of being and thinking in this unsettling climate. This earthy, real-world chaos is one of the reasons Brown (2011) refers to Ecclesiastes as a "theology from below" for the "theologically disillusioned" (p. 15). This is a theology for people in crises.

Despite their desperate attempt to control their situation, people were constantly bumping against the cold reality that the ways of this world were not under human control. And so, they lived in a world where everything is "vanity and a chasing after wind" (Eccles 1:14).

But wait. It turns out that "meaningless" is an incredibly unfortunate translation of the Hebrew word *hebel*. The literal meaning of *hebel* is "breath, vapor, or breeze" (Gibson, 2017). James Limburg (2006), an Old Testament professor, speaks of bringing a cigar into the classroom when talking about *hebel*, slowly unwrapping the cellophane, striking a match, taking a draw of the cigar, and then puffing out the smoke. And in that puff of smoke is what

Qoheleth means by *hebel*: "(1) It is without substance. You can't grab onto it. (2) It is not lasting. Now we see the puff of smoke; in a few seconds we will no longer be able to detect it" (p. 11).

Just as smoke or breath is transient and momentary, and the dew on the morning grass evaporates away, so is everything else humans do: nothing is permanent, everything is "chasing after the wind," beyond human grasp (Eccles 1:14; 2:11, 17, 26; 4:4; 6:9). Everything isn't meaningless; everything is transient! In an unpredictable world, everything is *hebel*: a chasing after the wind. The obsessive toil we engage in offers an illusion of control, and yet at the end of the day all is *hebel*. The unfortunate linguistic choice to translate *hebel* as "meaningless" has evolved over twenty-six hundred years, involving transitions between multiple languages (Hebrew, Greek, Latin, and English, at least), and has significant consequences for how we interpret Ecclesiastes.

Qoheleth is an early existential thinker, lamenting the human problem of *hebel*. For Qoheleth, *hebel* is central to the very fabric of life. *Hebel* speaks to the tendency for human plans to simply evaporate in the face of life's unknowns only to be replaced with desire and misery (Brown, 2011). Interestingly, *hebel* is identical to the name of Abel in Genesis 4. Abel gained God's approval after offering an honorable sacrifice only to become the victim of sibling jealousy the next moment. Abel gained security but then turned around and lost his very existence (Brown, 2011). Any gain in life, no matter how secure, can be *hebel*: transient, momentary, temporary. Any security one can hope to gain in life is but a temporary sense of security. Through and through, Qoheleth's lens is one of *hebel*.

This might easily drive a person into despair, except for this: God has not abandoned humans in their problem of *hebel*. As adamant as Qoheleth is about the precariousness of our position, he is equally adamant that God has not remained silent amidst the angst of *hebel*. God has responded. The divine response to the human problem of *hebel* is enjoyment (Eccles 5:20). This enjoyment is not a frantic, hedonistic searching for pleasure but a gift freely granted by God in *this* moment (Seow, 2001).

> And here he commends the joy of being together with friends at table and the enjoyment to be found in doing meaningful work. . . . These things, eating and drinking together with family and friends, bring us into contact with God! . . . In fact, good times with friends, days filled with meaningful and enjoyable

work—these are the best things in life, and they are God's gifts. (Limburg, 2006, p. 33)

This is not a message of optimistic platitudes, but a message of joy birthed from wrestling with life's messiness. Qoheleth never denies that suffering is part of existence.[3] As Seow (2001) writes, "human life inevitably comes with uncertainties and miseries. Still, [Qoheleth] believes that people may be able to cope with life—with all its miseries and pain" (p. 244). This is the case because God has given the gift of enjoyment to buoy us up amidst the hardships of *hebel*.

In addition to reflecting on God's response to the human plight, Qoheleth offers some insights into how humans may be able to slow down enough in order to be able to accept this gift of enjoyment (Gibson, 2017). When we are left chasing after security and control, it is difficult to slow down and appreciate the enjoyment of this moment:

> Indeed, those who long for perfection and certainty will not be able to function: "One who watches the wind will never sow; one who watches the clouds will never reap" (11:4). Farmers who constantly postpone what needs to be done for fear of inclement weather will be incapacitated by their unwillingness to risk; those who look for perfect conditions before they act will never do anything. . . . The times and seasons are ultimately unpredictable . . . and any attempt to find certainty is but a "pursuit of wind," a grasping of that which is ungraspable. (Seow, 2001, pp. 247-48)

The recipe for living well according to Qoheleth could be summed up in Ecclesiastes 7:14 (NIV): "When times are good, be happy; but when times are bad, consider this: God has made the one as well as the other."

One reason the recipe for contentment is important for Qoheleth is because it helps buffer against the danger of discontentment. Discontentment is depicted as a caricature, as one "whose toil is for his mouth and whose gullet (*nephesh*) is never satisfied (6:7)" (Seow, 2001, p. 245). Discontentment is a grasping monster: the person that takes in greedily but is never satisfied, never full. Seow suggests that this theological imagery would have been recognizable to Qoheleth's audience:

---

[3]The following section draws heavily from the work of Choon-Leong Seow (2001) on Ecclesiastes: "Theology When Everything Is Out of Control."

> In Canaanite mythology, Death is an insatiable monster whose mouth is wide
> open and whose gullet *(npš)* is never sated, threatening to swallow up Ba'al,
> the god of life. (*KTU* 1.5.2.2–4; 1.23.61–62)

In addition to depicting death, this same imagery is used to portray the
"threat of Death" as well as dangers posed by the "insatiable consumption of
oppressors" (Isa 5:14; Prov 27:20; 30:16; Ps 73:9, Hab 2:5) (Seow, 2001 p. 245).
By using this imagery, Qoheleth is suggesting discontentment can lead to
life-threatening, cosmic chaos. However, embedded in Qoheleth's theology
is the antidote to this threat. What protects humans from the threat of discontentment is the gift God freely gives—the possibility of enjoyment in this
moment (Seow, 2001). This is not about going out to seek pleasure for the
sake of instant gratification, but about accepting the gift God has freely
granted. In fact, accepting this gift is our responsibility, the appropriate response to the problem of *hebel* (Seow, 2001).

If enjoyment is not about a hedonistic pursuit, then what is it? Enjoyment
is "living life with full awareness of its ungraspable nature: eating, drinking,
[wearing] bright garments, anointing one's head with oil, and being with
one's beloved (9:7-9)" (Seow, 2001, p. 246). Eating and drinking would have
been communal activities. Perhaps another way of saying "eat, drink, and be
merry" is "be with the people you love, spending time mulling over the meal,
conversing, laughing, and being together." The future is unknown, the present
moment is here, and we can settle into the gift that is offered in the present.
Other expressions Qoheleth uses to describe enjoyment: "find enjoyment"
(2:24), "be happy" (3:12), and "be joyful" (7:14). The point here is not that we
should all wear rose-tinted glasses—only focusing on the good while ignoring
the bad. Rather Qoheleth's message is: "when times are good, 'be in good';
when times are bad, observe" (Seow, 2001, p. 246). We can only really live
when we give up a pretense of control; those who seek certainty and control
will struggle to function in a world marked by *hebel* (Seow, 2001). He is
making a keen psychological observation: the harder we try to grasp security
and control the more we suffer, the more anxiety and discontentment we
experience. But when we radically accept the uncertainty of life, we free
ourselves from chasing the ungraspable, which affords us the capacity to
anchor into this moment and the gift of enjoyment that waits for us here. Eat,
drink, and be merry: when times are good, be happy.

Integration Conversation Starters

1. We're about to observe some common themes between the time when Qoheleth was writing and contemporary times. Before you read ahead, what do you notice as similarities between then and now?

2. Ponder the last time you had a delicious meal and good conversation with friends. What felt enlivened in you? How did it help ease disillusionment? How do you feel about seeing times like this as gifts from God?

Ecclesiastes Today

You may have noticed that not many texts or journal articles on the integration of psychology and Christianity discuss Ecclesiastes. Yet here we are diving right into *hebel* in chapter two of this integration book. Some might argue we are making a strange choice, but our view is that Qoheleth's theology has profound implications for our current time and for how counselors and psychotherapists do their work.

Keep in mind that our goal is to model and promote conversation while integrating psychology and Christianity, which means that we will neither attempt nor succeed at giving a thorough theological analysis of Ecclesiastes or any other book of the Bible. Similarly, we can't discuss every possible implication and nuance for how Qoheleth's words apply to counseling and psychotherapy, and we won't build comprehensive integration models based on Ecclesiastes. But perhaps we can generate some conversation that carries forward into how we think about contemporary times and how the wisdom of Qoheleth might help us sit with troubled souls in our offices, and perhaps also with the rumpled places in our own souls. By the end of the chapter we hope you agree that these are important conversations, and maybe even that Ecclesiastes belongs in this book as it belongs in the Bible. If Qoheleth was writing in a chaotic time of uncertainty, we are doing the same. Consider just a few of the parallels.

A time of economic instability. First, economic chaos and upheaval characterized Qoheleth's era; don't we also live in such a time? The so-called Great Recession of 2008 has given way to a new economic confidence a decade later, but who's to say that we won't be in another financial downturn, or even economic tragedy, by the time you read this? Some predict bear markets, some bull markets, but the reality is that none of us knows, and the potential for rapid economic reversal is part of contemporary life.

While it may seem intuitively obvious, the economic crash of 2008 was one of the first times social scientists actually looked at mental health consequences. Christodoulou and Christodoulou (2013) reported increased rates of depression, suicide attempts, and alcoholism throughout Europe, including increased calls to an emergency crisis line in Greece. They note that for every 1% increase in unemployment, a 0.79% increase in suicides can be observed (among those younger than sixty-five years). In the United States, McInerney, Mellor, and Nicholas (2013) reported that those who lost wealth in the economic crash reported increased subjective feelings of depression and increased antidepressant use. Clearly, the instability and unpredictability of our economic systems has implications for emotional well-being, just as it did in Qoheleth's day.

As part of the baby-boomer generation, I (Mark) wonder if we have made ourselves vulnerable to economic downturns by caring overly much about professional success and accumulating wealth. I watch Megan Anna's millennial generation with interest. They'll spend more on a cup of coffee than my generation, and on Ubers and Ubering—words that were neither nouns nor verbs when I was young (or even when Megan Anna was!)—yet they are also less inclined to mark their identity by aggressive career development. In my generation we set out to make as much money as we could early in our careers and to establish ourselves so that we could progress in a career path. Megan Anna's generation cares more about finding work they enjoy and having a positive influence on society (White, 2015). Millennials have taken their share of criticism for their tendency to lack ambition and switch jobs, but I wonder if Qoheleth might commend them more than criticize them. I can imagine Qoheleth looking at my boomer generation and saying,

> You work hard all your life to build a career, to become stable and established, and then it all goes away with a corporate scandal or an unexpected health crisis. Your 401(k) balances aren't as stable as you think, and neither is the company that employs you. In fact, think of it as vapor that disperses in the wind. Here's an idea: Uber (verb!) to a local coffee shop, spend a ridiculous amount of money on a cup of fair-trade coffee, sit and enjoy the moment with your friends, and let a sense of connection, contentment, and joy wash over you.

Of course, I have overstated and oversimplified here. There is ample reason to work hard and save for retirement, but I sometimes wonder if those in my generation have elevated financial security to a place of idolatry. We have assumed a stability that is simply not true. I have a professional acquaintance who was about ready to retire from Enron with a huge portfolio, and then the scandal of 2000 broke. Three million dollars of stock options turned out to be *hebel*. I remember having this conversation in the locker room after enjoying a game of noon basketball with a group of aging men, and it occurred to me then, as it does now, that the joy of playing basketball with friends may bring more happiness than a large stock portfolio. Now this acquaintance is a Christian college professor with a meager salary and modest retirement account, a good jump shot, and deep joy in his life.

Life, death, and hebel. Ponder again Professor James Limburg's illustration of blowing a puff of cigar smoke to illustrate the fleeting nature of *hebel*. And now consider all those you hold dear who have passed from life to death, or are soon to do so. This is the world in which we live, where life itself is unpredictable, uncertain, and fleeting.

Kate Bowler's (2018a) memoir, *Everything Happens for a Reason: And Other Lies I've Loved* describes her diagnosis with stage IV cancer at the age of thirty-five. Bowler is a professor of Christian history at Duke Divinity School. Just out of graduate school and beginning her promising career at Duke, the diagnosis rocked her world. Describing the moments after her diagnosis, she writes:

> It is impossible. It is an impossible thought. I thought this life was only getting started, but now I am supposed to contemplate its sudden conclusion. I am supposed to imagine the end of my whirling mind, the slowing of my breath, a sunken vessel where my heart now beats. But, worse, it would be the conclusion of this thing I have built—a family. (p. 12)

In a powerful TED talk, she states:

> Aren't I good? Aren't I special somehow? I have committed zero homicides to date. So why is this happening to me? . . . I believed that hardships were only detours on what I was certain would be my long, long life. As is [the] case with many of us, it's a mindset that served me well. The gospel of success drove me to achieve, to dream big, to abandon fear. It was a mindset that served me well until it didn't, until I was confronted with something I couldn't manage my

way out of. . . . Anything I thought was good or special about me could not save me—my hard work, my personality, my humor, my perspective. I had to face the fact that my life is built with paper walls, and so is everyone else's. (Bowler, 2018b)

With each year of living it seems we accumulate more stories about life being built with paper walls. Life itself is like a puff of smoke, like a vapor, like *hebel*.

As I have now entered my sixties, I occasionally succumb to the life-expectancy calculators I find online. How many more years can I anticipate on earth? These calculators ask questions ranging from blood pressure, lifestyle choices, the longevity of my parents, exercise and eating patterns, and so on. At the end, after entering all sorts of information, I click the calculate button and learn I will likely have a long life. And then I remember Kate Bowler's words about life being built with paper walls. Like anyone else, I could be diagnosed with a terminal disease at any moment. We may try to grasp and hold on, and we may even succeed for a while, but life is fleeting. Sometimes the uncertainty of life seems to be our only certainty. Is it any surprise that our patients deal with anxiety about living and dying? What might we have to offer in the midst of these anxieties?

Professor of Old Testament William Brown (2001) offers a compelling anecdote of Qoheleth's invitation to enjoyment amid life's uncertainty.

> Since death, the final sabbath, serves as the starting point for Qoheleth's work ethic, I cannot conclude without reflecting on the untimely demise of a close friend. A gifted pastor and devoted spouse and parent, Lee died in an absurdly tragic auto accident on Father's Day. During the last days of his life, he received the result of an informal survey conducted in his congregation as part of an evaluation process for the renewal of a grant. One question in the survey asked members to identity the most significant form of ministry the church had provided over the year. Lee was disappointed that scarce reference was made to worship, and nothing to his preaching and pastoral abilities. At the top of the list, rather, were potluck suppers! Through Lee's ministry and death, I have come to appreciate anew Qoheleth's sobering message. The giftedness of life, Qoheleth presages, is found at the table and the cross, not in accolades and rewards. If, as the gospels claim, the kingdom of God is a banquet of fellowship, then perhaps the highest form of service, next to hosting, is to help set the table and enjoy it with others. (p. 284)

Disillusionment. Many people in the United States are leaving organized religion. Religious "nones" are a growing part of our population, and 78% of these nones were raised in a religion (Lipka, 2016). And the rate at which people are leaving is growing, with the rate of nones in the United States rising from 16% in 2007 to 23% in 2014. Strikingly, 35% of millennials are nones (Lipka, 2015).

Why people are leaving religion is a complex topic that has filled the pages of many books, but even if oversimplified it seems clear that disillusionment with religious organizations is a substantial reason. Try a simple Google search with "love Jesus" and "hate church" as the search terms, and you will find hundreds of books, blogs, articles, and videos exploring how disillusioned people are with organized Christianity.

Two findings are crystal clear from recent research on the psychology of religion. First, many forms of religion and spirituality are associated with positive health markers (Koenig, King, & Carson, 2012). For example, those who attend church live longer than those who don't, even after controlling for lifestyle differences such as tobacco and alcohol use. Second, despite these general connections between health and faith, many people find religion and spirituality sources of conflict and struggle (Exline, Pargament, Grubbs, & Yali, 2014). These religious and spiritual struggles are associated with all sorts of negative outcomes, including poor physical health, emotional distress, depression, anxiety, and "even higher mortality rates" (Exline et al., 2014, p. 209).

Religion is good for us, but religious struggle creates distress (Exline et al., 2014). Yet this is how many people live today. Frustrated and disappointed in faith, they leave organized religion behind. Our natural inclination is often to woo people back, to remind them that they will live longer if they come back to church or that returning to faith will make them faithful, obedient souls rather than wayward apostates. And here is where Ecclesiastes stops us from resorting to our default. Confronted with similar disillusionment, a book in the biblical canon refuses to woo back the wayward. If anything, Qoheleth validates a degree of disillusionment and struggle.

Ecclesiastes addresses the challenging topic of disillusionment without avoiding it or trying to make it pretty. Qoheleth is discussing the experience of many people today, which means we still need to be listening to what he is teaching us, maybe especially those of us seeking to integrate faith and psychology amidst an increasingly religiously fluid context.

Other parallels could be mentioned between the situation Qoheleth addresses in Ecclesiastes and our contemporary times. We live with political upheaval, where polarization and debate have become the norm. The sociopolitical backdrop of Ecclesiastes was similarly chaotic. In our day we face gross inequalities between the privileged and those who are not. Similarly, in Qoheleth's day property grants (ability to own land) were given based on favoritism and privilege. If any of us were to make a world we would likely reward moral character with financial gain, but does it seem to anyone else that often these are utterly unrelated or maybe even inversely related? In the same way, Qoheleth muses that the righteous get what the wicked deserve, and vice versa (Eccles 8:14).

The chaos, uncertainty, instability, and disillusionment of Qoheleth's day feel familiar to us both inside and outside the counseling office. And this has implications for how we integrate Christian thought with our professional work.

Implications for Counseling and Psychotherapy

We began this chapter with Megan Anna sitting with a woman whose partner was in peril the day DACA was revoked and Mark sitting with a pastor whose longtime spouse had recently left him for a former high school flame. Each of us sat with our patients in a place of deep disillusionment, profound questioning, and struggle. *Hebel* shows up often in the therapy room, and Ecclesiastes has implications for integration conversations. We begin with the importance of empathy.

Deep empathy. Empathy is the first concept taught in almost every graduate program in counseling and psychotherapy. We distinguish it from sympathy, we debate whether it is both necessary and sufficient, as Carl Rogers (1957) argued. We teach skills to communicate empathy, including reflections, acknowledgments, restatements, and so on. We may even learn appropriate body posture to communicate empathy—how to lean forward in our chairs at strategic moments to communicate our concern for what the patient is experiencing. With time we learn to connect various theories with empathy. Client-centered therapists see it as freeing the patient to grow, cognitive therapists say we're paving the way for effective therapy techniques, psychodynamic therapists believe we're creating a new sort of relationship that will help our patients heal.

This is all good, but notice that empathy is typically conceived as instrumental. In other words, we see empathy as a means to a therapeutic end of helping a patient become less depressed or anxious, less bound up by shame and more connected to others. Empathy is a therapeutic strategy.

Ecclesiastes causes us to wonder if there is a deeper sort of empathy that is not intended as a means to an end. This is an empathy of presence, just being with one another amidst *hebel*. This sort of presence acknowledges the pain of the other, even shares in the pain, but without invading the other by tidying anything up or imposing hope when hope is hard to find.

If you have ever had this sort of deep empathy connection with another, you'll likely recognize that it could not be easily taught in an interviewing skills class. There may be body postures that help, and it may or may not connect to particular diagnoses or treatment strategies, but all this misses the point. This is a deep experiential connection between two souls sitting together in the unanswerable questions of life.

WHEN ANSWERS ARE HARD TO FIND

Imagine going to a physician and describing a problem you are having with your health. The response you get back would likely fall somewhere on this continuum:

| That's easy. Here's what you do. | This might work. Let's give it a try. | This will be really difficult. | There is no answer for this. |

Of course, we hope for answers on the left side of the continuum, though we recognize that someday we will likely hear something on the dreaded right side. I (Mark) recently lingered on the right side of the continuum while sitting with an older adult with congestive heart failure, noting the desperation in his face as he described his shortness of breath and then asked, "What do I do?" I had no answer. No one did.

Psychologists and counselors find themselves sitting with people in anguish and sometimes having no answers to ease the pain. Perhaps this is why we learn client-centered skills first in graduate school—to keep us from rushing toward easy answers when there are none.

When we find ourselves on the right side of the continuum, this is an Ecclesiastes moment, when we accept hard questions about life's fleeting and unpredictable nature, lean into deep compassion and empathy for one another, and somehow learn to look for the gifts offered us in whatever precious moments remain.

AUTHOR DIALOG: SITTING STILL WITH DISILLUSIONMENT

Mark: Megan Anna, I recall a time in your own faith development shortly after your seminary internship in Ghana where you had some profound questions about your faith. You seemed deeply disillusioned at the time. I'm curious about what you found helpful and not so helpful during that time.

Megan Anna: Indeed, in Ghana I contacted deep and unnamable darkness, which led to some difficult and painful questions. Previously I had experienced crises of faith that were cognitive in nature. However, this was a different sort of crisis. These questions arose out of touching terror and darkness and being unable to find God in the middle of it—I suppose in a sense they were emotional questions. "Questions" is likely a misleading label, because "question" implies there were words and names for my experience. Perhaps it's better to say I had unformulated emotional responses to the darkness I'd touched. And the theological frames I held at the time could not hold this level of tension and pain. During this period it felt more honest to identify as agnostic than as Christian, and in fact opening myself up to the possibility of "not knowing" was incredibly freeing and healing. Giving myself a break from attempting to make sense of the senseless was what I needed to heal and restore my soul. I found it incredibly painful and difficult to sit with people who attempted to "prove" Christianity to me. Their arguments rang like deep, empty echoes through my body. It made me feel missed and my pain unseen. I recall a conversation with you that felt very different. At the time I hadn't been to church in a few years, and I was informing you about my identity as agnostic, something I imagine was incredibly painful for you. Somehow you created space for my pain amidst your own and you reflected, "Perhaps leaving your faith for this season is the most consistent—and perhaps even the most faithful—thing you could do right now." I don't know if you recall that conversation, or if you recall saying those words. I have often wondered what compelled you to give me your blessing to leave even when it must have caused you so much pain.

Mark: As you know now that you have your own children, the love between a parent and child has no measure. I imagine this is the way God loves us also, only much more so than what we can ever imagine. I have never questioned God's grip on you, which made it clear that my job was simply to be present with you in a place of deep empathy and connection.

Megan Anna: One thing I'm reflecting on as we write this is that it became uncomfortable to talk about religion with many people at that time. Likewise, when I was returning to faith you were one of the few people who felt comfortable to discuss this with. Your openness to my leaving made it so we could continue the conversation of my return to faith when I was ready. I imagine you aren't aware of what a meaningful gift this has been for me.

Mark: Thank you, Megan Anna. At the risk of being sappy in the pages of a published book, I also imagine you aren't aware of what a precious gift of grace you have always been to me.

At first this may seem contrary to Christianity. Isn't the Christian message one of hope and fulfilled promise? Shouldn't we always be bringing a good report of the active and present work of God in our universe? Perhaps. But as Qoheleth reminds us in the most famous part of Ecclesiastes, "For everything there is a season, and a time for every matter under heaven" (Eccles 3:1). And every seasoned clinician knows there is a time just to be present in a deep place of empathy and connection as tears stream down the cheeks of the one sitting with us. This is sometimes the work God calls us to—simply being present to the disillusionment of a confusing world and to the other who is nearly drowning in it.

In the biblical story of Job, his friends saw his great suffering amidst unparalleled *hebel* and they experienced deep empathy, sitting silently with no words for seven days and seven nights (Job 2:13). Then they opened their mouths and didn't do so well. Perhaps one of the most important starting points in clinical integration is simply knowing when to sit quietly and when to say something. And when we do speak, we do so in ways that acknowledge the uncertainty and disorderliness of life rather than trying to tidy up or explain away anything.

In the Gospel of John, when Jesus was confronted with the death of his friend Lazarus and the anguish of the community surrounding Lazarus, Jesus did what friends do: he wept (Jn 11:35). He then provided some amazing evidence of divinity by raising Lazarus, but first he wept. Those observing remarked how much Jesus loved Lazarus, not because he raised him from the dead, but because he wept.

Integration Conversation Starters

1. Think of a time when you didn't know what to say in a counseling session. What were you feeling and thinking at that moment? What might it be like to release any feelings of being incompetent or stuck in order to simply be present with the person you are sitting with?
2. What is it like to experience your own *hebel*? Try spending some time quietly sitting with your own disillusionment and questioning about life. Notice what feelings and instincts bubble up in the process. To what extent must a counselor learn to sit alone in uncertainty before competently showing deep empathy to another who experiences uncertainty?

The first task of good clinical work is to learn to sit still in the presence of pain. Qoheleth creates space for a deep sort of empathy rooted in presence more than solutions. This space is big enough to tolerate existential disillusionment.

Existential disillusionment. Toni first came to see me (Megan Anna) when she was sixteen, having struggled with crippling depression and anxiety for the last four years. Likely related to her early life trauma, Toni was hyper-vigilant about anything that might threaten her safety. Then just a week into our treatment a massive school shooting occurred in another part of the country. She found herself constantly scanning her classroom throughout the day and startling at loud sounds.

As I sat with Toni, I noticed an inner tension for how to approach treatment. Part of me wanted to offer reassurance, focusing on statistics to help her see how unlikely it is to be shot at school, even with the alarming increase in school shootings and the media attention it garners. But another part of me wanted to simply honor the pain and terror she experienced amidst life's unpredictability. Predictable pain is hard enough, but unpredictable pain has an excruciating quality.

Even if it's illusion, the mind likes to have a sense of control. The angst that comes with a terrorist attack or random violence can knock us on our knees in fear because of the unpredictable, chaotic nature of such pain. It reminds us of our existential vulnerability. This is part of being human—to touch this unpredictable pain that we would prefer to spend our life avoiding.

We need theology that can hold us when we touch this sort of pain, that can sit with us in the questions that arise when wrestling with the internal and external chaos.

Qoheleth gives voice to the uncertainty, lament, and pain of his people and to the vulnerability that inevitably results. Our patients also experience this sort of vulnerability, as we do as counselors and psychotherapists. My inclination to give probabilities and statistics may have been coming from my own sense of vulnerability and desire to help contain and control distressing thoughts. Part of the sacred work we do as therapists is create space where people can speak their disillusionment, where they can talk about life's paper walls. In a society otherwise obsessed with the illusion of control, having a space where one can put down illusion and address the existential terror that comes with being human can be healing.

Integration Conversation Starters

1. People often initiate treatment after an unexpected life event (e.g., relational, situational, onset of mood disorder). For many, in addition to the stressor they're facing, they may be feeling disillusioned about how the world works, either living in the disillusioning aftermath of realizing life is made of "paper walls" or working tirelessly to find an explanation to the life event so they can protect their sense of order. Both embracing life's fragility or working in overdrive to defend against it can cause problems. What is it like for you to work with these two very different responses to the human problem of *hebel*? Is one more comfortable to sit with? What does it evoke in you? How does this connect to your own experience with life's vulnerability?

2. In your counseling work, do you ever experience tension between wanting to help reduce a patient's angst versus simply being present to your patient in the present moment of intense emotion? Assuming there is an appropriate time for each of these approaches, when do you find it most useful to help reduce troubling feelings in a patient? When is it best to simply be present with the patient's deep questions and disillusionment?

3. Counseling often happens at the intersection of collapsing paper walls. What is it like to spend so many hours in the debris of *hebel*? What have you found to be helpful anchors in this work?

The renowned neuroscientist Daniel Siegel describes the experience of being empathetically connected and attuned as "to feel felt" (Siegel & Hartzell, 2003, p. 61). Science arising from interpersonal neurobiology is telling a compelling story: powerful things take place when a person feels felt. As we open up a space where people feel seen, heard, and felt this in return opens up a space within the individual to experience greater internal integration between their feelings, thoughts, and sense of self. It turns out external connection and internal integration are related to one another (Siegel & Hartzell, 2003).

Radical acceptance. At first glance, the conversation with Toni we just described may seem to pit cognitive-behavioral therapy (CBT) approaches against more relational and process-oriented approaches. Certainly the relational approaches to psychotherapy have always emphasized being present to the other without rushing to offer solutions, but as one who has written a couple of books about Christian approaches to CBT, I (Mark) also want to suggest there is ample room for CBT therapists to be fully present with whatever experiences and emotions patients bring, including those who come with deep existential disillusionment.

One third-wave approach to CBT is called acceptance and commitment therapy (ACT; see Hayes, Strosahl, & Wilson, 2012). ACT is not a form of therapy affiliated with any religion but can be easily adapted for Christian approaches to therapy (e.g., Knabb, 2016; Nieuwsma, Walser, & Hayes, 2016; Sisemore, 2014). It is a complex theoretical system based on relational frame theory, but to simplify it here consider just the descriptors in the title: acceptance and commitment. Commitment is about living according to our values. Acceptance is about giving up our various ways of avoiding life's pain and struggle and allowing ourselves to accept whatever is happening in the moment. So, if a patient like Toni is sitting with tears of anxiety, the ACT therapist is not likely to use a second-wave CBT strategy to get her to change her thinking and reassess the likelihood of getting shot at school. Rather, the therapist will sit with Toni just as she is and help her "feel felt" and validated, and more able to integrate and accept her feelings rather than deny or repress them. Rather than running away and avoiding those feelings, it is better to sit right in the middle of disillusionment with her, and even to see how these feelings make sense. Given her early life trauma, and in light of the prominence of school shootings these days, of course she is feeling hypervigilant and anxious. Her brain is doing just what brains do. Therapist and patient work together to radically accept whatever feelings show up in the room, and to stop avoiding them. It turns out these feelings don't have to run a person's life (thus, the commitment part of ACT), but still the first part of ACT is always to accept and be present to whatever is being experienced.

Recently I (Megan Anna) attended an intensive ACT training where the leaders engaged in "real plays," inviting participants in the training to volunteer to do real therapy work in front of some two hundred people. I squirmed in my seat a bit as I watched Dr. Robyn Walser work with volunteers on creative hopelessness. Creative hopelessness is about maintaining hope for the human being while giving up all hope that anything the person does in an attempt to control the problem will result in different outcomes. This involves a radical acceptance that there is no avoiding, outrunning, outsmarting, or outperforming our pain. Pain is unavoidable. Moving toward an enriching, meaningful life involves accepting this reality. It also involves transitioning the hope we have so that it's not about trying to *control* the pain but being able to *carry* the pain.

QUERIES FOR PATIENTS

Consider asking your patients questions in the following ways:

1. I see you working really hard to save this relationship even when she tells you it is over. What does that feel like on the inside to be working so hard with not much hope of bringing her back?

   Rather than directly confronting a patient to move toward radical acceptance, sometimes it is best to gain a glimpse of the inner experience first, which allows for a deep sort of empathy. In a safe place of empathy, patients are more willing to set down their strivings and accept the reality of the present moment.

2. When you called this week, you were punching in her name on your phone, wondering whether she would answer, and what she would say. You describe the vulnerability of that place. Can we take a closer look at that right here in the office? What is it like to feel so vulnerable?

   Bringing the patient into the present moment in the office can be a good way to help carry the pain rather than trying to control the circumstances that contribute to the pain.

Qoheleth spent a great deal of time and depth reflecting on humanity's plight: What are we to do in the face of this overwhelming uncertainty and chaos? How are humans to live in a world that is utterly out of human control and where everything that humans do is ultimately transient? What are we to do with a world that appears senseless and incomprehensible? How do we respond to *hebel*? His message is by no means that life is meaningless. Rather his message is one of radical acceptance, that there are "no fail-safe rules, no formulas that will guarantee success, nothing that one can hold onto, for everything is as ungraspable as vapor" (Seow, 2001, p. 243). According to Qoheleth, all of these unfortunate, unpredictable events will continue to occur despite how much humans toil and work to plan for the future and create a sense of security. People will be stuck on this treadmill of attempting to attain security, thus preventing them from abundant living until they are able to give up any illusions of control.

Those who cling to perfection and certainty will struggle the most, paralyzing them from action. "Whoever observes the wind will not sow; and whoever regards the clouds will not reap" (Eccles 11:4). Here Qoheleth is seeing that some farmers are postponing the work that needs to be done for fear of bad weather. In their attempts to avoid risk they are immobilized by fear. Qoheleth's message is that in accepting the conditions of *hebel*, people ultimately experience greater freedom; his message is essentially an ancient text about radical acceptance of our human predicament.

In Ecclesiastes we confront the inherent vulnerability of our humanity. Out of this vulnerability Qoheleth draws a deep appreciation for the gift of the present moment—gifts of relationship, food, drink, and joy. Only when one radically accepts their vulnerability do they become free to fully experience the gifts of any present moment.

Toni has difficulty contacting the present moment due to her desire to control future moments. She desires to control the chaos of her emotions, but the illusion of control causes her to toil ceaselessly. Toni is trapped: she wants to control her environment so that she feels safe enough to be present, but the more she works toward an illusion of control the more difficult it becomes to be present. If Toni were able to reach a place of radical acceptance of the human condition of vulnerability and the realization that control is but an illusion, it could help her become more present in her life, which would move her closer to her desired values of being in relationship with others.

> ### Integration Conversation Starters
>
> 1. What are some of the things your patients do to keep an illusion of control? What are some things you do? What do these things cost us?
> 2. What are some of the ways that our profession falls into the trap of creating an illusion of control (e.g., manualized treatment plans, symptom reduction checklists, etc.)? What does this cost us as a profession?

Valuing the present moment. I (Megan Anna) met Sam when he was struggling with his adjustment to married life. As a result of a tumultuous and abusive childhood, he formed some powerful defenses to protect himself. In addition to tending toward avoidance in relating to others, he also developed some obsessive and compulsive patterns. His home, and life in general, needed to be a certain way or he would become anxious and irritable. Similarly, he needed to stay busy. Slowing down was incredibly painful, as evidenced by the speed in which he talked in our sessions. His desire to control situations and environments was bleeding over into a desire to assert control over his partner's choices. In moments of vulnerability it was clear how desperately he wanted to be able to slow down and appreciate and be with his wife who loved him. When he did, he became paralyzed with pain and fear. Put simply, Sam had learned to avoid the present moment, but the avoidance increased his emotional and relational pain. One of our goals in therapy, then, was to slow down and help him identify ways he protected himself by staying busy and overly focused on the future, and to help change his relationship with the present moment.

Sam is not alone in having an anxious, future-oriented relationship to time. The industrial and technical revolutions that shaped modern society have leaked into how we think. It has become so much a part of contemporary life that we can hardly recognize it unless we have opportunity to step outside of our own culture for a season.

I anticipated that living crossculturally would change me—that it would affect some of my thought patterns and ways of understanding the world. However, one thing I didn't suspect is that it would change my relationship to time. After living in Malawi for two months, I began to notice my dreams shifting from future-oriented dreams to present- and past-focused dreams.

I also noticed my daily mind chatter began to shift. In the United States my thoughts are often preoccupied with the future: articles to write, papers to grade, goals to be achieved. In Malawi my mind became more focused on the present moment, as well as meaningful reflections of past events. Malawians tend to be much more present focused in their way of thinking about the world. It turns out this can be an incredibly powerful antidote to anxiety, as it is often said, "anxiety usually lives in the past or the future."

Another place where we might experience dissonance between present and future is in the work we do. Qoheleth was not opposed to work, but he rearranges our relationship with it. Rather than toiling to achieve monumental future results that in the end are like vapor, it is better to enjoy our work in the present moment:

> Unlike gain, which is gleaned *from* one's labors, enjoyment is found *amid* the toiling. Qoheleth's point is that the quest for gain invariably reduces work to the level of means and, thus, to toil. But stripped of the toiler's obsession with gain, toil takes on a different character. As enjoyment of the momentary pause comes to replace the ever elusive prospect for gain, work, thereby, is restored as gift and vocation. In other words, enjoyment resides beyond *and* within the realm of work. (Brown, 2001, p. 281)

Ecclesiastes reminds us that to escape the toil, the rat race, and the persistent anxiety, one needs to slow down and show up to the present moment. Qoheleth's call to "eat, drink, and be merry" is an invitation to be present. So is the invitation to enjoy our work: "There is nothing better for mortals than to eat and drink, and find enjoyment in their toil. This also, I saw, is from the hand of God" (Eccles 2:24). Anchoring ourselves to the present moment can be one of the best responses to our future-oriented anxiety that is beckoning to us and tempting us toward endless toil and illusions of control.

Integration Conversation Starters

1. Listen to how your patients talk. Where are they located in time? Where is their anxiety located? How do they respond to slowing down?

2. Where are your thoughts typically located during a therapeutic session: the past, present, or future? What pulls you into the past or the future? What is it like for you when you stay in the present with your patient?

In the introduction we identified our preferred approach to integration as conversation, which is done in the present moment. This sort of integration seems particularly fitting for clinical settings—where conversation is our primary means of treatment—and for a time in history where people are experiencing Qoheleth's wisdom that is born out of disillusionment. This is a wisdom to be present to the moment. Yesterday is gone, tomorrow flits away like the morning dew, but right here, right now, we have this moment of life to experience fully. Nouwen (1990) puts it beautifully:

> It is hard to live in the present. The past and the future keep harassing us. The past with guilt, the future with worries. So many things have happened in our lives about which we feel uneasy, regretful, angry, confused or, at least, ambivalent. And all these feelings are often colored by guilt. Guilt that says: "You ought to have done something other than what you did; you ought to have said something other than what you said." These "oughts" keep us feeling guilty about the past and prevent us from being fully present to the moment.
>
> Worse, however, than our guilt are our worries. Our worries fill our lives with "What ifs": "What if I lose my job, what if my father dies, what if there is not enough money, what if the economy goes down, what if a war breaks out?" These many "ifs" can so fill our mind that we become blind to the flowers in the garden and the smiling children on the streets, or deaf to the grateful voice of a friend.
>
> The real enemies of our life are the "oughts" and the "ifs." They pull us backward into the unalterable past and forward into the unpredictable future. But real life takes place in the here and now. God is a God of the present. God is always in the moment, be that moment hard or easy, joyful or painful. When Jesus spoke about God, he always spoke about God as being where and when we are. "When you see me, you see God. When you hear me you hear God." God is not someone who only was or will be, but the One who is, and who is for me in the present moment. That's why Jesus came to wipe away the burden of the past and the worries for the future. He wants us to discover God right where we are, here and now. (pp. 17-18)

Cracks in our meaning-making systems. Human beings make meaning out of the ambiguities of life. These ways of making meaning can be roughly divided into global meaning-making systems, such as how religion helps us see the world, and situational meaning-making systems, such as how

SOME WAYS OF GETTING PRESENT

Learning to attend to the present moment can be challenging, perhaps especially for the goal-oriented people who are most likely to read (and write!) a book like this. Here are some strategies for learning to stay present to the moment.

1. Wash your hands with warm water, specifically focusing on the sensations of the water and the soap. Many might find washing dishes to be the ideal time for this.

2. Sit quietly and pay attention to your breathing. Notice the rhythm and sensations as you inhale and exhale.

3. Contemplative Christians have practiced centering prayer for the last several decades. This Trappist practice was suggested by Thomas Keating and M. Basil Pennington in the 1970s but has roots that go back to the earliest times of Christian history. Centering prayer involves sitting quietly in God's presence and releasing any distracting thoughts (Bourgeault, 2004).

4. Try eating a meal mindfully. Slow down and notice the tastes and sensations of each bite. What sensations do you experience in your mouth and other parts of your body?

5. Gregory Boyd (2010), author of *Present Perfect: Finding God in the Now*, suggests putting sticky notes on your bathroom mirror, the dashboard of your car, your fridge, and computer screen that simply ask, "Are you awake?" as a reminder to attend to this present moment.

to understand parenting or financial practices (Slattery & Park, 2011). In Christianity, our global meaning-making systems have emphasized the triune God, the importance of Scripture in knowing God, the fallenness of all creation, being separated from God by our sin, the atoning work of Christ to end our separation from God, and our eternal hope of heaven. To many Christians throughout the world these are unquestionable foundations of our faith upon which meaning and hope rests.

But some Christians experience cracks in this foundation of faith. People debate whether Scripture should be considered inerrant or inspired or authoritative. Embedded in this is a sense of vulnerability and threat. If we were to question the inerrancy of Scripture, would our entire faith system crumble? We're not trying to address this question here; we are simply observing this crack in the foundation of how Christians construct a global meaning-making system.[4]

Similarly, we could look at almost any major Christian doctrine and see that questions are being raised now, and have been throughout Christian history. How do we understand sin? How big is grace? What about heaven, hell, and salvation?

We will see in chapter four that the atoning work of Christ can be viewed in various ways, and this may feel threatening to some who have always assumed one view of the atonement. Rather than fighting against the threat, can we radically accept and sit with the dissonance, seeking to learn from the wisdom traditions in our Christian past?

We're not arguing for particular views of theology but simply showing that the global meaning-making foundation of Christian thought can be easily cracked. It is important to remember that the students we teach and the patients we see may well be coming with profound questions and uncertainties, whether historical, generational, regional, or cultural. One option would be apologetics—to shore up the foundation by teaching what has been taught about evangelical Christian faith for the last hundred years. Another option would be the one Qoheleth took in Ecclesiastes—to allow, and perhaps even welcome, the deep, hard questions of life and death.

Several years ago, I (Mark) sat with Joy, a first-year doctoral student who had given up on faith. Raised in a Christian home, she attended a Christian college, then a faith-based master's program in counseling. Through all this she held onto faith, but as she began seeing the profound challenges of clinical work, she started questioning how God could be good amidst the chaos and suffering of life. She chose a Christian doctoral program, but mostly because she wanted to understand her patients who talked about faith and not because she herself held faith anymore. I recall sitting outside on the patio of a local coffee shop feeling heartbroken that this dear soul had lost her faith, wondering what I could possibly do to bring her back. Then I realized my job wasn't so much to bring her back as to stay present with her. She didn't need any proofs of faith I might have been ready to offer—she already knew all that and had rejected it. Instead, she simply needed my presence.

---

[4]Vanhoozer and Treier (2015) look at implications of divergent thought within evangelical theology in their book, *Theology and the Mirror of Scripture.* They explore the meaning of evangelical thought "now that (faux?) Reformed hegemony is over" (p. 35) while modeling a way forward.

These stories don't all have a happy ending, as Qoheleth would be quick to tell us, so I am hesitant to write what happened to Joy. Still, I will. After a couple of years of doctoral training, she discovered that an Eastern Orthodox view of Christianity resonated with her deeply, and she returned to faith. I remember the day Joy stopped by my office and invited me to her baptism in her new church. Tears of gratitude welled in my eyes, as they did in hers.

Back at that coffee-shop patio I could have tried to persuade her about one doctrine or another, but the greater gift was to simply accept the cracks in her meaning-making foundation and to be present with her in that moment, enjoying the Oregon sunshine on a warm autumn day, sipping good beverages, and enjoying one another's company. It turned out to be an Ecclesiastes sort of day.

Integration Conversation Starters

1. Do you notice any cracks in the foundations of your global meaning-making systems? What might it mean to sit with the uncertainties rather than rushing to fix them?
2. What do you notice in yourself when you sit with others who have profound questions about their faith? What inclinations and pressures do you feel?

Life as gift. Qoheleth doesn't leave us hanging after painfully describing the plight of humanity in gory detail. Though we live in an unpredictable and uncontrollable world, Qoheleth also outlines how God has responded to this problem, by offering us gifts to be enjoyed. The point of living well is not acquiring or obtaining, but learning how to notice and value God's gifts.

So the picture is beginning to look like this: neither the world nor your own life is completely within your control. If you spend your whole life refusing to accept that the day of your death is approaching, if you live and work 24/7 thinking that by doing so you can get ahead of the game and have a better life by making money or that you can understand the world by getting the right degrees or reading the right books, or if you think you can really leave a lasting mark on the world through what you do, then you are spending your life trying to punch above your weight. . . . We want to have it all, know it all, and be remembered by all for all time. No, says the Preacher; life is gift, not gain. (Gibson, 2017, p. 66)

In response to the fleeting nature of all things, God has provided the gift of enjoyment and delight in the material blessings of life, and the blessings of whatever work we are able to do in any given moment.

He has made everything suitable for its time; moreover he has put a sense of past and future into their minds, yet they cannot find out what God has done from the beginning to the end. I know that there is nothing better for them than to be happy and enjoy themselves as long as they live; moreover, it is God's gift that all should eat and drink and take pleasure in all their toil. (Eccles 3:11-13)

Enjoyment is not some selfish or hedonistic value but is the obedient and proper response to the difficulty of *hebel*. Yes, life comes with uncertainties, pain, and suffering, but humans are able to cope with this uncertainty in part because God has given us the incredible gift of being present to the moments that each day offers. God's response to the human plight is to gift us with gladness. This is both God's response to the human condition as well as humanity's telos—that which we can learn to grow into (Seow, 1997; Seow, 2001).

Qoheleth paints a picture of enjoyment as living a life open to pleasure even as we are fully aware of its ungraspable nature and have no illusions of control—illusions that feed our discontentment. This is not a mandate to live a Pollyanna sort of existence where we simply ignore the disillusioning parts of life and party to numb ourselves from the pain. Rather, it is paying attention to all of life. Life can be unpredictable and tumultuous and sometimes chaotic. Sometimes life simply takes our breath away. But if we pay attention, we also find divine gifts of pleasure scattered throughout every day—the smell of a freshly cut flower, the taste of key lime pie, the pleasure of touch, the delight of friendship. It's not that we can or should choose between the two—*hebel* and enjoyment—but that they coexist and comingle in every season of our fleeting life. Qoheleth is inviting us to enjoy the moments of pleasure, and to be grateful to God who is the giver of these gifts.

Integration Conversation Starters

1. Does it make you nervous that a book of the Bible places such a high premium on sensory pleasure? If so, reflect on where these types of discomforts may be rooted and how they may have been formed. It's interesting that some treatments for depression, such as behavioral activation, also focus on introducing more pleasurable experiences into people's lives. Also, the ancient word *acedia* (apathy) seems to be related to not spending enough time engaging in the gifts life offers. How might these various observations affect the way you sit with depressed patients?

2. One of the persistent heresies in Christian history is Gnosticism, which is the belief that the material world should not be trusted because it is prone to deception and evil, and that the world of the mind is more pristine and trustworthy. What does the book of Ecclesiastes have to say about the problem of Gnosticism?

Gratitude. Despite the instability and disillusionment of contemporary society, we seem to be living amidst a gratitude explosion. Gratitude serves as a fitting conclusion for this chapter because it brings together radical acceptance of life's circumstances, awareness that we cannot control much of what happens to us, and rich appreciation for the gifts of daily life. If Qoheleth were writing today, we suspect he might be quite taken by today's fascination with gratitude.

Positive psychology is the study of what goes right with people, as compared with psychology's more traditional emphasis on what goes wrong. The growth of positive psychology in the twenty-first century has been phenomenal, and the topic of gratitude has been one reason for this. Researchers Robert Emmons and Michael McCullough pioneered the idea of gratitude journaling in a series of studies published in 2003 and found that those who keep gratitude journals experience all sorts of health benefits when compared with others (see McMinn, 2017, for a summary of this study and other gratitude research). Since this landmark study, and scores of others that have followed, gratitude research has been touted in major media outlets, and gratitude journaling has become a mainstream practice (see Emmons, 2013, for a helpful look at gratitude practices).

Much of positive psychology has remained in academia as a topic for researchers, but gratitude is also finding its way into clinical offices. More and more we are seeing counselors and psychotherapists using gratitude interventions as part of their clinical work with patients (e.g., Emmons & Stern, 2013).

A GRATEFUL DAY

David Steindl-Rast is a Benedictine monk involved in gratitude work and interfaith dialog. He has written a number of books (see http://gratefulness.org/brother-david/about-brother-david/), and has also developed and narrated a short video on gratitude called "A Grateful Day" (Network for Grateful Living & Gnarly Bay, 2017). Brother Steindl-Rast encourages people to enjoy and share this video, which is available at http://gratefulness.org/grateful-day/.

Theologians and biblical scholars are weighing in on the topic of gratitude also. It turns out that gratitude and grace are closely connected, and the link between the two is the word *gift*. The New Testament word for grace can be translated as "gift," and gratitude is a natural response to a gift. Diana Butler Bass (2018) and John Barclay (2015) both challenge the quid pro quo manner of giving and receiving gifts that has been common throughout history. In this view we may receive a gift, but it is always with an expectation that we return the favor. The Christian view of gift and gratitude is different—we receive a gift and nothing is required in return. This is grace, and the most reasonable response is gratitude.

Gratitude is not just for our patients. We counselors and psychotherapists also are invited to enjoy the gifts life offers, and the more we do the more we can introduce our patients to the gift of each moment. Returning to Qoheleth's advice to eat, drink, and be merry, it seems important to notice this gratitude connection in the way we counselors live out our days. The point is not simply to eat or to drink, but also to be merry—to live gratefully in this moment because of the gifts God offers us. Theologian Norman Wirzba (2011) is fond of referring to food as "God's love made nutritious" and "God's love made delicious." Every time we eat or drink we have the opportunity to gratefully receive God's love.

How shall we respond to the disillusionment of life and to the hard work we do in the office each day? We gather with our friends, enjoy fresh, healthy food and perhaps a glass of pinot noir, and together we experience the joy of this moment—a moment replete with evidence of God's love and provision. Tomorrow is uncertain. Life evaporates quickly, as the morning dew evaporates. Life seems unfair when we look around and try to figure out who is wealthy and why. But today, right now in this moment, we see God's gift of presence all around us. This is a moment to be enjoyed.

Further Reading

Boyd, G. A. (2010). *Present perfect: Finding God in the now.* Grand Rapids: Zondervan.

DeCaussade, J-P. (1989). *The sacrament of the present moment.* San Francisco: Harper-Collins.

Warren, T. H. (2016). *Liturgy of the ordinary: Sacred practices in everyday life.* Downers Grove, IL: InterVarsity Press.

Wilson, K., & Dufrene, T. (2010). *Things might go terribly, horribly wrong: A guide to life liberated from anxiety.* Oakland, CA: New Harbinger Publications.

Further Listening/Watching

Bowler, K. (2018, December). *Kate Bowler: "Everything happens for a reason"—and other lies I've loved* [Video file]. Retrieved from www.ted.com/talks/kate_bowler_everything_happens_for_a_reason_and_other_lies_i_ve_loved

Bowler, K. (Producer). (June 3, 2019). "John Green: Chronic not curable" [Audio podcast]. *Everything Happens with Kate Bowler.* Retrieved from https://katebowler.com/podcasts/john-green-chronic-not-curable/

Steindl-Rast, D. (2013, June). *Want to be happy? Be grateful* [Video file]. Retrieved from www.ted.com/talks/david_steindl_rast_want_to_be_happy_be_grateful

TEDx. (March, 2013). *What makes life meaningful: Michael Steger at TEDxCSU* [Video file]. Retrieved from https://www.youtube.com/watch?v=RLFVoEF2RI0

FINAL CONVERSATION

Facing Difficulty

If you are reading this book as part of a class, a counseling staff, a study group, or in some other group context, consider having this final conversation before moving on to part two.

Early in my career, I (Mark) often came home from a day of clinical work with sharp headaches. After several years of this, a wise supervisor helped me figure it out. We live in a world where we expect solutions, but we work in a field where there sometimes are no solutions. If we expect to be able to fix the problems of our patients, or even to fix all our own problems, we are creating unreasonable expectations for ourselves and others. That amount of responsibility creates mountains of stress, and in my case, headaches.

Don't get me wrong. It's great when there are solutions to problems, and sometimes there are. The right medication can often fix an infection. Sometimes a strategic counseling technique can fix a relational or anxiety problem. Deep forgiveness truly can heal a broken relationship at times. These are beautiful to behold, but if you have over thirty-five thousand clinical conversations in your career (see the introduction to be reminded of the math), only a small fraction of these sessions will involve fixing anyone. Most of them will feel more like sitting with people in pain, bearing witness to their journeys. And here is where my supervisor was so helpful.

Often it is better to help people grieve well than to try to resolve their problems. Some problems can't be fully solved. Maybe an adult patient had a parent who struggled to express love or grace well, and while that can be grieved, it cannot be fixed. Perhaps the patient is struggling with anxiety or sadness about an irresolvable health problem, touching the reality that Kate Bowler describes—that life is built with paper walls. Sometimes a depression is so persistent that no treatment can fully resolve it. Or consider how often we sit with those who have lost a child or a partner or a meaningful love relationship. Grief work will help, but life will never be exactly the same after such a thing.

The problem is that people typically come to us thinking we can fix them when we cannot. Christianity can sometimes add to this by teaching that if we try the right spiritual practice, or adopt particular beliefs, or memorize certain Scriptures, or find the perfect church, then all will be well again.

We need lament and Ecclesiastes. Sometimes our patients need to cry out in anguish to God (or to us) more than they need the latest therapeutic strategy or optimal spiritual advice. Sometimes we all need to remember that life is like a puff of smoke, that it is unpredictable and uncertain. In these times, it doesn't matter so much whether we are trying a twelve-week treatment protocol or even what approach has the most empirical evidence. These are times simply to sit with a person in pain and to see the gift of this moment, the gift of tears, the gift of grief, the gift of being together in uncertain times.

Final conversation: How much pressure do you feel to fix people in your role as a counselor or psychotherapist? When is this helpful? When is it not?

PART TWO

Pondering God

Life changes us, perhaps especially when we navigate seasons of pain. When given the chance, many patients want to consider their views of God, and how those views may be shifting. This is both theological and psychological work.

Pondering God is theological work because theology provides the structure, language, and history to consider the nature and interconnections of God, self, others, and nature. Accordingly, in these next two chapters—on imaging God and narratives of the cross—we address some theological presuppositions and questions. These need to be considered for informed conversation. But these theological explorations are not enough for the conversations we are hoping to encourage.

It may seem shocking to suggest that theology is not enough, but consider again the book you are reading. First, we are not theologians. Yes, one of us has a seminary degree and the other loves and reads theology, but we are trained as mental health professionals, not theologians. Second, this is a book about integration conversations, and conversations open up spaces and dialog rather than seeking certainty. Third, the community of people reading this book is diverse. Some are evangelical, some identify as mainline Christians, some are questioning religion or have left religion. As such, our goal is not to reach places of certainty with any particular theology, but rather to probe how we ponder God and to create spaces for meaningful conversation.

This is also psychological work. We humans are active construers. We bring our own histories and experiences and presuppositions into how we ponder God, and it seems best to name this as part of healthy conversation rather than pretend it isn't so. Also, it is important to recognize that people change over time. How we understand God today may well be different than our understanding from a decade or two ago. This doesn't mean that God has changed, but just that we see through a mirror dimly (1 Cor 13:12) and our understanding of God may shift as we move through life and encounter one another.

We address quite a lot of theology in the next two chapters, but if you are looking for a precise articulation of what is correct theology and what is not, you will probably be disappointed. Instead, we open up these theological spaces and questions, along with some from psychology, to promote meaningful conversation about how we see God and how God may see us.

3

Imaging God

WHAT DOES MY VIEW OF GOD HAVE
TO DO WITH MY WORK AS A COUNSELOR
OR PSYCHOTHERAPIST?

AT TIMES SEMINARY FELT TO ME (Megan Anna) like walking in the Chamber of Secrets (yes, a Harry Potter reference in an academic book). We learned the nitty, gritty, and sometimes dirty details of how Scripture, orthodoxy, and the church came to be. I often wondered why we don't teach these things in church. A professor once commented that seminarians tend to learn the complex background of faith and then not know what to do with it when they get to the pulpit. Pastors might find the complexity intimidating, and many feel a tension as they walk the delicate line of prophet, truth teller, and comforter.

Perhaps another reason we keep some of these things quiet is that it feels disorienting to think of the human dimensions of how Scripture was developed. Many times, I experienced this peek behind the curtain as shocking—for example, when I learned that the creation stories found in Genesis drew from imagery and themes from older Egyptian and Mesopotamian creation stories. While I was increasingly comfortable encountering the humanity of Jesus, I felt less comfortable encountering the human dimensions of Scripture. In her book *Wrestling the Word,* Hebrew scholar Carolyn Sharp (2010) draws on the story of Jacob wrestling with God (Gen 32:22-32) as a useful metaphor for interpreting Scripture. It is arduous and challenging, and a big part of the struggle is understanding how the cultural context of both writer and reader is interlaced with divine authority as we make sense of Scripture.

Understanding the Bible calls us to acknowledge "the situatedness of authors, textual forms and languages, and readers in particular historical contexts" (Sharp, 2010, p. 5). Scripture is embedded in culture and draws from particular historical imagery, metaphors, and literary devices.[1]

While threatening at first, this way of looking at Scripture eventually opened up new avenues of meaning, creativity, and theological poignancy. As I became more comfortable with the Bible as a cultural document, I was freed to be curious about ways the Bible is both similar to and distinct from the dominant culture of its time—and it turns out this has exciting and rather profound theological significance. Hebrew Scripture transforms common cultural imagery to say something distinctively different about God. By exploring how the God of Israel differed from dominant concepts of gods, I gained a deeper appreciation for God's distinctively loving and gracious essence. Seeing the juxtaposition between the Genesis creation accounts and other ancient Near Eastern (ANE) accounts, I stood in awe of the bold countercultural claims presented in Genesis. We see a God who creates from abundance, who creates in freedom and love. It turns out this is a radical, audacious claim. When we read the Genesis creation narratives from within the context of the ANE cultural backdrop, the significance of being made in the image of God takes on new life. For this reason it may be helpful to meander through the Chamber of Secrets and explore some of the ANE creation stories.

Intrapersonal Conversation Starters

1. I just shared about feeling disoriented when learning that the Bible is a culturally embedded document. What are your reactions to this idea? How does this fit or not fit with what you've learned about the Bible?
2. How does this fit within your faith tradition? This is a great chance to notice and be curious about your reactions to some of these ideas. What is at stake for you in this conversation?

---

[1]To learn more about the Bible as a culturally embedded text, see Jared Byas and Pete Enns's podcast episode "God's Children Tell the Story" found in further listening at the end of the chapter.

Substitute Workers

The creation stories arising out of the ancient Near East (including Mesopo-tamia, Egypt, Canaan) tended to borrow from and build on one another, often sharing imagery and themes. While there are different iterations, many of these creation narratives follow a similar arc (Dalley, 1989). At the risk of oversimplifying and condensing these creation accounts, the narrative goes something like this: This is a world with higher gods and lesser (worker) gods. The worker gods labor to meet the needs of the higher gods. They become tired of toiling and rebel, declaring that they are done serving the higher gods. This leaves the higher gods in an uncomfortable predicament, as they are kind of lazy and don't want to do any work. The solution to the predicament is to create humans to do the work. The humans are created as substitute workers for the gods (Brown, 2001; Clifford, 1994). Humans exist to bear the toil that the gods refuse. In other words, the gods create humans to serve their need. In *Atrahasis*, one of the more developed creation accounts, human beings succeed in being helpful, but also in procreating, thus be-coming noisy and disturbing the gods. Because of the pesky noise the gods send a series of plagues to wipe them out. Only Atrahasis, who is clever enough to build a boat, escapes the last plague—a flood. However, once most of the humans are gone the gods realize that despite their noise they were quite useful, and they revise the human population by setting limits. In this new, limited world, humans can die, have limited fertility, and so on. But notice that the gods were happy to wipe out the humans until realizing they needed them.

This devaluing of humanity continues throughout ANE creation narratives. In the Egyptian account *Instruction to King Merikare*, humans are referred to as "cattle of the gods" (Clifford, 1994, p. 116). The role of the king and the temple also take on special meaning within this narrative. In order to keep these worker-humans in line, there is need for a king. In the Akkadian creation narratives—and later in Egyptian creation stories—the king is created to oversee the "human servants." And the temple is imperative to the gods be-cause this is where they come in order to collect their goods from the humans. Batto (2013) writes: "A temple was less a place of worship than a palace from which the deity ruled and maintained right order in the world" (p. 17). Humans and their sacred spaces are all intended for the service of their gods.

Another significant distinction is that in Genesis humans come from life not death. In the Akkadian account humans are created out of moistened clay mixed with the blood and flesh of a slaughtered god who had rebelled. Human life comes from mixing the flesh of a sacrificed god, whose ghost forever intermingles and intermixes with human life (Simkins, 2014). The Judeo-Christian account in Genesis 2 has God creating humanity out of dust, but the additive ingredient that brings life is Yahweh's life-giving breath or spirit. God brings clay to life through *life*, not *death*.

AUTHOR DIALOG: CREATION AS SCIENTIFIC HISTORY OR MYTH

Mark: It seems like you're talking about the creation account as mythical. Is that right?

Megan Anna: I'm cautious using the word *myth* as I think it can easily seem dismissive. I'm also cautious reading creation as scientific history. What I find most helpful is thinking about how the Hebrew people would have heard the creation account, and to think about the questions that were important to them. Brueggemann (1982) says that within modern epistemology there is a pull to place the creation narrative within a binary (either scientific or mythical), and yet the story doesn't fit either of these two camps. The Israelites were more concerned with exploring God's intentions than God's methods or techniques. Thus, the text is neither scientific history nor myth, but *theological proclamation*. This is news about God's gracious and powerful transforming Word. God has chosen to bind Godself to the world for the purpose of the creation's wholeness, redemption, and growth. The creation account is declaration of the gospel: the good news that God's mysterious, gracious presence now transforms and changes creation.

Mark: I wonder if modernism has inclined us to ask questions such as whether the stories in the Bible are true or not. It seems like you're suggesting the creation accounts in the Bible hold important truth even if creation didn't unfold in exactly the way the words suggest. Do you ever worry that this perspective undermines the authority of Scripture?

Megan Anna: One of my struggles with modern thought is the narrowing of truth that has happened. Truth became reduced to factual information. In order to keep up with the pressures of science, we began applying the same criteria to Christianity—most notably Scripture. We

Given this cultural backdrop, one can see how dramatic the theological statements of the Hebrew creation narratives are! *God created humans out of surplus of goodness, not out of need.* Human life comes from God's life, not from death. The Hebrew creation narrative is not a story of deficit but one of abundance. While other ANE accounts serve the purpose of the gods, the Hebrew creation narrative explores a God who is distinct from creation and yet *chooses* to be intimately bound to creation by graciously moving toward creation (Brown, 2001; Brueggemann, 1982). God is both transcendent

made Scripture jump through modernist hoops to prove its authority (Catholicism did this less than Protestantism). Biblical authors were less concerned with factual truth than with getting at essential truths—broad truths about the world and about who God is (relational truths, truths about God's character and essence, how to be in the world, and so on). I think this narrowed view of truth can be detrimental to how we view the authority of Scripture.

The Bible is not a modern text, so when we apply modern criteria to it we do it a disservice and potentially miss some of the beauty of the essential truths it offers us. I also think we make it easier for people to dismiss the Bible altogether when we insist on a modern criteria of truth for this premodern book. When I first learned about factual discrepancies in the Gospels, I felt pulled in one of two directions: either engage in mental gymnastics to explain away the factual discrepancies or disregard the idea of authority altogether.

I did some of both, and neither felt very satisfying. Similarly, many of my peers who have difficulty trusting Christianity can point to moments where they discovered factual discrepancies in the Bible. Sadly, they lacked a framework that would allow them to remain interested in and engaged in the truths of Scripture.

Through the work of Karl Barth and others I was introduced to a way of thinking about Scripture that held the tension—a human book, divinely inspired, that does not align with scientific facts yet speaks to profound human truths. This is a view that takes seriously the authority and sacredness of Scripture without requiring it to meet the criteria of a modernist framework.

There are many other views on this, which makes me glad the goal here is to stimulate conversation and not argue for a particular perspective on how to approach Scripture. See the further reading list at the end of the chapter for people I recommend engaging with on this subject.

(above and beyond creation) and immanent (invested in and present to our material world). In Egypt, humans were the "cattle of the gods," but for Yahweh humans are worthy of being imprinted with the image of God. The Hebrew creation narrative inverts the common cultural conceptions of God and humans. Rather than being mere cattle, humans become representatives of God on earth—agents called to do God's good work (Brueggemann, 1982, 2002).

EUGENE PETERSON AND THE GOOD CREATION

The creation story held by Christians affirms that creation is good. Throughout the Genesis 1 account, God stops to reflect multiple times, consistently concluding, "This is good."

At the memorial service of renowned Christian author and pastor Eugene Peterson, his son Leif Peterson noted how God stopped at the end of each day of creation to pronounce that it was good, and then reflected on a similar pattern in his father:

> I think my dad did that a lot. He was always looking around, at the mountains, at the flowers, at the birds, and at the relationships forming and playing out all around him, and you could tell from the twinkle in his eyes what he was thinking. "Oh man, that's good. That's really good." (Peterson, 2019, p. 2)

With all the complexity and challenge life offers us, it is helpful to return to this original truth as often as we possibly can, remembering that everywhere around us is the sort of beauty that reflects God's favor, and that we ourselves are part of this good creation.

This has implications for the practical lived reality of our faith. Later in the same service Leif Peterson mused that his father really only had one sermon and that he simply found different ways of saying the same thing week after week for thirty years. What was his sermon? "God loves you. He's on your side. He's coming after you. He's relentless" (Peterson, 2019, p. 4).

Notice the stark contrast between this message and the ANE accounts. We are not here as substitute workers. We have nothing to earn. God's goodness is seen all through creation and in every human heart. God is with us.

Imaging God

Being created in the image of God is distinctive of the Hebrew creation account (Gen 1:26-27):

> Then God said, "Let us make humankind in our image, according to our likeness; and let them have dominion over the fish of the sea, and over the birds of the air, and over the cattle, and over all the wild animals of the earth, and over every creeping thing that creeps upon the earth."
>
> > So God created humankind in his image,
> > in the image of God he created them;
> > male and female he created them.

Jewish and Christian scholars have spent thousands of years sorting out what this means. And it turns out there is good reason for confusion, as the Bible does not speak much about the image of God (*imago Dei*) after this initial passage in Genesis (Middleton, 2005). Thus, the construct has been left to theologians and philosophers to muse for a couple millennia, which is always a good way to stir up a variety of opinions.

While the theological implications of *imago Dei* are profound, neither of us has ever had a patient seek therapy to better understand what it means to be created in God's image. Most people, including the patients who seek our help, are much more likely to question how they view God than how God's character may be imprinted in their lives and relationships.

Theology informs the work we do in the counseling and psychotherapy office, but when it comes to imaging God, we need to consider both the psychological work of how humans image God as well as the theological work of how God's image shows up in humanity. One option is to look in the theological direction: the triune God creates humanity to reflect God's image. This is the arrow pointing downward from God to humanity in figure 1. The other direction—a psychological one—is also important. How do we infer particular ideas about God based on our own experiences, beliefs, and sociocultural context? This is what many psychologists have referred to as "God image" and "God concept," represented by the upward arrow in figure 1.

I (Mark) recently attended a lecture where religious scholar and bestselling author Reza Aslan (2017) began by stating that throughout all human history, we have created God in our image. While I felt dissonance with much of his lecture, I often return to that opening line and nod. Psychology has a lot to

VIEWS OF THE *IMAGO DEI*

Views of the *imago Dei* (image of God) offered by theologians, philosophers, and biblical scholars have emphasized different qualities over time. These are known as the functional, substantive, and relational views. Rather than try to argue for a particular view of the *imago Dei,* we are taking a different approach. Because the *imago Dei* has meant many different things throughout Christian history, we suspect it may, in fact, hold multiple meanings—or at least the various perspectives make for good conversation that does not require firm resolution. We offer a brief reference map here and provide additional resources for those interested in a more in-depth conversation on the philosophical and biblical underpinnings of these concepts.[a]

Functional. Many Hebrew scholars hold to a functional view of the *imago Dei*, emphasizing that humans image God through how we function in the world. The Hebrew worldview was an incredibly concrete worldview, so locating the meaning of *imago Dei* within concrete actions seen in human behavior made a lot of sense within this cultural context. This view understands humans as representatives of God's rule here on earth, invited to participate in ushering in shalom.

Substantive. Perhaps the most dominant view throughout Christian history, this view of the *imago Dei* holds that humans share essential or ontological characteristics with God. The likeness to God is located within ourselves (such as human reason, our ethical nature, the ability to be relational).

Relational. In the last half century, since the writings of Karl Barth, many theologians have begun to think about relational components of the *imago Dei*. Here, the emphasis is not on the ontological capacities we humans may share with God, or on the functions we are asked to carry as God's stewards, but on the dyadic, relational nature of being human. Humans emerged from a relational God ("Let us make humankind in our image" [Gen 1:26]), and humans are created as relational beings, flourishing in the context of relationship. Here the emphasis is not on our capacity for relationship (that would be substantive), but the relationship itself is what images God.

Emerging views. Trying to pinpoint views of the image of God can be challenging because new ideas emerge quickly. One recent attempt is what might be called a proleptic view, which suggests that the image of God is still unfolding through the long, slow process of theistic evolution. The *imago Dei* is an invitation forward toward transformation and fullness that is the ultimate telos of the process of becoming that God set in motion

---

[a] In an earlier draft of this chapter we described these different perspectives of the *imago Dei* in some detail. At some point we determined this deep dive into theology might cause some boredom in our readers, and boredom is never good for meaningful conversation. If you would like to see and consider more about these four perspectives, feel free to download it at meganannaneff.org/embodyingintegration.

(Peters, 2018). As Ecclesiastes reminds us, "there is nothing new under the sun" (1:9), and so it should be noted that this proleptic view bears some resemblance to the work of Irenaeus in the second century and Origen in the third century.

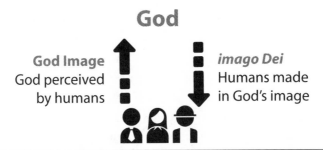

God

God Image
God perceived
by humans

imago Dei
Humans made
in God's image

Figure 1. *Imago Dei* and God image

IMAGE OF GOD AND EMOTIONAL VALENCE

Figure 1 demonstrates the relationship between *imago Dei* and God image, demonstrating a sort of relational and perceptual loop between God and humanity. It is worth noting that the emotional valence shifts in different parts of the loop.

The arrow pointing downward from God to humankind reflects the theological notion that humans are made in God's image. We argue throughout this chapter, as we do throughout the book, for a positive emotional valence here: creation is good, God creates us from life rather than death, we are made to be in relationship with the divine and not merely to be substitute workers, and God is always with us.

The arrow pointing upward, from humanity to God, reflects the psychological notion that we humans image God in particular ways that are related to our own backgrounds, worldviews, and relational history. Whereas the arrow from God to humanity is overwhelmingly positive, the arrow back the other direction is complex and multifaceted. Sometimes this upward arrow is characterized by gratitude and love and awe, and sometimes it is tinged with anger and disappointment and frustration (see chapter one on lament).

This is not so much a problem to be solved as an observation to be made. Love flows downward from God to humanity, and the circle closes with a host of emotions—both positive and negative—being directed back toward God. This paradox of unequal valences is often the work faced by Christians in the counseling office.

say about the ways we create God in our image. This need not be a matter of shame or embarrassment; it is simply how we perceive everyone and everything in our world, and indeed it is made possible because of the capacities God has given us. We do our best to perceive the other, but we typically transpose and project our own experiences and expectations in the process. We do the same thing with our friends and spouses and parents and children. We presume we understand the other based on our insights and observations, but we also bring our personal histories and assumptions into the process. Psychologists and counselors know the concepts of transference and countertransference, which refer to our natural tendency to place the expectations and emotions of past relationships onto current relationships in the counseling office. In the same way, we tend to transfer past experiences onto how we understand God. To explore the notion of God image, we need to take a brief detour into how we know what we know.

Over the last thirty years, social and cognitive scientists have learned a great deal about how we process information—rather automatically it turns out (Hofmann, Gschwendner, & Schmitt, 2005). It's a bit like getting in the car and driving away, knowing the car works, and knowing there is a good deal of complexity under the hood, but not needing to understand much of the complexity for our daily purposes. Similarly, when we think about something we engage in complex processes quite automatically without much need to stop and ponder what the processes may be. Mechanics and neuroscientists make their livelihood looking under the hoods and working with the complex parts of systems that seem quite automatic in everyday life.

Current neuroscience research suggests we have two different ways of knowing: explicit and implicit (Hall, 2007). Explicit beliefs are the things we consciously know we believe, even as implicit beliefs, attitudes, and biases hum along beneath our consciousness. Neurocircuitry is complex and defies simple taxonomy, and some have grossly oversimplified the brain by attributing particular ways of being to precise neuroanatomy. But whether it is metaphor or neurology, explicit beliefs seem to involve the prefrontal cortex and left side of the brain. These beliefs include linear, abstract, verbal, and analytic thought processes. Explicit beliefs are sometimes called "high road" brain circuits. In contrast, implicit knowledge tends to be more experiential than cognitive, often showing up as emotional states and unconscious stories that weave through our lives. This "gut level" knowledge may involve more right-side activity in the brain, and perhaps structures that exist at a lower level of evolutionary development, such as the amygdala. Because implicit knowledge is storied and experiential, it both emerges out of relationships and influences our present relationships. These templates, emotions, and unconscious stories influence how we are with others, and how we are with God (Hall, 2007).

Many have had the experience of holding a positive or negative attitude about someone even before knowing the person. Perhaps we know the person's name and it reminds us of someone else we have known with a similar name, or we see a certain facial characteristic that reminds us of someone else. Maybe the cadence of speech or tonal qualities of the other remind us of a beloved grandmother, a fierce competitor, or a belligerent former neighbor. These implicit ways of knowing the other affect us even without us deliberately deciding about the trustworthiness, safety, or character of the other.

Hall (2007) explores the concept of "unthought knowns," first proposed by British psychoanalyst Christopher Bollas. Unthought knowns refer to a deep sense of relational knowing that is not accessible through linear, rational thought. Our implicit knowledge is a world of these unthought knowns—knowledge that is not yet consciously accessible to us yet influences much of our daily existence and relational patterns. This implicit system involves templates and filters that influence our everyday life, often without our awareness of their presence. Not surprisingly, our relationships with one another are deeply influenced by implicit knowledge, though we have no words or thoughts to adequately describe the implicit things we know. While we are quite aware of our explicit beliefs, and many of us assume these beliefs drive our decisions, it turns out that implicit beliefs are also quite influential in shaping our daily decisions, relational patterns, and behavior.

This distinction between implicit and explicit knowing has implications for how and who we imagine God to be for at least four reasons. First, because language is the economy of explicit beliefs, we can talk and write quite a lot about God's character, and these theological discoveries and propositions help shape what we know while also creating a cognitive frame for how we want to live in the world. This is a good and important way to form and transmit a God image to future generations, but it can be misleading if we presume it to be the primary or exclusive way we come to know God.

Second and related to the first reason, the explicit knowledge we use to understand God has implications for both forms of knowing. That is, cognitive beliefs are held, discussed, and lived out in particular ways that shape both explicit and implicit ways of knowing God. For example, a devout Christian couple may hold particular faith beliefs about virtuous living. These explicit beliefs will, in turn, guide their daily interactions with their children. They may attend religious services, pray before meals, and read devotionals after. Their family beliefs will likely also shape how the parents view obedience and discourage disobedience, and how they model honesty, self-restraint, patience, and love. How their children come to know God will be both a function of the explicit beliefs they are taught and the implicit, lived stories emerging from how this family interacts with one another.

Third, if explicit knowing has implications for implicit knowing, the opposite is also true. Though we like to think that we base our daily experiences on the rational beliefs we hold in our heads, hundreds of studies in social cognition demonstrate that it often works the other way around: we shape our ideas based on our experiences. With something like God image, we will likely be drawn to explicit beliefs and doctrines that seem consistent with our implicit experiences of God. For example, let's start with an assertion with which most Christians agree: God forgives our sin. People who hold implicit beliefs about God's commitment to justice may be more prone to emphasize the word *sin* in this assertion. Those who experience God as benevolent and gracious may be more inclined to emphasize *forgives*. So often we sit side-by-side talking about God without recognizing that each of us has a story that undergirds our words and our beliefs.

Fourth, even as we try to match our implicit beliefs with our explicit ones, and our explicit beliefs with our implicit ones, the gap between explicit and implicit beliefs remains (Moriarty & Hoffman, 2007). Our explicit theological beliefs and ideas about God make up our God concept, whereas our felt, embodied and lived relational experiences make up our God image (Davis, Moriarty, & Mauch, 2013). To the extent that our relationships with God and others match or do not match the frame of our explicit beliefs, we ourselves will be shaped and influenced. Often in the work of counseling and psychotherapy we see patients who have quite a large gap between their implicit and explicit God image.

God creates humans in God's image (*imago Dei*), humans create God in their image (God image), and counselors and psychotherapists sit in this complex interplay with their patients and help them find meaning and direction for life. Both theology and psychology are essential parts of this conversation. In contrast to ANE creation accounts—where humans are substitute workers for the gods, where human life emerges out of death—the Christian story calls creation good and directs us toward harmonious relationships with God, others, and nature (Hoekema, 1994). This is a story of abundant life (e.g., Jn 10:10), experienced through connected relationship.

We also see this instinctual, God-given call to relationship in human attachment and relational neurobiology. Infants are born to connect with their caregivers through gazing into their eyes and expressing pleasure in their presence, and this instinct to connect never goes away unless it is beaten out of a human being through unspeakable trauma. Both our explicit and implicit ways of knowing, but perhaps especially our implicit ways, call us to be in harmonious relationships with one another.

We make it sound easy to be connected and singing in harmony, but we all know better. The German word *Sehnsucht* has no perfect translation in English, but it speaks to a deep yearning for something that is elusive and impossible to fully attain. Even as we are created for harmonious relationships with God, others, and nature, we still notice a gnawing within us that things are not fully right. Almost anyone with even a casual gaze toward the events of the world would agree that things are not right. This is the context of counseling: in the absence of harmonious relationships, we have the good sense to feel unsettled and upset. Each of us comes from families and communities with unique struggles and areas of brokenness. We come to one another and to God with our implicit and explicit ways of knowing, yearning for wholeness and completeness even as we question whether these ideals can be fully attained. And so we face spiritual struggles, emotional pain, and relational turmoil, even as we glimpse the possibility of harmony and shalom. Poets, artists, novelists, musicians, ministers, spiritual directors, physicians, teachers, and many others join with counselors and psychotherapists to help attune people to their inner desire for harmony and the impossibility of fully attaining their deepest longings.

1. What are some of your explicit beliefs about God? How do they differ from your implicit beliefs?
2. How have you seen counseling and psychotherapy influence your patients' implicit beliefs about God?

Implications for Counseling and Psychotherapy

One of the basic assumptions we make in writing this book is that theology and psychology both matter for how we sit with people in the counseling and psychotherapy office. For many hundreds of years Christians have pondered the *imago Dei,* and in recent years we have learned a great deal about how humans perceive and experience God. But how are these findings from theology and behavioral science relevant for the day-in, day-out work of counselors and psychotherapists? We offer five suggestions in the remainder of this chapter.

A theological and psychological anthropology of goodness. What do you do for a living? When we hear such a question, many of us respond that we are a counselor, a psychologist, a clinical social worker, or a pastor. But implicit in this answer are many other roles that we play. We ponder human nature. We form theories about what makes for healthy living and unhealthy living. We transmit our beliefs about how people become healthier. We choose particular tests to assess health and ignore others because they do not align with our views of health. We work with our patients to determine goals for the outcome of our work together. We help people consider which relationships are worth pursuing and which are not. In sum, we are continually evaluating human nature and exerting benevolent influence for how to make the world a better place.

We may hear in ethics workshops that we are not to impose our beliefs onto others, and certainly it is true that we need to be exceptionally cautious not to take advantage of others for our own sake, but if we honestly look at our work, inevitably our beliefs guide every interaction we have. We transmit our values to others despite our best efforts to respect them as autonomous agents. As Christians doing this work, it behooves us to know our view of persons, what makes for health and unhealth, what helps people move toward health, and how we can best be in relationship with one another and with God in this process. These worldview assumptions are contained in our theological anthropology (i.e., our view of humanity in relation to God). In turn, our views about the *imago Dei* form the core of our theological anthropology.

Just as theology offers us a particular anthropology, so also our psychological theories give us a particular way of looking at humanity, including what goes wrong (unhealth), what goes right (health), and how to help people to places of health. Client-centered therapists focus on self-actualization, third-wave cognitive therapists on psychological flexibility, second-wave cognitive therapists on right thinking, psychoanalytic therapists on restorative relationships, and so on. Each of these approaches contains an implicit view of persons, and so does Christianity. Some have viewed this as evidence that psychology and religion are competing worldviews, but we prefer to think of this as one of the intriguing adventures of integration. How can we bring the anthropology implicit in Christianity together with the anthropology of a particular psychological theory in a way that transforms both? It certainly involves more than sprinkling a few Bible verses atop a psychological theory or using a little psychological jargon while pronouncing a theological anthropology. True integration involves working from theological and psychological anthropology. This is why the arrows in figure 1 go both directions, with both theology and psychology informing who we are in relation to God and one another.

The starting point for a theologically grounded view of persons is that humanity is fundamentally good, even if not entirely good. We are both created in the image of God and fallen creatures, struggling to love God and neighbor as much as we naturally love ourselves. But the first truth of humanity is that God is delighted with us. The Hebrew phrase *tov, tov, tov meod* reflects the language of God in the first chapter of Genesis, reminding us of God's assessment that creation is good, good, very good.

During times of complexity and pain, it can be hard to hold onto this belief. During the exile the Israelites faced despair, bombarded with messages of their worthlessness. One of the truths that anchored the community during this time was that God had promised to preserve the *imago Dei*. Despite the huge challenges and struggles humans caused in the first eleven chapters of

Genesis (e.g., expulsion from garden, sibling murder, flood), the *imago Dei* persists. It has been stamped onto humanity and cannot be washed off. The construction of Genesis 1:1–2:4 is commonly dated among this exile and postexilic period (Brueggemann, 1982). So precisely when the world attempted to convince Israel of their worthlessness, this beautiful theological proclamation of the dignity, worth, and goodness of all humanity, even the Babylonians, arose.

This goodness, at times, can be difficult to remember in the counseling office. Benjamin came to my (Megan Anna's) office shortly after enduring a contentious divorce. He had struggled with anger and depression for years. Still, I wasn't expecting the chilling story that came next. Through shame-filled tears, Benjamin described the hours after his wife informed him that she wanted a divorce. Benjamin, unable to imagine life without her, described taking his gun from the safe and loading it with the intention of shooting his young son and then himself. He went to gather his sleeping son, but as he held his son in his arms he began sobbing and aborted his plan.

Here, in some of the greatest complexity I have ever encountered in another human being, I was left pondering the notion that humans are fundamentally good. Sitting right in front of me, in the person of Benjamin, the choice of whether to believe in human goodness or not confronted me.

As I sat with Benjamin, I noticed fear creeping in. Part of my mind busily scrolled through liability, ethics, and safety issues: Will he do this again? Is his son safe? Another part of my mind questioned my own safety. Will Benjamin ever experience me as abandoning him like his wife? If so, how might he respond?

While these safety concerns had merit, it is right to see the image of God in others even when flooded with fear. I needed to let Benjamin know I wasn't repulsed, afraid, or scared of him. I needed to be able to see his badness while also holding onto his fundamental goodness. I suspected Benjamin rarely felt comfortable with himself, and so I wanted to communicate that I felt comfortable with him.[2]

---

[2]While it is rare, there are times in this work that clinicians come across personal safety concerns. In this case there was no indication of imminent danger. If you are in imminent danger, it is critical to listen to these cues and respond appropriately to protect yourself and others who may be in danger.

Benjamin was having difficulty holding onto any semblance of belief in his goodness. The Hebrew people likely also faced difficulty holding onto their sense of goodness during the Babylonian exile. The thing about being held captive is that there is often an overt mission to break one's humanity and sense of dignity, but in the words of Scripture we see God's unrelenting commitment to humans as created in the *imago Dei*. Perhaps there are times we hold the hope of the *imago Dei* for our patients—to see the sacredness and honor that they cannot currently see.

Psychologist Carl Rogers (1957) used different language while identifying a similar concept. Rogers identifies the importance of having unconditional positive regard for the people with whom we work, in part because this regard from the therapist helps the individual cultivate self-regard. It's hard to imagine one could ever have positive self-regard without first experiencing positive regard from another. Similarly, we can hold hope in the sacredness, dignity, vocation, and relational goodness in our patients while they are developing the capacity to remember and hold onto these truths.

Stepping into Benjamin's chilling moment of planned homicide and suicide was dreadful, but I needed to step into that moment in order to glimpse his terror. Perspective taking increases empathy (Hooper, Erdogan, Keen, Lawton, & McHugh, 2015). By experiencing his mind, as best I could, I could sense the intensity of betrayal, pain, hurt, and chaos churning inside him. While the image of him lifting his son and moving him toward the garage brought chills, the image of this hurting man who felt utterly powerless at the thought of losing his family brought me to a place of deep empathy and compassion and enabled me to give words to what had gone unnamed for Benjamin. I experienced positive regard for him, believed in his desire for relationship,

Integration Conversation Starters

1. Do you find it difficult to see a fundamental human goodness in certain people? How do you hold a belief in the *imago Dei* in these times?

2. Some views of the *imago Dei* suggest the image is contained within each person. Another view, called the relational view, sees the image as existing in the relational space between two persons. How might this change the way you perceive human goodness in the counseling office?

and saw in his tears an implicit awareness of life's sacredness. I held the belief in *imago Dei* for Benjamin, inviting him to borrow from my belief until he, too, had the capacity to have hope in his sacredness.

Trauma as a bridge between implicit and explicit beliefs. A psychologist, colleague, and mutual friend of ours, Kenneth Logan, explores implicit and explicit belief structures with particular interest in how trauma can be a transformative event in integrating the two. During trauma we largely operate from our fight-or-flight or sympathetic nervous system. During these moments our brains don't spare precious energy for explicit meaning-making activities, so we tend to operate from more automatic, implicit perspectives. Recalling moments of trauma in an experiential way can break through our explicit beliefs, revealing our core implicit beliefs. By being exposed to these moments we increase our awareness of implicit beliefs, and this greater awareness opens up the possibility of transformation (Logan, personal communication, May 30, 2018).

Ken's ideas are fascinating, and the implications far-reaching. What does it mean to have both a God concept (theology) and a God image (relational-experiential) that influence how we experience the world, ourselves, and God? How do these come to bear on the daily experience of life in stressful times? In calm times? How might we as counselors and psychotherapists adequately empathize with the awful traumas our patients face while still holding the possibility that these same traumas might lead to growth and self-awareness?

As awful as trauma is (no matter the cause), it is remarkable that those who study trauma are also beginning to pay close attention to the experience of growth and positive change that sometimes occurs in the wake of these horrific experiences. Two psychologists at the University of North Carolina at Charlotte, Richard Tedeschi and Lawrence Calhoun, initially suggested the concept of posttraumatic growth in the mid-1990s, and the concept has grown rapidly in the scientific literature (Tedeschi & Calhoun, 1995). Tedeschi and Calhoun suggest that life crises can sometimes result in "increased appreciation for life in general, more meaningful interpersonal relationships, an increased sense of personal strength, changed priorities, and a richer existential and spiritual life" (Tedeschi & Calhoun, 2004, p. 1). Spiritual writers allude to something similar—that suffering can bring growth and even joy. While an intriguing construct, posttraumatic growth research is still in its infancy and is beset by a number of methodological and concept challenges (Jayawickreme & Blackie, 2014). Still, it is worth considering that growth and increased spiritual awareness may be an indirect outcome of experiencing trauma, and perhaps one of the mechanisms at play might be that in crises we glimpse our implicit beliefs in ways that everyday experience does not allow. Growth is not an automatic outcome of trauma, but counselors and psychotherapists are often blessed to see a surprising beauty growing from the ashes of past trauma.

Jenny came to me (Megan Anna) following an acute crisis that left her destabilized. As a first-generation college student and the glue that held her struggling family together, she worked tirelessly yet felt she was never good enough. She tended to find herself in asymmetrical relationships where she was the giver, and yet in her mind, she was never a good enough sister, daughter, friend, or partner. While introducing her to the concept of self-compassion, with tear-filled eyes she reflected, "That's impossible, I could never do that." She received strength from God, she believed God loved and delighted in her, yet she was functioning from an implicit belief that she could never be good enough for God, that God's grace was not *for her*. She was working hard to please God and gain God's favor, just as she was doing with everyone else.

Trauma had been a constant backdrop in Jenny's life, from disjointed memories of childhood trauma to reexperiencing sexual trauma in adulthood. Jenny tended to minimize the role trauma had played in her developing sense of self. Her mentality was, "It's in the past, people have it much worse, this shouldn't still be impacting me." In these words, we see a wide gulf between Jenny's implicit relational knowledge and her explicit knowledge and beliefs. The implicit relational patterns were continuing to disrupt her life—impacting her relationship to self, others, and God—but lacking the ability to talk about these experiences with words, she was not able to bridge her intrinsic and extrinsic beliefs. This gap left her with fragmented and jarring symptoms of anxiety.

Ken Logan's concept is encouraging—that perhaps through gaining access to our implicit beliefs, as happens when reexperiencing times of crisis or trauma, there is space to have these beliefs opened up to bridge implicit and explicit beliefs, and thus to redemption and transformation. In times of pain our belief structures are cracked open and we gain access to deeply held internalized beliefs.

There was nothing glorious about Jenny's acute stress, and yet, it was the current crisis that was opening up space for her to explore the disconnect between her implicit and explicit beliefs. As a child Jenny didn't have anyone to help her consolidate her story, leading to increased fragmentation and terror. Lacking the ability to integrate her implicit stories of relationship with her explicit knowledge, Jenny found it difficult to construct a coherent story about herself, others, and God. But now as an adult, in the context of a safe psychotherapy relationship, she could go back and retell the stories of trauma. Especially as she learned to move past a cognitive telling of the stories, and into an embodied, visceral reexperiencing of her pain, this opened up the possibility of her intrinsic and extrinsic beliefs looking each other in the eye. Telling stories is an ideal way to integrate intrinsic and extrinsic beliefs because it creates a sort of knowledge spiral where explicit knowledge and implicit knowledge are interpreting and building off one another (Hall, 2007). And it turns out this knowledge spiral is key for revising our patients' spiritual stories (Hall, 2007, p. 40).

Jenny had the good sense to be anxious when things started spiraling out of control. This may seem a strange way to think about emotional distress, but recall that we humans are drawn toward flourishing and harmony. This is how we are made, so it seems quite good and reasonable that we have warning signs when things are going poorly. For Jenny, her anxiety served as an alarm system. Her intellect could not deliver her from the angst she experienced. Notice how the discrepancy between Jenny's explicit and implicit beliefs raised important questions about how she experienced God. While Jenny explicitly believed life is sacred and that she is made in God's image, she implicitly held a view more akin to ANE creation accounts—that her worth was found in being a substitute worker, that her life emerged out of death. Her self-concept was ridden with shame, causing her to find herself in a constant rat race of "never good enough" as she frantically attempted to prove her goodness.

Jenny had internalized the message of her shame, her badness. As we opened up space for her to explore her story, her implicit beliefs came to light, opening up the possibility of transformation. She began opening up to the possibility of a God who could look upon her with love and grace, enabling her to be more compassionate with herself.

Conversations such as these can lead to difficult places where trauma and self-doubt lurk, but these are also places that can be transformative. Becoming aware of our implicit beliefs can be liberating and empowering, freeing us to live into the life-giving power of our Creator.

1. In your own clinical work or personal life, how have you seen encountering or recalling trauma as helpful in bridging implicit and explicit beliefs about God?
2. Talking about a belief isn't the same as encountering it. What helpful ways have you found to help patients access their implicit beliefs about God?

The self-offering nature of the **imago Dei.** As depicted in common creation cosmology in ANE accounts, humans existed for the purpose of the gods. The gods coexisted and intermingled with humans; they weren't worried about having "multiple relationships" with their servant-humans.

In contrast to the ANE accounts, in the Christian creation story we meet a God that can satisfy God's own needs—God creates out of abundance not deficit. God is separate and exists independent of creation. And yet, from this distinctive, separate place God chooses to be connected to creation. The creation account is not a story of coercion or tyranny. God invites rather than obligates (Brueggemann, 1982). Humans are ushered into a noncoercive relationship with God for the betterment of all of creation, not for the purpose of meeting God's needs. God does much more than the Babylonian gods who simply put up with the pesky humans. God delights in humans (Ps 149:4).

In this Christian account, humanity emerges out of God's generosity, not God's need. This, in turn, has implications for how we live in the world. As those created in God's image, do we relate to one another from a generous, self-offering place, or do we slip back to a more primitive place of seeing others as means to our own ends? Counselors and psychotherapists occasionally hear stories of colleagues who take sexual advantage of their patients. These situations feel akin to the Babylonian creation story—gods who created for their own pleasure. And one need not look to such extreme examples to recognize our vulnerability to thinking first of our own needs even as we care for others. Both Alice Miller (2008) and Michael Sussman (2007) have explored the unconscious motives of therapists and the tendency for "wounded healers" to be drawn to the field with a desire to be needed by others. For many of us being needed provides a source of meaning that helps us navigate the world. It can be captivating and enticing to have others need and desire us. Why else would we be crazy enough to submerge ourselves in people's darkest moments repeatedly? We aren't suggesting this is inherently wrong; it is, however, important to be aware of underlying motivations and what we gain from the therapeutic relationship.

The self-offering God who creates humanity to reflect God's own image teaches us about balance as we walk in the psychotherapy room. God is distinct and yet committed to creation, in grace. As representatives of God we are invited to remain distinct from one another while also being bound together in grace. As we hold hope for our patients and invite them into nourishing, supportive relationships, we embody God's image, representing and extending God's way of being in relationship with the world.

Experienced counselors know the nagging tension between self-focus and self-offering. Perhaps you have just received a text or phone call with disturbing news, maybe your car is in the shop and costing way more than you imagined to repair, or it could be that you have just received a troubling medical result that requires more tests. When you walk to the waiting room to greet your next patient you have a choice to make. Will you remain in the mental space of recounting your troubles, or perhaps even look to your patient for some comfort (a role reversal that can be quite harmful to patients)? Or will you set down your own personal worries and enter into that generous, self-offering place of hosting a meaningful conversation about your patient's concerns?

As we ourselves become accustomed to living from generous, self-offering places with patients, we can also invite them into similar places in their relationships with others.

QUERIES FOR PATIENTS

Consider asking your patients questions such as:

1. What is it that your partner/friend/child most needs from you right now?

   This question helps get one's mind off of personal needs and desires, helping them focus on another.

2. I notice how deeply concerned and compassionate you are for [name]. What is that like for you?

   This is a way of noticing compassionate self-offering in a patient, and allowing the patient to notice as well. We are about to explore relational selves, and this question may also help a patient feel connected in a larger relational web.

Relational selves. What is a self? And how does our view of God inform our answer? How has culture impacted how we think of selves? How does the intersection of culture and Christianity influence this? How we answer these questions has a significant impact on how we sit with ourselves and other selves.

Western philosophy is heavily influenced by Descartes' famous words: "I think, therefore I am" (Descartes, trans. 2016, p. 10). This modern, self-contained understanding of the self marks a dramatic shift from how humans historically thought. Contemporary theologies in Africa, Latin America, and Asia are translating Christianity through a contextual lens that bears similarity to many of the biblical contexts.[3] In juxtaposition to Descartes' words, an African understanding of the self is more akin to "I am because we are, and since we are, therefore I am" (Mbiti, 1990, p. 141). This distinction provides a glimpse into how culture influences our understanding of Christian anthropology.

The Canadian philosopher Charles Taylor (2007) captures the shifts and turns that have occurred in how we conceptualize the self in his book *A Secular Age*. Taylor identifies the premodern to modern shift as highly significant when it comes to the understanding of selves. Prior to modernity, the self was seen as more of a "porous" self (p. 27). These selves existed in an enchanting, magical world where the boundary between the self and outside was permeable. The self could be taken ahold of by external forces such as passion, excitement, depression, sickness, and external spirits. The porous self was linked to other selves: "I am because we are."

After the Enlightenment we experienced a shift to more "buffered" selves (p. 27). These are self-contained beings with impermeable boundaries separating one person from another and from the external forces in the world. There is even a boundary between mind and body. Emotional states, beliefs, and thoughts originate through internal processes. Given that psychology was birthed in modernity, many of its core concepts are built around this idea of a buffered self, where each individual is self-contained and distinct from others.

---

[3]Kwame Bediako (1994), for example, has brought forth significant theological contribution reflecting on Christianity from within a primal worldview, a worldview that holds many similarities with the Hebrew worldview. Philip Jenkins (2008) also explores the importance of this in *The New Faces of Christianity*.

The strongly rooted assumptions of the buffered self are beginning to be challenged in the behavioral and neurosciences, and the premodern view of the porous self is regaining momentum. For example, scientists have discovered mirror neurons and the power of relationships to reduce perception of pain and regulate difficult emotions (Coan, 2010; Coan, Schaefer, & Davidson, 2006). It seems we are rediscovering that humans are intrinsically relational. Our nervous systems are connected; they are not buffered from one another but are porous, impacting and being impacted by the other. To describe this as new knowledge is perhaps simplistic, or maybe even silly. Lisa McMinn, our sociologist spouse (to Mark) and mother (to Megan Anna), points out that we have always known this truth, even before neuroscience discovered it. Whether of a laboring mother or a dying soldier, pain and emotion is reduced and regulated by a companion who is actively present. It seems we have intuitively known and practiced this through most of human history.

Psychiatrist Daniel Siegel has been at the forefront of much of this contemporary research. I (Megan Anna) learned from Siegel and Bryson (2012) that when my five-year-old becomes upset the best thing I can do for him is not to establish a firm external boundary around his self, but rather to link my nervous system to his, allowing him to borrow my executive functioning. And so I kneel down, looking him in the eye while naming his experiences and emotionally attuning to him. As we connect selves, I am making the intensity of his emotions more tolerable as we metabolize them together.

Siegel isn't suggesting we ditch the buffered self completely and return to porous selves. In fact, there may be some risk if we were to embrace a completely porous self, such as losing a sense of personal responsibility and agency. For example, imagine the difficulty if patients were to start reporting that the external force of depression had so engulfed them that they could no longer be responsible for personal choices. There is something important to hold onto about the embodied self who holds agency. Siegel (2014) beautifully integrates a buffered self with a porous self by highlighting the importance of holding onto both a "me" and a "we." He even suggests a clever "MWe" to describe how the self is shaped by both. On one hand, we have an embodied internal identity (me), and we also have an interpersonal and interconnected identity (we). These both shape our sense of self.

Powerful things happen when we refuse the temptation to reduce our sense of self to either the *me* or the *we* and embrace the integration of the two (Siegel, 2014). This marks a shift in thinking about the human mind. Rather than simply being a self-contained object that is reduced to the brain's activity, the mind is active and changing as it is influenced both by energy within and without. The mind is both embodied and relational. It is this relational component of the mind that makes joy so contagious, causes us to yawn when another yawns, and makes deep empathy possible.

In a talk given at the Wisdom 2.0 conference in San Francisco, Siegel (Wisdom 2.0, 2017) tells the story of visiting a village in Namibia. While in a country stricken with drought, famine, and diseases, he felt amazed by the amount of joy and happiness in the village he visited. One night sitting around a campfire with villagers, Siegel asked his translator: "Can I ask you to ask this tribesman a question: They've got drought, they've got famine, they've got disease, and they are so happy. . . . Can you ask him why his fellow villagers look so happy? Are they really so happy?" After a moment the translator responded: "He says his people are happy because they belong. They belong to each other and they belong to Earth." After a pause the villager asks Siegel: "In America, do you belong?" In his talk, Siegel goes on to suggest that in America we have cast ourselves out of belonging.

With industrialization and modernization we have gained much freedom: from being at the mercy of the weather for food, from diseases and many hardships. And yet there may be some hidden costs to these advances. Is belonging one of those hidden costs? Have we pulled ourselves out of belonging as Siegel suggests?

> We have pulled ourselves out of belonging in the most unhealthy way you can imagine. . . . We've created this culture that has a lethal lie that the self . . . is separate and that relationships don't really have anything to do with it or maybe they're icing on the cake. They're not icing on the cake—they are the cake. (Wisdom 2.0, 2017)

How does one find deep, enriching selves living in a society built on the assumption of buffered selves, a society that has pulled itself out of belonging? Perhaps belonging to others, belonging to land, and belonging to community requires a level of porousness, a sense of "MWe."

The relational view of the *imago Dei* can be difficult to wrap our minds around (see sidebar "Views of the *Imago Dei*"), but perhaps there is some

"MWe" happening at the heart of the *imago Dei* that doesn't quite fit into our modern binary of "me" versus "we." And this may have profound implications for counseling and psychotherapy.

Traditionally, the psychologist or counselor is the expert in the room: a self-contained being who holds knowledge and passes it along to the other self-contained person in the room. With the rise of interpersonal therapy, relational psychoanalysis, and third-wave cognitive-behavioral therapy, we are seeing more discussion of relational, intersubjective spaces. Relational psychoanalysts use the language of "cocreated space"—the idea that two selves are always bringing something to the room and together create something new. There is a willingness to be impacted and affected by the other. As we meet with our patients we link our nervous systems together, and our linked nervous system takes in difficult emotions, metabolizes them, and offers them back to our patients in a way they are able to better integrate with their other experiences and emotions.

Being mindful of how our nervous systems are linked is also helpful in establishing safety within the therapeutic room. Geller and Porges (2014) explore biobehavioral explanations of how therapeutic presence works in cultivating a sense of safety. Safety is cultivated at a neurological level—a process that often takes place outside of our awareness. Our safety systems are constantly evaluating tone of voice, facial cues, and gestures, assessing for safety and risk. When presence is detected on a neurological level we lower our defenses, creating a space of vulnerability where meaningful therapeutic work can occur. Geller and Porges describe these encounters as cutting through all therapeutic orientations. Creating presence for others—linking our nervous systems to theirs—is sacred work. And, of course, it is work that affects us also as we are deeply present with other souls.

Integration Conversation Starters

1. How might the notion of porous and buffered selves translate to your understanding of God?

2. How we think of selves may influence what theoretical orientation we are drawn to. As you think of your own theoretical persuasions in counseling or psychotherapy, how might your view of selves be related?

BUFFERED SELVES, POROUS SELVES, AND BURNOUT

Christina Maslach (1982) and her colleagues developed a widely used scale to measure burnout among helping professionals. They identified three main components to burnout: emotional exhaustion, depersonalization, and reduced personal accomplishment. Burnout has been an extremely useful concept in the helping professions, and we applaud the work that has been done. Still, it is interesting to note how closely tied each of the three dimensions of burnout is to the modernist understanding of the buffered self.

The notion of emotional exhaustion is related to a sense of being overextended and depleted by the demands of human service work. Implicit in this is an assumption that energy and compassion are primarily located within the self and then flow outward to others who are in need of services. When the self is depleted, we are told it needs to be recharged by sitting by a fire and reading a novel (for introverts) or spending a weekend with friends (for extroverts). This is not all wrong, but notice how much the notion of a buffered self is assumed: we charge up our individual selves and then spend down our emotional energy helping others. If we spend more than we recharge, we are vulnerable to burnout.

Depersonalization occurs when we stop having compassion for the people we serve. We become impersonal and unfeeling, as if they are a needy object more than a precious human being. Again, notice the isolation of the self from the world around: "I am a helper, and you are a need that must be met."

Decreased personal accomplishment is the sense that one is no longer competent or that whatever is being accomplished is trivial and unimportant. The word "personal" even shows up in this description, marking how self-contained we perceive our presence in the world to be. We have resumes and degrees and honors to demonstrate our accomplishments, and when we start questioning their importance, we are vulnerable to burnout.

Both premodern views of the person and contemporary neuroscience point us toward more cocreated spaces in our helping efforts. Yes, the work can be depleting, but when we are fully present to the other, we also open the possibility of deep emotional and spiritual connection that is life-giving to both the helper and the one being helped. The *we* joins the *me* in the counseling office and something beautiful emerges. These moments cannot be marked by lines on a vita, but they leave both the helper and the one being helped with a sense of standing together in a place of grace and hope.

Grasping and sabbath. We have reflected on the *imago Dei* and on God image, and we close this chapter by considering how these may be impacted by our pace of lives. Living into God's image almost certainly requires reflection beyond the production mindset of contemporary life.

In ANE accounts, humans were created to work for the gods, but in the Christian narrative God is fully sufficient without humans. Creation emerges from a self-offering God rather than from gods who need more workers. This must have some bearing on the lives we live as mental health professionals.

Honestly, this does not come naturally for either of us. Even as we write this section of the book we recognize a tendency to take on multiple projects, work feverishly to meet our commitments and deadlines, and be available for anyone who may need us. Like so many in our academic and cultural contexts, we are worker bees. We admit our vulnerability here, imagining that many other counselors and psychologists may resonate with this struggle. There are always more patients to see, more articles and books to write, more classes to teach, more bills to pay. Meanwhile, even as we struggle to keep from pedaling too fast, we find pondering God's character calls us to slow down and seek places of perspective and rest.

Our colleagues and patients struggle with this too. Have you noticed if you ask a friend in the coffee shop, a colleague in the hallway, or a patient at the beginning of a session how they are doing you are likely to hear about how busy they are, perhaps followed by a litany of activities that currently feel overwhelming? This reflects an anxious restlessness to how we live. The technological advances that were supposed to free up our time and capacity have somehow made us busier and added to our stress load. If we're lucky we frantically squeeze "self-care" and "personal time" into our busy lives. Even the way we frame these respite activities as utterly separate from ordinary life suggests how restless regular life has become for many of us, even for counselors.

Our externally busy lives often contribute to increased internal noise that is difficult to escape. Poet and writer Christian Wiman (2010) reflects on how this contributes to the scattering of our very selves and ponders the following question:

> How does one remember God, reach for God, realize God in the midst of one's
> life if one is constantly being overwhelmed by that life? . . . But the reality of

> contemporary American culture—which often seems like a kind of collective ADHD—is that *any* consciousness requires a great deal of resistance, and how does one relax and resist at the same time? (p. 63)

How do we remember God when we can barely keep up with our lives? How do we cultivate a restful, embodied presence?

The gods of the Babylonian creation narratives were grasping gods: grasping for more, grasping for power (Brueggemann, 1982). Similarly, when the Hebrew people escaped slavery in the exodus, the culture of Egypt was a grasping culture: more, more, more. Build the bricks without straw, work seven days a week. Do more. Do it faster. Be productive. Do it now (Brueggemann, 2017).

The Hebrew God does not grasp. This is also seen in Jesus, the one who did not think of equality with God as something to be grasped (Phil 2:1-11). Early in the creation account humans are called to vocations of shepherd and gardener. This calling stands out against the backdrop of a culture marked with exploitive grasping and invites us into a new way of being—to live into our vocation modeled after the "Good Shepherd who does not grasp" (Brueggemann, 1982, p. 38). And when God gives Moses the Ten Commandments, after the Hebrew people left the grasping culture of Egypt, sabbath shows up in the middle of the list, right after three commandments about how we ought to relate to God and just before six commandments about how we are to treat one another (Brueggemann, 2017).

An alternative to grasping is sabbath: a rest from work, a reprieve from grasping, a deliberate resistance to the ubiquitous assumption that more is better. Taking a day of rest during the exilic period was a powerful statement. While the Babylonian gods were anxious about creation, the Hebrew God rests in the knowledge that creation is *tov* (good). This God is at ease (Brueggemann, 1982).

When we practice rest we proclaim that "life does not depend upon our feverish activity of self-securing, but that there can be a pause in which life is given to us simply as a gift" (Brueggemann, 1982, p. 35). This is much more than an activity engaged in once a week, and in fact history is replete with examples of how we humans have turned sabbath into a feverish set of rules rather than an invitation to rest. Sabbath infuses the totality of a person's way of being in the world. Instead of grasping, there is rest. A sabbath-infused existence is a reflective, grounded life. Sabbath is relaxing our grasping hands, our clinched fists, and trusting the hands of God. It asserts that the deepest life is one of peace and satisfaction, not exhaustion. Sabbath is devoted to awareness.

> We parcel out our moments of devotion—a church service here and there, a walk in the woods, a couple of hours of meditation a week—all the while maintaining the frenzy of our usual existence outside of those moments. This is inevitable . . . but it is not sustainable, for the soul is not piecemeal. (Wiman, 2010, p. 69)

Sabbath rest is not something we simply do, but something we embody. Psychology uses different language, but it also identifies the power of embodied rest. In psychology we often talk about this in terms of regulation and being grounded, and what we are learning is that our centeredness can help create an environment where our patients find a calm repose. The image of God involves adequate space for rest. Out of this rested place we can offer centered relationships where feelings of safety and security arise as the therapist is present and fully engaged (Geller & Porges, 2014). In this, we image God in relationship with one another.

While we often equate rest with sleep, and this is partly right, another dimension of rest is balance. As Heschel reminds us (1951), sabbath is not a method by which we "recharge" so we can keep sprinting through life, sabbath is "for the sake of life" (p. 14). A Christian view of persons, founded in the theologies of the *imago Dei,* suggests we are created to experience connection with God, others, and nature (Hoekema, 1994). These connections form us; they grow us into the wholeness of what it means to be fully alive and human. For those of us who are counselors and psychotherapists, how are we resting in ways that promote connection with God, others, and nature?

I (Mark) have been finding rest in nature over the past decade. Lisa and I love to walk and hike and grow plants. We have even developed a small farm where we grow vegetables, berries, apples, chickens, and goats. At this stage of life we find ourselves talking quite a lot about "downward mobility," which means we write fewer books than we once did and spend more time on the porch, in the kitchen, and in the hammock. I am trying to learn how to be a better friend, and to make better friends. Lisa is becoming a spiritual director after years of being a sociologist, and I am learning a lot from her as she quiets herself before God. My mental pace can still be a problem—I'm always generating new ideas and new projects—but my aging body is reminding me to slow down, to be quiet, to notice the breeze, to see a cedar tree in ways I have failed to do before, to be present to the gifts of the moment.

As I am at the beginning of my career, I (Megan Anna) notice how difficult it is to transition away from a "grasping" mentality. While navigating clinical training and the start of my career with young children, it's taken considerable resistance to keep from succumbing to a sprint mentality (my husband would likely tell you I often fail at this). Personally, I have found sabbath in reading, creative writing, and moving my body in ways that feel pleasurable, such as shooting baskets after a long day. My husband, Luke, and I have made choices to try to embrace sabbath as a family by protecting our weekends as a time for our family to reconnect, slow down, and anchor ourselves between busy weeks. In a culture where it would be easy to spend our weekends shuffling kids from activity to activity, we limit our family commitments and enjoy one another's presence as we all slow down together.

What about you? How are you finding ways to experience sabbath despite the complex lives that mental health professionals lead?

Integration Conversation Starters

1. How do we cultivate rest within ourselves so that we can provide our patients with a different kind of experience when they step into our offices?
2. Is it possible that you have particular views of God that make it difficult to rest? If so, can you imagine another way?

Further Reading

Brueggemann, W. (2017). *Sabbath as resistance: Saying no to the culture of now.* Louisville, KY: Westminster John Knox.

McMinn, M. R., & Campbell, C. D. (2007). *Integrative psychotherapy: Toward a comprehensive Christian view.* Downers Grove, IL: InterVarsity Press. Chapter one considers *imago Dei* as a foundation for an integrative approach to psychotherapy.

Sharp, C. J. (2010). *Wrestling the Word: The Hebrew Scriptures and the Christian believer.* Louisville, KY: Westminster John Knox.

Further Listening/Watching

Byas, J., & Enns, P. (Hosts). (2019, February 11). "God's children tell the story" [Audio podcast]. *The Bible for Normal People.* Retrieved from http://thebiblefornormalpeople .podbean.com/e/episode-74-pete-jared-god%E2%80%99s-children-tell-the-story/

Wisdom 2.0. (2017). *A truly connected life: Dan Siegel, Wisdom 2.0 2017* [Video file]. Retrieved from www.youtube.com/watch?v=zF8nBDKxAQI

4

Considering Atonement

FROM WHAT ARE WE BEING SAVED?

MARIA FOUND HERSELF in a season of disorientation when I (Megan Anna) met her. On the roller coaster of an "in-and-out" marriage with a man who was abusive, like many survivors of intimate violence she experienced symptoms of posttraumatic stress disorder (PTSD). Underlying this, she experienced a rigid narrative about self and world, with a number of "stuck points" (cognitive beliefs that make it hard to move into a new narrative) that left her immobilized and spiraling in shame and depression.

It is common for survivors to get stuck with self-blaming beliefs (*I could have stopped it, If only I'd been better,* and so on). This is a particularly sticky stuck point, one that requires much care. On one hand, the belief that she could have done things differently provides a sense of agency and empowerment, providing a contrast to a chaotic relationship in which she lacked agency and control. In other words, these beliefs provide her a sense of being able to make choices that protect her in the future. On the other hand, when these beliefs are taken to an extreme they can lead to self-deprecation, self-blame, and shame that can be difficult to escape. For Maria, her self-blaming beliefs isolated her from her community of faith, family, and relationships that might have been healing for her. Fraught with conflict, she frequently brought in examples of how she must have caused her partner's abuse, while holding onto the hope that if *she* changed, she could return and things would be better.

Intertwined with these dynamics was a theological narrative. A devout Christian, Maria struggled with the moral implications of initiating divorce.

She spoke of her call to forgive, the importance of obedience, and the call to follow Jesus in his example of taking on suffering. Amidst tears and confusion, she looked at me searchingly and said, "But Megan Anna, aren't I supposed to forgive?" Her narrative had little space to move, and it was taking a profound physical, psychological, social, and emotional toll.

The Power of Story

"If you want to know me, then you must know my story, for my story defines who I am. And if I want to know myself, to gain insight into the meaning of my own life, then I, too, must come to know my own story" (McAdams, 1993, p. 11). This opening line of a foundational book in narrative psychology reminds us that the stories we tell ourselves underlie our concept of who we are.

For reasons I (Megan Anna) will likely never fully unearth, when I was young I was fused to a painful narrative about who I am in the world. The narrative I told myself was that I didn't really matter, the fact that I breathed and had life wasn't enough to reserve my "mattering." I needed to earn it. Through my accomplishments, being good and accommodating, and attuning to others I might somehow be able to earn my "mattering."

When I (Mark) read these words from Megan Anna, I have two reactions. First, I feel a profound sadness for her narrative and what it must have been like through her childhood years. Even as her father, I did not fully glimpse the inner angst she carried—and likely her two sisters as well. Second, I resonate and identify with this narrative myself. I suppose it is reasonable that narratives cascade down from one generation to the next, and so my way of explaining myself in the world must have been contagious in various ways to Megan Anna throughout her childhood years. Plus, she faced some unique cultural challenges that she is about to mention.

Those who have researched the unconscious motivations of therapists would suggest that some of (perhaps many of) those reading this book may resonate with this narrative (Miller, 2008; Sussman, 2007). Of course, narrative doesn't form in a vacuum (personal or theological). It is formed within a complex interface of interpersonal relationships, cultural and social location, community influence, and so forth. For me (Megan Anna), this narrative was compounded by my context—coming of age in the affluent and high achieving, evangelical pocket of Wheaton, Illinois, during the purity culture movement. This narrative I told about myself intersected with a particular way of understanding God in such a way that it reinforced fears about never being enough. Throughout this chapter, I'll draw on my experience to reflect on how personal and theological stories intersect. It feels important to note I am not suggesting one causes the other, nor am I particularly interested in looking at causal links. Instead, I'm curious about how our narratives show up in a complex and intricate web, and how we respond as counselors and psychotherapists.

If our stories are integral to our views of ourselves, then understanding our clients becomes an intricate task of understanding the stories they tell about themselves alongside life circumstances. For Christians, our narratives are interwoven stories of self and the Christian gospel. And though the word *gospel* means "good news," it is curious to see how the implications can sometimes turn out to be less than fully good. The story of the Christian self is always more than an individual story—it is the story of an individual embedded in a larger story of tradition that stretches back thousands of years. How these stories intersect for good and for harm is of utter importance for the Christian psychotherapist.

A growing body of research demonstrates that religion is connected to health and well-being. It can protect against depression through difficult times by helping people make meaning of life, and can encourage altruistic and prosocial behavior, which have a positive impact on mental and physical health (Koenig, 2018; Post, 2005; Schwartz, Meisenhelder, Ma, & Reed, 2003). But not all forms of religion are helpful. For example, those studying the psychology of religion note an important distinction between intrinsic and extrinsic religion—a distinction that goes back as far as Gordon Allport in the 1960s. Those with intrinsic religious beliefs see their faith as the primary organizing principle of life, whereas those with extrinsic beliefs see religion more as a means to an end. Extrinsic religiousness in the United States has been linked with rigid thinking, prejudice, and narrow-mindedness (Hood, Hill, & Spilka, 2018). Also, negative religious coping (also called "spiritual struggle") is associated with various risk factors for poorer mental health (Koenig, 2018). Spiritual and religious distress often includes struggles with religious and moral guilt, as well as anger toward God (Exline et al., 2014).

It is encouraging to look at how the Christian faith anchors us as therapists, provides our clients with strength, and can be profoundly experienced *within* the therapeutic relationship. It's less comfortable to think about how Christianity can be a source of distress and fuel unhelpful patterns. In the same way that religion can both contribute to well-being and to harm, Christian narratives that overlay and interweave with our stories can both be beneficial and harmful.

In this chapter we're zooming in on atonement theology. How God saves us often becomes interwoven with how we imagine God to be (God's character and attributes) and how we imagine God to perceive us.

A Word About Approaching This Chapter

This has been our most difficult chapter to write, as made painfully evident by the number of revisions it has endured. The primary challenge we encounter is getting lost in the complex and heated theological conversations about atonement that stretch over two thousand years. Continually, we have worked to pull ourselves back to the therapy room rather than get lost taking an evaluative stance toward atonement theology. Atonement theology matters; it has profound implications for how psychotherapists and Christian counselors sit with themselves and their patients. Our aim is to look at atonement narratives, how they interplay with our personal narratives, the narratives our patients bring, and how this influences the work we do. Given the heat, depth, and history of the atonement conversation, it can be hard to resist the pull of diving into an evaluative conversation about the theological content.

Salvation can be a challenging topic to discuss while holding a humble and generous space. We've worked hard to hold this space, but have done so imperfectly even after multiple revisions. Surely you'll notice our leanings, informed by our personal stories and how they've intersected with theological narratives. To try to pretend that we do not have biases would be disingenuous and potentially harmful. While we find strengths in all the views, we lean toward a nonviolent view of the atonement. Still, we try to treat other views with generosity, and ask for grace where we have failed to do so.

Given our challenge in writing this chapter, we have thought carefully about its title. "Considering Atonement" contains two words—one a verb, and one a noun. We suspect that however you're engaging this chapter, as an individual or in the context of a small group, you may notice a pull—as we have—toward entering into an evaluative conversation of atonement theories. This is approaching atonement as noun (a theory to be analyzed, evaluated, and understood). In contrast, what we attempt here is to focus more on the verb. *Considering* atonement moves us toward the stories our patients tell themselves and an opportunity to enter into meaningful places of conversation and transformation. We are not aiming to articulate the ultimate atonement theory that solves the two-thousand-year mystery, but are more interested in how atonement moves in our cultures and our lives. How has it moved across the two-thousand-year history of Christianity? How does it move in the life of the therapist, and the life of the patient? To accomplish this goal, we attempt two things. First, we provide a general theological map, because discerning movement requires understanding the larger contextual landscape. Second, we highlight six implications of how atonement theory and psychotherapy interplay.

God as Disapproving Father

When I was three, I (Megan Anna) shared a room with my five-year-old sister Sarah. One night as we lay awake, she explained personal salvation and told me about the prayer that could invite Jesus into my heart, resulting in my sins being forgiven. In the darkness of our bedroom I prayed this prayer with Sarah. I went on to pray that prayer another thousand times throughout my childhood. Whenever I sinned I would quickly follow up with the salvation prayer, wanting to make sure I was *really* saved despite my continued badness. I felt immense guilt when I sinned. Part of the story I inherited about salvation was that in that critical moment on the cross Jesus took on all of the world's sins (past, present, and future), and that it was the taking on of this sin that was the greatest pain for Jesus—even more than the physical pain of crucifixion. In my mind, every time I sinned, I increased Jesus' pain and suffering. This resulted in a sort of binary relationship with God. I felt incredibly grateful for and close to Jesus the Son, but God the Father frightened me. God the Father disapprovingly gazed at me as I struggled to be good enough. Jesus was the buffer, making it so God the Father could *tolerate* being in my presence.

I was reassured knowing that "through Jesus' blood I was made pure," but I experienced God the Father as wrathful, disgusted by my sin, and unable to look upon me without the blood of Christ. I wanted more than just being *okay* with God. I wanted God to *like me*. This theology, intersecting with my personal narrative, fueled a "not good enough" mentality. This led to years of engaging in what Brené Brown (2010) refers to as "hustling for worth," which she describes as the tendency to prove our worth through "performing, perfecting, pleasing, and proving" (p. 23). In my narrative, I frantically tried to prove my worth to God the Father, frustrated that no matter what I did God still seemed disgusted by my sin. This made it difficult to experience divine grace, acceptance, and connection with God the Father.

My rigid narrative about God's saving work interwove with my personal narrative around worthiness and identity. Thankfully, my narratives became kinder and more self-compassionate once I was introduced to additional understandings of atonement, such as nonviolent models. These views helped transform how I saw myself in relation to God, providing me with hopeful movement within both my personal and theological narratives.

But here I pause to reflect on the complexity of this conversation. What I am referring to as a violent view of atonement (known as the penal substitution view, to be discussed more later in the chapter) was not helpful to me as a child or as a Christian, but an anonymous reviewer of an earlier draft of this chapter gave us a beautiful gift by unpacking their own Christian narrative and explaining how life-giving this penal substitution view had been, especially during the reviewer's early years of faith.

Perhaps the penal substitution view settled poorly with me because of my near obsession with sin and salvation. Though I may be a bit unique in this, it turns out I am in good company. Throughout his life, Martin Luther struggled with questions of sinfulness and salvation. Luther's early life included struggle and pain. He was treated harshly by his parents and struggled with depression and anxiety throughout his life (notice the context that gave rise to a self-deprecating personal narrative). Stuck in the middle of a ferocious thunderstorm, Luther—terrified by death and the possibility of damnation—vowed to become a monk. This existential angst around salvation and damnation continued. Luther's overarching narrative, informed by the monastic life, was that the only way one could hope to stand before God was through striving for perfection (Gillespie, 2008). From within this narrative, Luther constantly doubted his worthiness despite his strenuous efforts for perfection. Painfully aware of his sin, he constantly fretted about his salvation in the face of a wrathful God (Gillespie, 2008). Years later, through studying and teaching Scripture, Luther's narrative began to expand. As he lectured on Romans, he began to see the meaning of the text "the just shall live by faith" anew (Rom 1:17 NKJV). Luther began to understand justification as resulting from God's faithful actions. The just live by the faithfulness and righteousness *of God*. Righteousness is not something actively achieved, rather, it originates in God and is freely given to those who live by faith (Gonzalez, 1985). With this profound shift in narrative he could finally put away his frantic toiling to be among the "just," which was likely Luther's own version of hustling for worth.

Moving from Rigidity to Flexibility

One can hear the freedom, expansiveness, and joy that emanates from Luther as he shifted narratives: "I felt that I had been born anew and that the gates of heaven had been opened. The whole of Scripture gained a new meaning" (Gonzalez, 1985, pp. 19-20). Luther grasped that in Jesus' life and death healing took place and we no longer live estranged from God. This truth revolutionized Luther's life, which contributed to a revolution within the church as new narratives around grace and salvation were offered by Luther and other Reformers.

Though separated by five hundred years of history, it's comforting to know that Luther and I encountered similar struggles, tied in frozen and rigid narratives. The opening lines of John Calvin's *Institutes* start with the bold claim that any wisdom we possess, "consists of two parts: the knowledge of God and of ourselves" (Calvin, trans. 2008, p. 4). Given the intertwining nature of self-knowledge and divine knowledge, it is no surprise that particular narratives of God correspond with certain views of self. Stuck points in this blended narrative can complicate and exacerbate suffering while also interfering with our knowledge and experience of God.

Like Luther, I experienced God and self with more abundance as my narratives shifted. You'll notice we didn't land at the same destination. Luther found hope in focusing on Jesus' substitutionary act, and others later built on this to develop the penal substitution theory (discussed below). I find hope in nonviolent models that emphasize Jesus suffering *with*.

While theological content matters, for purposes of conversation the point is not so much about correct destination as the ability for us to move within story. We realize this may sound dangerously close to a free-for-all spiral into relativism, but we are not suggesting that a shifting narrative around atonement means we discard the idea of universal religious or theological truth. As will be discussed below, a rich and varied array of atonement metaphors can be found in the New Testament. The idea of fluid narrative lives in the dialectic of anchoring into the theology of the New Testament while recognizing how the context of people's lives will make certain metaphors more accessible and meaningful than others. This is not a rebuttal of truth but rather an acknowledgment of the diversity of theology represented in the Christian tradition and an appreciation of the complexity that emerges when our social context intersects with our attempts to understand the mysterious truth of the atonement.

The context from which we seek God means that we may be drawn to different metaphors. One metaphor may speak to us in a way that allows for deep encounter with God, while others may cause encounter to be stifled.[1] One of the reasons we have confidence in highlighting the fluid narrative process for individuals is because it finds resonance in Christian history, which has involved a shifting, multidimensional, and contextually informed narrative of atonement.

The Complex and Shifting Story of Atonement

The atonement, or the process of coming to wholeness and reconciliation with God, is one of the most central concepts to the Christian tradition (Maimela, 1986).[2] The truth of the atonement is mysterious and poetic, inviting us into deeper relationship with God. We started this chapter by

---

[1] For a personal example of this, see Brock and Parker's book *Proverbs of Ashes* (2001). Two female theologians draw on their personal stories of sexual and racial trauma to show how trauma intersected with a view of atonement in a way that interfered with their ability to experience God.

[2] We're focusing the conversation around atonement theology, but you'll notice that it's difficult to talk about atonement without also weaving in views of salvation, God image, and other topics. Therefore, what follows is a conversation that runs the risk of conflating atonement with other key theological ideas.

FINDING FLUIDITY IN SMALL STORIES
AND BIG STORIES

In this chapter I've used my example of being locked in a frozen, intersecting personal and theological narrative, and how movement led me to experience freedom and deeper connection to self and God. What I haven't shared is that this experience made me vulnerable to be locked into a different form of rigidity.

Projecting my experience and trajectory onto others, I was frozen in a story about theology having good (empowering) and bad (disempowering) views. Stuck in a rigid and evaluative place, it was difficult to hold space for generosity, compassion, and genuine curiosity for others'

views. That is the thing about frozen narratives—when we are stuck it becomes difficult to engage in true conversation with the other.

It was in "taking my own medicine" that my larger story was able to thaw. As I listened to students and peers and the anonymous reviewer of an earlier draft of this book, I heard stories of how the penal substitution theory had provided them with profound moments of grace and encounter with God. I offer this not to be overly self-deprecating but to observe the essence and power of good conversation.

exploring the power of story, and indeed theology could be seen as an attempt to tell a story about ungraspable, infinite truth.

In telling the story of redemption, we have historically employed a multitude of metaphors. These metaphors arise at the intersection of culture and gospel, helping us to see with "wider scope and truer depth perception" (Sharp, 2010, p. 26; Gunton, 2003).[3] One of the profound aspects of the Christian gospel is that it takes seriously its intersection with culture. God's desire to come close, to address new frontiers and cultures, is evident in Abraham's calling and throughout the Hebrew Scriptures, culminating in the divine translation of *Logos* into human flesh (Jn 1:1). This means that truth, and our understanding of truth, is not limited to abstract and universal statements

---

[3]Gunton (2003) discusses how metaphor is much more than a technique for communicating understanding. Rather, it is a means of understanding. Metaphor and understanding exist in a dialectical process: "finding new language and discovery happen together, with metaphor serving as the vehicle of discovery. . . . We comprehend aspects of the world as we find the new words to use in our search for understanding" (p. 31). In this sense, metaphor is not simply a way of conveying truth; rather, it is a hermeneutic by which we come to understanding.

but rather comes clothed in cultural particularity, metaphors, and imagery (Sanneh, 2004). Since the beginning we've used metaphor anchored in culturally embedded imagery in our attempts to grasp the ungraspable.

Even with a wealth of metaphors for atonement theology, we will always remain limited, as British Reformed theologian Colin Gunton (2003) writes: "Metaphor claims only an indirect purchase on reality, bringing to expression some but not all aspects" of what it is attempting to grasp (p. 34). This suggests that all the atonement metaphors capture part—but only part—of the mystery of God's saving grace. Each of the metaphors grasps unique dimensions and speaks to unique contexts about the truth of atonement, and because they are all attempts to grasp infinite truth in human terms, they also all have strengths and shortcomings.

A wide array of images is used throughout the New Testament to understand God's saving work (Green, 2006). Parenthetically, we also note that God's saving work is evident in the Hebrew Scriptures, but here we will limit ourselves to the New Testament. John emphasizes the importance of the "saving work of Jesus" and gift of eternal life, the author of Hebrews focuses on access to God, Peter underscores the importance of "a living hope by the resurrection of Jesus Christ," James highlights the "the law of liberty" (Smith, 1919, pp. 51-52). This vast collection of metaphors is not simply due to different writers, because even individual authors provide varying images. The apostle Paul, for example, uses a wide range of metaphors to talk about the saving work of Jesus, from substitution to triumph over powers to sacrifice and justification (Green, 2006).

New Testament metaphors of salvation speak to the particularity and contexts of people's lives, and can be roughly grouped into six general categories that draw from the audience's sociocultural context: forensic, commerce, personal relationship, worship, battle, and medical (Green, 2006; Reichenbach, 2006). When a metaphor looks like a court of law and deals with concepts such as guilt or innocence, a forensic metaphor is being used. The word *redemption* (literally, "buying back") suggests a commerce metaphor. Personal relationship metaphors emphasize reconciliation. At the time the New Testament was written, animal sacrifice was still part of the prevailing worship practices, so references to sacrifice draw on a worship metaphor. Battle metaphors emphasize the triumph of good over evil, and medical metaphors emphasize healing.

Theologians continued this tradition of using metaphor to understand Christ's saving work as they drew upon culturally relevant imagery to try to make sense of the atonement. This led to three dominant metaphors that have been employed throughout Christian history.[4]

Christus Victor/ransom theory. A dominant view for the first thousand years of Christianity, the Christus Victor view casts atonement through the lens of a cosmic battle where Christ conquers evil, sin, and Satan, thereby setting humans free. Sin is conceptualized as an overarching state representing our alienation from God. Christ's victory over the enslaving powers of sin, death, and the devil brings reconciliation and overcomes our state of alienation (Aulén, trans. 2003; Crisp, 2020; Maimela, 1986). In the age of the Roman Empire, early Jewish believers found solace in how this imagery draws on the familiar cosmic battle language of the Hebrew Scripture (Gunton, 2003). There were variations of this classic motif, such as the ransom theory, in which the death of Jesus served as a ransom price paid to Satan. In a time of fear of robbers who routinely interrupted trade by holding travelers ransom, this would have held meaning (Weaver, 2001; Smith, 1919). Proponents of this view included Irenaeus, Origen, Athanasius, and Gregory of Nyssa (Aulén, trans. 2003; Beilby & Eddy, 2006; Green, 2006; Hardy, 1954; Smith, 1919).[5]

Moralistic theory. God's love is at the forefront of the moralistic model (Crisp, 2020). Jesus' life and obedience to death on the cross demonstrate God's sacrificial love which has the power to move people toward repentance and moral transformation. This theory is a subjective model of atonement (whereas the other two are objective) because it emphasizes the subjective experience of reflecting on God's love which leads to transformation of one's spiritual life. In contrast, objective views emphasize who and how people are in relation to God. This model is represented by Peter Abelard, Faustus Socinus, Immanuel Kant, and Friedrich Schleiermacher (Crisp, 2020; Green, 2006; Maimela, 1986).

---

[4]These three motifs were outlined in Gustav Aulén's (trans. 2003) work, *Christus Victor,* and have remained a helpful typology in understanding the history of atonement theology. It is outside the scope of this chapter to cover all of the atonement theories presented throughout church history. We sketch out a few of the significant atonement metaphors that have been meaningful to the church historically. For deeper study, check out further reading at the end of the chapter.

[5]While many, such as Aulén, have put ransom theory and Christus Victor together, typologically there are some important differences. For a more nuanced conversation about how these theories overlap and or differ, see Oliver Crisp's (2020) book, *Approaching the Atonement.*

Satisfaction/penal substitution. In the twelfth century, chivalry became an important cultural concept, and atonement was cast in imagery of honor and "satisfaction." When a person's honor was broken, there were two options: satisfaction by offering something greater in kind to the insult, or punishment. God chose the path of satisfaction rather than punishment as demonstrated by Jesus' obedience in his life and climaxing in his obedience to death on the cross (some proponents of this view include Anselm of Canterbury, Thomas Aquinas, and John Calvin) (Crisp, 2020; Green, 2006; Gunton, 2003; Maimela, 1986; Smith, 1919). Luther and Calvin emphasized Christ's death within a legal and penal framework, which then evolved into the substitutionary or penal substitution theory of atonement in the following centuries (Weaver, 2001).

The penal substitution theory has remained the dominant model for the last five hundred years and remains so pervasive within American Christianity that: "many Christians may wonder whether the saving significance of Jesus' death can be understood in any other way" (Green, 2006, p. 169). The irony is that while this model is the most popular, it also provokes the greatest amount of negative feedback. Complicating the conversation, this model is the most vulnerable to misrepresentations and misinterpretations (Schreiner, 2006).

New Testament scholar N. T. Wright (2018) suggests that penal substitution can mean vastly different things to different people, depending on the larger narrative in which it is couched:

> The penal substitution theory can be expressed in very damaging ways, and even when preachers don't intend to do this, it is quite clearly the case that this is how many people, particularly many young people, hear it. . . . So now, if that is what people have heard and are hearing then we have some serious work to do. Because we have taken John 3:16, "God so loved the world that he gave his only son," and what people have heard is that "God so hated the world that he killed his only son." And then, when you say that in a world where there is child abuse and domestic violence, people think, I know that bully of a God and I hate him, and then the whole thing goes horribly, horribly wrong.

Wright goes on to talk about how this fails to consider the complexity of the New Testament and provides a distorted view of both this theory and God's saving work. This nuance feels important to note, as narrative fluidity does not simply mean moving from one metaphor to another—it can mean redeeming and reclaiming a distorted narrative.

As the center of Christianity shifts south and east to the Majority World, and as voices from marginalized groups in the West are increasingly entering the theological conversation, concerns about the penal substitution view increase, and we're seeing a new shift in the atonement conversation. While it would be easy (and tempting) to get lost in this complex conversation, treating atonement like a noun, we attempt to keep an eye on atonement as a verb by highlighting how individuals have subjectively experienced the penal substitution theory. These experiences lead to some of the concerns as well as some of the strengths of this perspective.

Current critiques of the penal substitution model. Many of the concerns regarding the penal substitutionary model of atonement arise from feminist, womanist, black, liberation, and peace-oriented theologians. We outline five concerns here.

First, the most central criticism is that at the heart of this model is a God complicit in violence, which seems inconsistent with a loving God (Crisp, 2020). This view provides theological justification for taking a life, which sets a precedent for theological justification of violence. Critics point to the link between this model and systems of retributive justice, suggesting this theory runs the risk of perpetuating violence and alienating the poor (Brock & Parker, 2001; Cone, 1997; Maimela, 1986; Weaver, 2001; Williams, D. S., 2013; Williams, J. G., 2007).[6] Second, with its emphasis on the individual, it risks decontextualizing and overemphasizing sin. When sin is decontextualized, it is taken out of the complex social-cultural context that contributes to human behavior. And by failing to focus on systemic and contextualized sin, the transformation of institutions is not addressed (Maimela, 1986; Stoltzfus, 2012). Third, this view emphasizes an abstract salvation, outside of history, and therefore fails to address the injustices that take place within history (Brock, 1988). An ahistorical, abstracted model of atonement runs the risk of divorcing salvation from ethics and therefore lacks resonance for the poor and oppressed as it fails to address the complexity of human suffering in the face of injustice (Maimela, 1986; Weaver,

---

[6]To see a review of this criticism as well as a response, see the chapter "The Problem of Atoning Violence" in Oliver Crisp's *Approaching the Atonement* (2020).

2001). Fourth, it emphasizes a punishing and remote God, characterized by wrath and judgment (Brock & Parker, 2001; Maimela, 1986; Stoltzfus, 2012). Fifth, it appears antitrinitarian in that God the Father appears to be functioning differently than God the Son: God is the Judge demanding justice, and Christ is the Savior satisfying God's legal demand (Johnson, 2005; Weaver, 2001).

We offer these concerns as they may be helpful considerations when working with clients who are struggling with a "stuck" theological narrative. Recall Maria introduced at the beginning of this chapter. In addition to her current relationship, Maria, a Latina, experienced social and cultural oppression and marginalization. Given the concerns raised above, we can see how her theological narrative intersected with her personal narrative in a way that was disempowering and placed her at greater risk (both actual risk and the harm that comes with internal shame).

Maria and I made little progress with cognitive processing therapy for trauma. Any attempts to crack, question, or shift her story by entertaining alternative thoughts led to a rebound effect where she would reinforce her core beliefs with Bible verses about her "bad" behavior or need to forgive and return to her partner. My job was not to correct her theology. But still, understanding her concept of God, salvation, sin, and violence were integral for having a full conceptualization of Maria. My awareness of concerns arising from liberation and womanist theology about the penal substitution view, as well as my own journey of making sense of atonement, helped me more deeply understand the complexity of her personal and theological narratives. My treatment plan shifted from a cognitive processing model toward a relational and interpersonal approach. We could not adjust her narrative at the cognitive level, but perhaps we could touch these themes on an experiential level—and perhaps a new relational experience would provide her narrative with wiggle room.

Strengths of the penal substitution model. When we used the first draft of this chapter in an introductory integration class, the conversation felt a bit off. I (Megan Anna) was expecting students to experience some of the liberation I did when I learned there were multiple ways of looking at atonement. I (Mark) came prepared with some brilliant metaphors and illustrations for the penal substitution view of atonement, and for how limiting these views can seem. Well, at least I thought they were brilliant. The students didn't seem quite as compelled as I expected.

It occurred to us as we were debriefing from the classroom conversation that we were not connecting with students, and the quality of the conversations felt off. We think this is because we offered a polarized view and our students were either not connecting to our perspectives or feeling somewhat defensive of a view they had come to hold as central to Christian thought. Some students spoke of how this metaphor had given them a glimpse of God's grace carrying them in difficult times. Just as this metaphor has potential to cause problems, it can also lead to deeper encounters with God, self, and others. Here are five ways this may happen.

First, Jesus' atoning death leads to an awareness of the radical forgiveness of God as represented in Jesus' obedience and willingness to take our place in suffering and death. Stepping out in vulnerability, God takes on the risk, suffering the breach for us (Sanders, 2007). Second, reflection on God's risky and radical forgiveness can lead to greater self-acceptance and help one be more forgiving to others (Brock, 1988). Third, the penal substitution metaphor takes the problem of human sin seriously (Schreiner, 2006). It causes us to recognize the harm we've done, a necessary condition for healing broken relationships (Sanders, 2007). Relatedly, emphasizing our need for salvation can foster relational humility. Fourth, the justice of God is emphasized, protecting us from the risk of overemphasizing love at the cost of underemphasizing righteousness and justice. Both are integral to a covenantal relationship with God. Fifth, both God's holiness and love meet at the cross (Schreiner, 2006).

Our point is not to determine the rightness or wrongness of this view, but rather to look at how it shows up in our lives and the lives of our patients. As is true of narratives, our understandings and explanations sometimes move over time. When we are stuck in one metaphor, we risk limiting our access to and understanding of the infinite truth and our ability to experience God fully and truthfully. Conversely, we experience vitality and flexibility when we embrace the level of movement modeled for us in the New Testament.

Reflections on the Atonement Conversation

Hot topic conversations in Christianity are places where it's easy to miss one another. In reflecting on atonement narratives, we've noticed how the conversations are framed quite differently, fueling the tendency to talk past one another. For example, those critical of the penal substitution theory of atonement tend to rest their eyes on God the Father and use language of "wrath," "transaction," "appease," and "child abuse" (Brock & Parker, 2001; Weaver, 2001). Those more favorable to this model tend to focus their eyes on the Jesus who sacrificially and lovingly steps in to take a punishment deserved for us (Crisp, 2020). One way of framing the conversation leads to God doing something *to* Jesus; another way of framing the conversation emphasizes Jesus' agency and choice to do something *for* us in forgiveness and sacrificial love (Crisp, 2020; Green, 2006; Sanders, 2007).

It's difficult to have searching conversations across differences when we frame the conversation narrowly and rigidly. A difficult but important task is to also frame the narrative from "the other side" with generosity. When we engage a conversational approach, the language we employ to frame our narrative and the other's narrative becomes critically important.

Integration Conversation Starters

A classroom or small-group activity that is helpful for increasing capacity in perspective taking and fostering hospitality is known as the "five-minute rule." For five minutes you are invited to take on an unpopular or differing perspective than what you would naturally hold while entertaining it with hospitality and generosity. As a classroom or individual, do the following: If you are a critic of the penal substitution theory, spend five minutes considering some of the benefits and merits of this view. If you find yourself a proponent of this view, take five minutes and consider some of the critical reflections we have offered. As you take on a new perspective for five minutes, ponder these questions.

1. In what sense and in which contexts may this view be helpful?
2. How does this view expand your understanding of God?
3. How might this view help you see your patients with more complexity or more compassion?

Having outlined the classic atonement metaphors, we briefly offer two newer views of the atonement that have arisen from the rubble of many historical debates.

Kaleidoscopic view. A kaleidoscopic approach acknowledges the limitation of any one metaphor for engaging the important task of proclaiming the meaning of Jesus' life and death, and encourages us to "drink deeply from the wells of our own tradition" (Green, 2006, p. 169).[7] Drawing from early church examples, Green (2006) recommends an expansive way of looking at the atonement:

> The church has worked faithfully to embrace the message of the atonement without presuming that one image subsumed or trumped the others. In other words, the biblical narrative, which we seek to inhabit and to put into play in our lives . . . authorizes an expansive range of images and models for comprehending and articulating the atonement. (p. 170)

This approach considers how metaphors emerged from the context and situation of people's lives. These metaphors were not developed abstractly but arose as a theological response to concrete situations. Green (2006) writes:

> We find in the New Testament an abundance of terms and phases for conceiving the condition that characterizes human existence apart from God: slavery, hard-heartedness, lostness, friendship with the world, blindness, ungodliness, living according to the sinful nature, the reprobate mind, the darkened heart, enemies of God, dead in trespasses and more. How we articulate the saving significance of Jesus' death is tied to our conception of the human situation. People who are blind need illumination. Slaves need liberation. The lost need to be found. (p.167)

A kaleidoscopic approach is fluid, active, and contextual. An expansive range of metaphors allows for movement, providing an expansive narrative with room to breathe.

A nonviolent view of atonement. A nonviolent view of atonement emphasizes the Jesus who bears suffering and embraces weakness. God allowed Jesus to be drawn into a world of sin "and thus made sin" (Marshall, 2000, p. 591).[8] Jesus' ministry laid bare the evil and oppressive political forces, and now these evil forces are confronting him with death; his commitment to be with and for the poor by speaking out against an oppressive political system ultimately leads him to the cross (Padilla, 1983; Schwager, 1999). Responding

---

[7]For a comprehensive review of this model see Joel Green and Mark Baker's (2011) *Recovering the Scandal of the Cross* or Joel Green's chapter "Kaleidoscopic View" in Beilby and Eddy's *The Nature of the Atonement: Four Views* (2006).

[8]A nonviolent view of atonement emerges from several streams of thought, including peace-oriented traditions, and contextual theologies such as feminist, womanist, black, and liberation theologies. This model draws themes from Christus Victor while also expanding it.

to violence with active nonviolence, Jesus chooses to die "rather than compromise with violence," and the cross stands as the "ultimate paradigm of nonviolence" (Wink, 1992, p. 141).[9] The cross is a subversive act, inverting the old model of power and oppression, revealing that nonviolence is integral to God's being (Wink, 1992).

As Jesus is drawn into the darkness he embraces and transforms it, taking up the violence of the whole system (1 Pet 2:23), sacrificially entering into the oppression (Wink, 1992). Jesus exposes and endures the horrific violence, speaks forgiveness (Lk 23:34), and triumphs over death and violence with love and forgiveness, transforming it: "God takes upon himself all the pain and suffering of history and then reveals himself as the God of love who opens up a hope for the future through the most negative side of history" (Padilla, 1983, p. 17). Jesus shows a profound love through this complete taking on of weakness and darkness, and in this act of love Jesus identifies with all the victims of torture, violence, and oppression (Wink, 1992).

The resurrection plays an important role in this view also, as it demonstrates that violence does not have the final world. Jesus rises again, demonstrating the inability of social evils to destroy him. He has broken the power of death and violence, and now we are invited to participate in this saving work. Salvation is understood as dynamic and comprehensive, rooted in a contextualized, comprehensive understanding of sin (Maimela, 1986). It is personal and communal, involving concrete social-political dimensions—such as challenging oppressive cultural systems—and making persons more human and the world more humane (Bediako, 1994; Cone, 1997; Nasimiyu-Wasike, 1991). Salvation occurs within history and therefore has *here-and-now* implications.

Why Atonement Matters for Christian Counselors and Psychotherapists

This is not just academic quibbling. Atonement theology has profound implications for psychotherapists and Christian counselors. Volumes could be written on this, but for the purpose of promoting integration conversations we limit ourselves to six implications: the availability heuristic, how therapists

---

[9]The employment or nonemployment of violence and God is another complex conversation. To see a comprehensive approach to Scripture that makes an argument for God as nonviolent, see James Williams's *The Bible, Violence, and the Sacred* (2007).

view patients, how patients view themselves, how therapists view themselves, how we view suffering and darkness, and finding hope in the face of suffering.

Availability heuristic. Cognitive psychologists study, among other things, the thinking shortcuts we take in order to make sense of our complicated world. One of these shortcuts is called the availability heuristic: we pay attention to the ideas most readily in our mind rather than attempting to understand a matter in all its complexity. A silly example of this is how fast food companies try to plant an image or a jingle in your head so that when you are deciding where to go to lunch you don't have to sort through all the complexities of your various options. You just head to the place that is most available in your mind.

Hold this thought and prepare for a brief tangent. One of the key characteristics of integration—as opposed to other ways of relating psychology and theology—is mutual transformation. If we are integrating two things, then each of them is capable of influencing the other. It's not just that theology informs our understanding of psychology; true integration requires the possibility that psychology may also influence our understanding of theology.

The church has had many different views of atonement over the centuries, all of them developed and argued by intelligent people, passionate about following Jesus. Given the complexity and nuance involved in these atonement theories, how do we go about choosing one, or should we even try to choose one? Psychology can influence our understanding of theology in this case because the answer seems to be that we will choose the view of atonement most available in our minds. The views prominent in a particular historical period, or a certain denomination, are the ones that will be most available to us, so we naturally assume these are true and correct views. But what if that's just our mind doing what minds do—choosing the most available idea to shape our thoughts and behaviors, like going to a fast food restaurant that happens to have a catchy advertising campaign? After going to that restaurant long enough and frequently enough, we may even forget the alternative choices.

We live in a time where the penal substitution (i.e., forensic) view of atonement has gained greatest availability to most Protestants (Green, 2006). As such, we read the Bible through this assumption, teaching our children—as Lisa and I (Mark) taught Megan Anna—that Jesus saves us by taking the punishment we deserve, and often failing to consider other perspectives offered by godly men and women over the centuries. We may not even realize there are other ways of understanding orthodoxy and Scripture. I was at a Christian counseling conference recently where thousands of us sang beautiful praise songs to God before hearing from leading Christian counselors. It was a positive experience, but at the same time it was striking to see how almost every one of the songs assumed a penal substitution view of the atonement. "Jesus paid it all, all to him I owe." "Until on that cross as Jesus died, the wrath of God was satisfied." "Bearing shame and scoffing rude, in my place condemned he stood." "How great the pain of searing loss, the Father turns his face away." "Now my debt is paid; it is paid in full by the precious blood that my Jesus spilled." These lovely songs help us understand the weight of our sin, and the magnitude of God's grace—and these are powerful and essential concepts to grasp—but having a singular view of the atonement also creates some problems for contemporary Christian counselors and psychotherapists.

Here are two of the problems. First, simple certainties that cover complex realities are barriers to curiosity and searching conversation. Today's Christian wants to understand the nuances, the messiness, and the historical alternatives. Holding generous space for multiple views expands our understanding of God and salvation. Second, our views of atonement have profound implications for how we understand the nature of God, and that, in turn, affects how we sit with troubled souls during their most difficult seasons of life. If we can only see the atonement through one metaphor, then we may remain limited in our understanding of the work of Christian counseling and psychotherapy.

Integration Conversation Starters

1. To what extent do you find it necessary to settle on a single "correct" view of the atonement? In other words, might it be possible that different views speak to the various ways that God works in the world?

2. How might your views of the atonement affect the ways you view and interact with the patients you see in your counseling or psychotherapy office? Does it make a difference? Why or why not?

How therapists view patients. If integration is lived out in conversation, as we are suggesting in this book, then it's helpful to explore alternative views of the atonement and their clinical implications, because they hold profound implications for how God looks at us in our weakness and vulnerability, which in turn, carries implications for how we look at one another.

One option is that God loves the essence of us while despising our sin, and that we should be the same in our interactions with one another. When I (Mark) first became a Christian psychologist, I recall a phrase we often used in the church: "Hate the sin, love the sinner." This worked fairly well in a binary modern framework, but it turns out not to work as well in today's context. Making a clean conceptual slice between a person and how the person behaves isn't as easy as it may seem. Being a person is a complex mix of choices, emotions, thoughts, social connections, biological predispositions, and much more. To somehow imply we can neatly parse and love the essence of a person without considering the complicated amalgam of that person's behaviors, thoughts, and emotions is quite unrealistic. Also, "hate the sin, love the sinner" often carried an invisible postscript which was to be sure the sinner knew about the sin. The message seemed to be that I can love you as long as I make it clear to you how you are sinning, and that I cannot accept that part of you.

I recall working with a client, Richard, early in my career who started having an affair with a coworker midway through therapy. In my zeal to hate sin and love the sinner, I tried to be as kind as possible in referring him to another therapist. At the time I justified the referral because one of our therapeutic goals was to help his marriage and I believed I couldn't help with that while Richard was choosing another relationship. A referral seemed like the best option, as I hoped another therapist could help him with his other treatment goals (depression, life adjustment issues). Plus, I felt a strong need to communicate something about his wrongness, even as I treated him kindly. Hate the sin, love the sinner. I shudder now to wonder what this must have communicated to him. Knowing I was a Christian psychologist, what did my rejection of him communicate about how Christians view people, and about how God views us when we make disloyal and selfish choices?

An alternative narrative, and one that holds complexity: "Love the person even as we recognize how muddled our world can be." This may appear to be just a matter of semantics, but consider how much better this might play out in the counseling office. I could have entered into my patient's angst and uncertainty rather than shunning him because of his sin. Perhaps I could have reflected (privately and silently) on my own muddling in life, and how easy it is for all of us to lose our way. Richard's choice to have an affair could have been a tragic opportunity for empathy and compassion, a way to demonstrate the gracious presence of God in our broken world, to love both God and neighbor.

A more flexible understanding of atonement might have helped me experience my patient's sin differently. Perhaps if my atonement narrative had been attuned to the cross as ultimate evidence of God's enduring love, I could have better held my values of righteousness alongside the muddled spaces where we all live.

How might I have responded differently by considering how Jesus entered willingly into the darkness?

> Jesus at his crucifixion neither fights the darkness nor flees under cover of it, but goes with it, goes into it. He enters the darkness, freely, voluntarily. The darkness is not dispelled or illuminated. It remains vast, untamed, void. But he somehow encompasses it. It becomes the darkness of God. It is now possible to enter any darkness and trust God to wrest from it meaning, coherence, resurrection. (Wink, 1992, p. 141)

Holding a view that places faith that God understands the darkness with us, once having entered it, creates the possibility that darkness is redeemable. I wouldn't be walking into the muddle alone; God would be there waiting for us.

This ability to enter into spaces of sin while holding the hope of redemption was beautifully modeled for me by one of our colleagues who works in the field of substance abuse, where she regularly encounters patients stuck in cycles of sin.[10] Prior to Doug beginning his sixth round of treatment for substance abuse, he experienced a shattering trauma as he witnessed his partner severely beating their son. In addition to witnessing his son's abuse at the hand of his partner, he also had a lifetime of traumatic events. Doug's

---

[10]When we talk about sin in this context, we're talking about a contextualized, intersecting understanding of sin. Particularly with substance use, which is often linked with trauma, we are looking at something more complex than an individual's sinful choices. These are choices often made in the context of family and systemic injustice.

therapist was the first to address his shame and trauma as it connected to his addiction, and he began to make progress in healing.

He left treatment for a week in order to testify at his partner's trial. But Doug never made it to the trial; instead he relapsed, remembering little of that week. His family and friends cut him off, telling him, "this was the last time." In disgust, Doug's family turned away from his "sin" and darkness. Doug's therapist took a different approach: rather than discussing his failure, she made efforts to enter into and connect amidst his darkness. She observed, "It makes sense that you relapsed. Alcohol is your oldest and most trusted defense in this world." With this, Doug's therapist communicated a deep commitment to being with him inside the muddled mess of sin, pain, and darkness. Similar to how Jesus entered into the world's darkness and suffering, taking it all in, the therapist entered into Doug's suffering.

Today, with a more flexible, conversational, and dialogical understanding of integration, I could have provided better treatment than when I was trying to hate the sin and love the sinner. I wish I could rewind time and help Richard cast a vision for how a loving and complete way of living might look.

Integration Conversation Starters

1. Consider your own experience of entering into (rather than moving away from) the "muddled" parts of life (your own, others', your patients'). When you've entered into these spaces, what has it been like for you? What theological and personal resistance do you notice when going into the muddle?

2. Does the idea of a God who is already there in the muddle waiting for you change how you might experience or think of these moments?

How patients view themselves. I (Megan Anna) recently had an exchange with Amanda, who lives in complexity and pain, as well as in deep faith in God.

Megan Anna: I'm curious, where do you feel God is amidst this pain, this suffering?

Amanda: Well, I know he has a plan. Sometimes I just have a hard time seeing it. I should pray more.

Amanda has a newborn, born seven weeks premature, and a four-year-old struggling with behavioral and emotional dysregulation, and a husband who experiences crippling depression. She experiences acute anxiety and depression exacerbated by her struggle to manage her diabetes. It took us months of working together before she became comfortable talking about how painful and hard life was, in part because Amanda felt she was being ungrateful whenever she discussed hardship. With that background in mind, let's look again at what was happening at this moment in therapy:

> **Megan Anna:** I'm curious, where do you feel God is amidst this pain, this suffering? (Notice that my desire was to help her find God in her suffering, an idea which emerges from my belief that on the cross God entered into the darkness of her suffering.)

> **Amanda:** Well, I know he has a plan. Sometimes I just have a hard time seeing it. I should pray more. (Notice that Amanda responded with shame.)

Amanda's response told me a great deal about her theology: suffering and pain are here for a reason, because God has an endgame or purpose. She sees it as selfish to be angry or to lament and grieve her hardships. As Amanda paces the wooden floors of her bedroom, wringing her hands, trying to avoid another panic attack, is God a distant critic who sees her as weak in faith, or does God fully enter in and pace alongside her?

Listening to Amanda talk about her experience of God also gave me insight into her perception of herself. I heard "shame talk" and noticed how her experience of God (God image) brought both protective and risk factors. It soothes Amanda to know someone bigger than her is in control, and it simultaneously makes her vulnerable to think that this bigger someone is quite disappointed in her, and perhaps capricious in how the pain of the world is distributed.

This reminds me of several exciting research frontiers in integration looking at how our view of God impacts our perception of self and psychological well-being.[11] These conversations include research on God image (experience of God) and God concept (ideas about God), looking at authoritarian versus benevolent concepts of God, and how these concepts relate to shame and vulnerability, attachment, and so forth. In this chapter we're

---

[11]For a comprehensive conversation that looks at the interplay between God image, God concept, and psychological well-being, see Moriarty and Hoffman's (2007) book, *God Image Handbook for Spiritual Counseling and Psychotherapy.*

interested in how one's God image, God concept, and subsequent relationship to self may be deeply influenced by one's narrative about Jesus' work on the cross. In other words, views of the atonement are not isolated chapters in theology textbooks. These views weave into our understanding of God, self, and other, and really do matter in our daily lives and in our vocation as counselors and psychotherapists.

The point of counseling is not to correct wrong belief or to help patients more closely align to orthodoxy, but it is still essential to understand that our patients' views of God have a direct bearing on how they experience psychological and spiritual pain. We echo the intent of Moriarty and Hoffman (2007):

> [We] do not intend to suggest that there is a correct way that all people see God; rather, we are concerned that many people distort their experience of God in a manner that causes unnecessary psychological and spiritual suffering. (p. 6)

It is clear that our God image and self-perception are intimately mingled together. A multitude of studies have evaluated the link between people's God concept (intellectual definition of God), God image (subjective emotional or relational experience of God), and psychological and spiritual wellness. For example, Alavi, Amin, and Savoji (2013) evaluated the link between depression, pathological guilt, and God image among cancer patients, finding a significant correlation between people's God image and depression, and that pathological guilt played a significant role in predicting depression. Similarly, self-esteem is positively correlated with positive God images and negatively related with punitive views of God (Francis, Gibson, & Robbins, 2001).

Our patients' God image has a significant impact on how they view themselves, specifically their sin and how they relate to their sinfulness (pathological guilt). Understanding how our patients view God and particularly how God relates to their sin provides helpful information about how they may relate to their own sin and potential vulnerabilities to guilt and shame.

We have made the point that theology, such as views of the atonement, shapes God image, and yet there is much more than theology at play. Theological and personal narratives are always intersecting, forming one another. For example, early attachments and relationships have a significant influence on one's internal representation of God. As such, the task of the counselor is rarely the cognitive task of correcting theology, but instead the interpersonal task of living out a godly relationship with the patient in the context of counseling. Noffke and Hall (2007) note that the work of shifting a God image has less to do with changing theological content and more to do with "the power of emotion, metaphor and therapeutic bond" (p. 69). Being in an attuned, empathetic, securely attached relationship helps rewire one's God image.

My instinct when I heard Amanda describe her God image was to have a theological "righting reflex." While, thankfully, I know getting into a theological dialog would not be helpful or ethical, I did notice this instinct. My fix-it response oriented me to the cognitive realm. I silently ruminated on whether there were other ways to bring an alternative view of God into the room. Ironically, me detaching from Amanda's affect, going into cognitive fix-it mode was moving me farther away rather than closer to helping Amanda have a more relational, attuned view of God. Rather than talking about the atonement (noun), I drew from my own narrative of the atonement to shape how I could be with her (showing up in her suffering and being attuned to her pain, while not allowing her pain, shame, or sin to compromise the security of my presence). It turns out living the atonement (verb) was more helpful in creating the neural pathways necessary for the rewiring of her God image than any theological concepts I could have brought into the session.

Six months later, Amanda was in session, standing, rocking, and soothing her infant son as we talked. I wondered out loud if she ever wished someone would hold her like that. Amanda teared up and described a moment that week where she experienced a powerful image. She described seeing God hold her as an infant, staring down compassionately into her eyes. She described how it continued to be rare to experience God this way, but these occasional glimpses of grace provided her with an anchoring image of God's love to return to during times of pain.

Amanda's history of having unattuned and disconnected parents makes it difficult to experience Jesus pacing alongside her on those bare, creaky wood floors, but perhaps as she experiences enduring connection and empathy from her Christian therapist her internal representation of God will slowly shift.

QUERIES FOR PATIENTS

To access your patients' self-perceptions, consider asking questions such as:

1. When do you feel connected to God?

   Listen for qualifiers. Is the person's connection to God based on doing enough or being good enough? Do they feel connected amid their messiness?

2. When you notice brokenness in your life, how do you imagine God responding to this? Viewing you?

   Listen for their God concept.

3. When the shame-storm hits (i.e., struggling with feeling worthy or good enough), what would I see you doing?

   Are they disconnecting and isolating? Are they connecting with others? With God?

How therapists view themselves. I (Megan Anna) found it a bit intimidating to learn that the most important tool I bring into therapy is *me*. Utilizing the self of the therapist requires exploring the significance of therapists as "wounded healers." How we integrate and use our wounds makes a difference, more so than technique (Aponte & Kissil, 2014; Lum, 2002; Satir, Banmen, Gerber, & Gomori, 1991; Sussman, 2007). Early in my training I recall thinking I would be more confident if I could simply master therapeutic techniques to address my patients' troubles. It felt overwhelming to see *myself* as the primary agent of change. Over time, I am finding comfort with this reality.

Counseling is relational; who I am in relation to myself and others matters a great deal. Some of my best work and some of my most timid work comes from my own wounds and areas of healing (Aponte & Kissil, 2014, refer to these core issues as therapists' "signature themes"). When I work with patients struggling with shame dynamics, I notice an increased sense of weightiness. At times this causes me to be avoidant and at other times to enter into the heaviness and terror with them. When my woundedness and the woundedness of my patient overlap, this brings up a mix of vulnerability, risk, and opportunity.

How I navigate my woundedness influences how I will work with my patients in their woundedness, particularly when our areas of woundedness overlap. Similarly, how I navigate and think about my own muddle (sinfulness and relationship to God as a broken human) influences how I relate to my patients' experiences of these spaces. When locked into my "hustle for worth" narrative, I may recoil in shame at my own sinfulness and skirt away from the muddled spaces, likely struggling to be present to the pain and shame my patients are expressing about their experience of brokenness. My hustle for worth could also show up as frantic attempts to "fix" my patients. But when I am able to experience God's gracious presence with me in my sin, it enables me to be a gracious presence with my patients' pain, modeling an ability to tolerate their distress.

As I was able to draw from my profound experiences of Jesus with me in pain, darkness, and brokenness, I felt empowered to enter into Amanda's and Maria's confused and muddled spaces. And so, if it's true that the self of

FALLING APART WHILE HOLDING IT ALL TOGETHER

Graduate work is demanding and invokes personal change. While all education brings an element of challenge and change, this is heightened for those entering mental health professions because of the personal exploration it requires. Most graduate students in counseling and psychotherapy programs probably wonder at some point why they didn't just go get a degree in business or theology or thermonuclear physics.

As students enter training, they will likely hear some version of the following informed consent: "It will be hard. You will come out of this a different person." While we all hear it, I suspect few of us actually understand what it means at the time. If I were to attempt to describe this experience to students coming into this field, I'd describe it this way: *Clinical training exists in the precarious tension between falling apart and holding it all together.* And while this intersection may be most intense during training, this is not a dialectic that is ever fully resolved. Seasoned therapists—at least the best ones—continue to live in a dialectic between brokenness and healer.[a]

Trainees aren't simply undergoing the usual deconstruction-reconstruction that occurs in the education process. They are deconstructing their very selves. If we take seriously the notion that we ourselves are a therapeutic tool in the room, then training

---

[a] Psychotherapist and bestselling author Lori Gottlieb (2019) provides an intimate look into this complex intersection as she chronicles her experience as both therapist and patient in *Maybe You Should Talk to Someone*.

the therapist is the greatest tool we bring into the therapy room, then as Christian psychotherapists and counselors we need to reflect on our own experience of darkness and how we relate to ourselves and God in our personal experience of sin and shame.

Like Megan Anna, I (Mark) have grown to see the importance of my own presence in the room, and how I view myself, to be more important than the techniques I have mastered. Despite having written a couple of books and many articles on Christian approaches to CBT, and teaching classes on the topic for decades now, I am more convinced than ever that the theory and techniques of a particular approach are less important than the genuine person who shows up in the counseling room.

It wasn't always this way. Like Megan Anna, I can be quite vulnerable to the "hustle for worth" paradigm. I remember early in my career I assumed

for this work involves sitting in and reflecting on our brokenness and woundedness. This requires self-reflection, vulnerability, transparency, and a process that can at times feel akin to "falling apart."

At the same time, trainees need to *hold it all together.* They hold the trauma, complexity, and pain of their patients. Professionally, they hold it together as they work to impress professors and peers with keen insights, publications, and achievements. This pressure can make it difficult for trainees to talk about the fact that while they are busy *holding it all together,* they are also *falling apart.* This season of life calls for complex and fluid narratives (i.e., I can both be a professional who is able to hold complex and painful things and I can be a vulnerable and confused patient myself struggling as I work through deep-seated emotional pain).

An expansive and fluid Christian narrative around brokenness, sin, and redemption can be a helpful frame for the trainee's experience. Theology that draws our attention to the universality and seriousness of our brokenness while also drawing our attention to the hope of redemption and reconciliation can hold together the tension of the both/and: brokenness and healing, sin and salvation, death and resurrection, falling apart and holding it together. As trainees (and seasoned therapists) embody the dialectic of falling apart and holding it together, perhaps they can find hope in the Christ who encounters and embodies the dialectics of sin and redemption, darkness and light, death and life.

my patients wanted to be in and out of my office as quickly and efficiently as possible, so I would make a diagnosis, propose a crisp treatment plan, and implement the plan as efficiently as possible. Curiously, I recall not needing to replace the box of facial tissue in my office over the first few years of my clinical work because patients never needed it! A few years later when I got into personal therapy I recognized that I was not looking for efficiency as much as connection. Thankfully, I found a psychotherapist who connected with me in compassion and care, and sometimes in confrontation, and who valued relationship above efficiency. This transformed my understanding of psychotherapy more than all the books I had read and workshops I had attended. What I discovered is that my patients yearn for the same thing I wanted—to be connected in a real relationship where empathy and human compassion are the centerpiece.

The best outcome researchers estimate is that about 15% of the variance in counseling outcome is related to the techniques we use, and much of the rest has to do with the personal, lived experiences of the patient as well as the so-called "common factors" of psychotherapy (Lambert, 1992). These basic dimensions of human civility and relational warmth play out in any effective counseling, whether psychodynamic, CBT, or almost any other theory one may be inclined to follow.

Perhaps the greatest relevance for the atonement theology we have discussed in this chapter is how we as therapists view ourselves. Are we locked into rigid narratives that fuel shame, or do our atonement narratives allow for movement to hold the complexity of being human: muddled and deeply loved, imperfect and agents of transformative work? The story we hold about how God sees us will shape our lives, both personally and professionally. This, in turn, will affect how we sit with patients in the messiest moments of their lives.

Intrapersonal Conversation Starters

1. When I notice the presence of sin in my life, what is my first response (physical sensations, emotions, thoughts)? What does my self-talk/mind chatter look like? Similarly, when I ponder God's love, what are my first responses?

2. For most of us it is more common to think that God loves us than to think that God likes us. If you imagine God liking you, what responses do you have?

Views of suffering, darkness, and violence. Even as we argue that God's love abounds, and is all around us, we also acknowledge that suffering persists in our world. We recognize that as therapists we come into close contact with the brokenness and sin of the world (sin done to our patients, sin of our patients, sin in the social structures that we and our patients exist in). We believe that love abounds in the biblical story, and persists through all history, but this does not discount the reality and consequences of living in a broken and fallen world.

With speedy access to information, nearly any moment can be invaded by news of horrific suffering resulting from the world's brokenness. I (Megan Anna) have had horrific traumas invade both mundane and sensitive moments: learning of the Sandy Hook school shooting while playing a game with my three-year-old daughter, the news of the murder of a mother and her children in my community as I get my kids ready for school, learning of children severely neglected in migrant detention centers right before diving into a full day of being with patients. We live in an age where we are bombarded with human suffering on a massive level.

On top of this, we take on and listen to the suffering of our patients as we sit with them in their stories of pain: past and present. Being bombarded with suffering on a global and a personal level prompts the question: How are we to respond to human suffering? A view of atonement that considers Jesus' role in taking on human suffering, pain, and violence has implications for how we understand our response to the suffering of others.

Many people who go into the field of counseling are already attuned to the suffering of others and committed to the call of being with those who suffer. And so, we fear that writing about the significance of the Christian call to "suffer with" may be akin to preaching to the choir. At the same time, we also wonder how many of us in the helping professions struggle, like Amanda, with being present to, responding to, and taking seriously our own suffering. After sitting with some of the deepest traumas this world has to offer, it is tempting to minimize and discredit our own experiences of pain and suffering. Might not responding to our own suffering—not recognizing the presence of God in our pain—limit our ability to sit with others in their suffering?

1. How do I respond to suffering in the world? Do I shut it out, drown in it, experience numbness?
2. Do I respond to my own suffering? How?
3. How do I experience God in the world's suffering, my patients' suffering, and my personal suffering?

Finding hope amidst suffering. While there are many differences among the atonement metaphors, we believe they can all agree on these: Jesus death saves, and hope arises from the ashes of suffering. All views of the atonement give us hope that suffering is not without meaning.

I (Megan Anna) have had more conversations than I would like with patients discussing posttraumatic stress disorder secondary to sexual assault, interpersonal violence, and loss. When discussing trauma, I am extremely cautious about how and when to bring in the idea of posttraumatic growth (also discussed in chapter three). I've noticed a trend. Patients tend to feel empowered when they learn about the research and concept of posttraumatic growth. I've been witness to incredible transformations as patients begin to name and live into the growth and resilience gained through their suffering. An atonement narrative that holds the suffering God, who embraced our suffering, is a narrative that can hold hope, providing the clinician and patient with a renewed confidence in hopeful suffering.

Gregory of Nazianzus, one of the patristic theologians, was committed to articulating the importance of taking seriously the full humanity of Jesus (in addition to Jesus' divinity). He famously wrote "for that which he has not assumed he has not healed" (Ford & Higton, 2002, p.92). It was through the process of assuming the totality of our humanness that God brought redemption. Similarly, in the process of assuming suffering it becomes possible for it to become a hope-filled suffering. Human suffering is no longer a suffering without hope; it is no longer a suffering without God (Johnson, 2005).

I met Beth two weeks after her pregnancy loss. She and her husband had been trying for over two years to conceive, and she was ecstatic about her pregnancy. With news that a little girl, "June," would be joining them, she and her partner got busy putting together a nursery. At twenty-six weeks Beth lost

June. She and I spent weeks together sitting in her pain and confusion, pondering the significance of this loss. After a few months of sitting in the muck together, Beth began to bring in new insights: "I struggle to be present. My whole life I'm jumping from one thing to the next." Grief had forced Beth to slow down, and she was beginning to reflect on the quality of her existence. A successful lawyer well on her way to partnership at her big city firm, she worked grueling weeks. She was so used to pleasing others, always saying yes to people's requests without pausing to consider her own feelings. When hosting a dinner party with friends, Beth described feeling disconnected, so consumed by the details of managing all of the things (food, chairs, drinks) that she was unable to slow down and *eat, drink, and be merry.* This way of life had never bothered Beth before. But grief forced her to slow down. As Beth looked at her life, she reflected on the values guiding her and how disconnected these were from the things that gave her life, vigor, and purpose. As Beth was moving through her grief she began to pace out her appointments more.

At a follow-up appointment Beth began with a life update: she had quit her job at the prestigious law firm and was working for a small practice in her rural town. The cost in pay and prestige felt worth it to her for what she got back in quality of life. Beth also noticed that when people made requests of her she was pausing to check in with herself and listen to her voice. She described feeling more present and engaged in life—she highlighted noticing the sunset, birds, and the sensations that paired with gardening, swimming, or reading a good book in the sunshine. Midway through the session Beth returned to the topic of June, her mind continuing its attempt to make sense of this.

After a heavy pause I interrupted the silence with an observation that felt risky: "You have discovered a vibrancy, engagement, and connectedness that wasn't there before. You have utterly changed your way of being in the world. It feels like this may be a gift June has given to you. By living this way, you are continuing to integrate her into your life. What a powerful gift June gave you."

Beth's eyes welled up with tears as she fumbled, "I hadn't thought about it this way before. But yes . . . she gave me this gift." Beth continued to return to the significance of this meaning in future visits. At our next visit she talked about "June's gift" with ease. Reflecting on how she continued her attachment with June through living a good life continues to be an anchoring point of hope throughout her suffering.

Beth's story is an example of how God shows up during suffering. God doesn't promise that suffering won't happen. God showing up in this case didn't save June from dying. God showing up doesn't make things neat and tidy; it's God showing up to be with us. And this means that we counselors don't have to go home with headaches because we have failed to make our patients' lives neat and tidy.

God showing up doesn't even mean making sense of the suffering. Some suffering can never be fully understood. But God helps us find the hope amidst the suffering, and that informs our clinical work. God, whose redemptive presence is evident through all history, continues to show up in the messiest times of life. And the presence of One who loves us brings hope during suffering.

Integration Conversation Starters

1. Suffering can be senseless. When exposed to some of the most senseless suffering, what thoughts, sensations, and emotions show up for you (e.g., powerless, angry, anxious, retreat)?

2. Reflect on a time that you have experienced God or another person showing up amidst your suffering. What was your experience of this? What was this like for you? What about it felt helpful or unhelpful?

AUTHOR DIALOG: WHAT ABOUT THE WEIGHT OF SIN?

Mark: We've been pretty tough on the penal substitution view of atonement in this chapter, Megan Anna. Like you, I've been compelled in recent years by some earlier views of atonement, but one aspect I have always appreciated about the penal substitution view is that it demonstrates how much God grieves sin. All around us we see a world suffering under the weight of greed, selfishness, exploitation, and unfettered hedonism. We don't use the word *sin* much these days, but it's hard to deny that something is terribly broken and wrong with the world. In moving away from a penal substitution view, are we vulnerable to minimizing the significance of human sinfulness?

Megan Anna: I appreciate this image of God grieving sin. While I think it takes on a different form and is perhaps emphasized less in some other atonement theories, God's grief about the human predicament is still present in other views. Some of these other theories move away from an individual focus of sin and more toward a collectivistic view of sin. While I think it is important to look at collective views of sin, you are right that we could lose an emphasis on individual responsibility. I'll highlight this tension through story:

I grew up going to an evangelical youth group, and our winter retreats often involved speakers who addressed issues related to personal piety. We would often leave with a renewed vitality and passion for the sanctified and holy life. It was incredibly moving and powerful, though it lacked connection to collective sin. Fast-forward ten years to when I was in seminary and leading a youth retreat for a mainline church where the winter retreat topic was about water and resources. They highlighted the importance of being ecologically responsible. While it helped the teens connect to an idea that salvation was also about the earth and the poor, it didn't seem to ignite their passion or interest. The message about water was a bit . . . dry.

These accounts reflect a tendency within the church to either focus on personal piety or public piety, evangelism or the social gospel. With today's polarization we run the risk of separating individual and public ethics. I long to see the Western church embody the gospel in its fullness, which will include a comprehensive view of atonement and salvation. I wonder if there is a way to keep an eye on the seriousness of sin and the responsibility of the individual, but without God needing to be punishing Jesus on our behalf?

Mark: I love your answer and how you use story to explain it. And yes, I agree that we need to think about sin both collectively and personally. Still, given what social psychologists teach us about the fundamental attribution error—that we tend to have generous thoughts about ourselves and blaming thoughts toward others—what's to keep us from seeing sin as someone else's problem? In other words, a collective view of sin, coupled with our self-justifying tendencies, might make it easy to assume the sin problem in our world is someone else's doing. It's the political system or the corporations or the criminals who cause the problems in the world. But what about our personal responsibility? I remember reading Donald Miller's (2003) *Blue Like Jazz* and being so drawn to his idea that he would like to show up at a protest someday with a sign that reads, "I am the problem." If we lean too far toward a collective view of sin I wonder if we may miss the opportunity to see our own contributions to the problems of the world.

Further Reading

Beilby, J. & Eddy, P. (Eds.). (2006). *The nature of the atonement: four views*. Downers Grove, IL: InterVarsity Press.

Crisp, O. (2020). *Approaching the atonement: The reconciling work of Christ*. Downers Grove, IL: InterVarsity Press.

Weaver, J. D. (2001). *The nonviolent atonement*. Grand Rapids: Eerdmans.

Zahnd, B. (2017). *Sinners in the hands of a loving God*. New York: Waterbrook.

Further Listening

Rohr, R. (2019, March 30). "Nonviolent atonement" [Audio podcast]. *Another Name for Every Thing with Richard Rohr*. Retrieved from http://cac.org/podcasts/episode-7-non violent-atonement/

Rosa, E. (Producer). (2019, May 27). "Unshackling the imagination: J. Kameron Carter on structural injustice, misery and melancholy, and the theology of race" [Audio podcast]. *The Table Podcast*. Retrieved from http://cct.biola.edu/witness-possibility-j -cameron-carter/

Rosa, E. (Producer). (2019, April 22). "Patchwork redemption: Suffering and joy in racial perspective [Audio podcast]. *The Table Podcast*. Retrieved from http://cct.biola.edu /patchwork-redemption-ethics-race/

Wright, N. T. (2018, November 27). "Qs on sacrifice, crucifixion and atonement" [Audio podcast]. *Ask NT Wright Anything*. Retrieved from www.premierchristianradio.com /Shows/Weekday/Ask-NT-Wright-Anything/Podcast/2-Qs-on-sacrifice-crucifixion -and-atonement

FINAL CONVERSATION

Pondering God

If you are reading this book as part of a group, here is a final conversation to have before moving on to part three.

Sometimes we may think the theological task of our time is to find some hidden truth, like we're scrambling through a maze looking for the treasure of correct belief at the end. This view has some merit, because what we believe is important insofar as it shapes our relationship with and actions toward God, others, nature, and ourselves. But in this part of the book, we have attempted to provide a different way of looking at theology.

Rather than questing for a particular correct belief, we have tried to open up conversations about the relationship between psychology and theology, because doing this allows for insight, personal awareness, and meaningful conversation. So yes, there are doctrines of what it means to be made in the image of God and about how atonement happens, and these doctrines matter. But for counselors and psychotherapists, it is also important to remember that our patients don't come for private lessons in theology. They come in pain, and many come with big questions, and with the hope that we might be hospitable and generous enough that they might eventually voice these questions of ultimate meaning. Within a few sessions people typically figure out whether we are able to host these big, difficult questions or whether it's best just to talk about symptoms and solutions.

When big questions emerge in counseling, it is typically after trust has been established and patients are confident that we can engage in true conversation without trying to educate or fix them. When deep questions come, they are not academic questions about theology but profoundly personal questions about the nature of who God is, and how God perceives them, and how they feel about God, and how to make sense of pain.

Final conversation: Metaphysics is a branch of philosophy that deals with the nature of reality. It's concerned with questions such as: What does it mean to be human? How do we know things? How are mind and matter related?

As you ponder this, how do you think the work of a counselor or psychotherapist is similar and dissimilar to the work of a metaphysician? To the work of a theologian? To the work of a physician? To the work of a pastor or priest?

PART THREE

God in the World

One of the questions we hear in our work as counselors and psychotherapists is "Where is God?" Pediatric and child psychologists likely hear this in the cutest of ways, as young children try to make sense of whether God lives in their neighborhood or maybe in the sky or maybe in Australia. But this is a question that persists far beyond childhood curiosity.

When an adolescent faces profound questions of sexual or gender identity, where is God in this confusion and uncertainty and social alienation? When young adults struggle with addictions or eating disorders, where is God in the longing for control and stability? When families are ripped apart by premature death or enmity or infidelity, where is God in the chaos? When bigotry triumphs in our communities and people are marginalized and wounded as a result, where is God in the injustice?

Where is God?

If you're hoping for a precise answer, you'll probably not find it here. But we think the question is terribly important anyway, even if answers are hard to find. These are questions that show up in the counseling room, so we should become familiar with the conversations. These are integration conversations—not ones with clear answers, but conversations that bring value to the question and the one who quests.

Even in the absence of a precise answer to the question Where is God? we do offer a more general answer. While our answer may seem vague, we try to unpack it in these final two chapters. Our answer to where is God? Here. Active. Present, even when difficult to discern.

5

Mission of God

WHAT IS GOD UP TO IN THE WORLD?

HERE'S A QUESTION I (Mark) have been asked many times over the course of my career: "How often do you share your faith in the context of counseling?" Of the many integration questions I have received over the years this is perhaps the most difficult, and my answers have always felt clumsy and inadequate. Indeed, this question is so common and intimidating that I have come to think of it in uppercase terms as "the Question."

Even as I sputter out some words in reply, my mind spins with the complexity of it, and the only thing I feel certain about is that my answer isn't very helpful. Recently, with Megan Anna's help, I have been able to place the Question in the context of a much bigger question: What is God up to in the world? At first glance speaking of religious beliefs in counseling may not seem very connected to this bigger question of God's activity in the world, but we attempt to make this connection clear in this chapter. And, as is true of every chapter in this book, we hope our ideas will promote further conversation among those who read this book such that our collective wisdom will evolve into something much greater than the two of us can offer here.

Early in my career, my answer to the Question tended to be guilt based. I included a general statement about my Christian faith in my informed consent form, and occasionally I would venture into conversation about how Jesus can save us from our self-focused ways and offer a more abundant life, but most often I did not. With almost every patient who did not identify as a Christian I had this nagging feeling that I might be doing something pallid and shallow in my therapeutic work. I pondered whether I was colluding with them to look at the little stories of human life without considering the bigger story that could ultimately lead to abundant and eternal life.

Midcareer, during my years as a psychology professor at Wheaton College, I taught professional ethics in our doctoral program. Ethics standards look closely at issues of power and persuasion, so in those days I would often stumble through some answer about balancing ethical practice with our calling as Christians to spread the good news of Jesus. This already-tricky balancing act is further complicated because our professional licenses make us accountable to state regulatory bodies and national professional organizations. Being a licensed psychologist or marriage and family therapist or professional counselor means we are expected to act in ways that are congruent with what our jurisdiction mandates and our patients expect. If you were to ask the Question in those days, I would probably say something about attending to the deep spiritual questions of our patients, offering what we can while staying congruent in our roles as licensed professionals, and then referring people to clergy to further address these questions. Still, even as I offered these words I would feel internally guilty for not sharing enough about Jesus with my patients who seemed to be searching for some greater meaning in their lives.

Now in my late-career years, and in conversation with Megan Anna, I have come to a place of personal peace with this. In all those prior years I tended to nuance and parse the answer to the Question without spending much time pondering its connection to the larger topic of God's character and activity in the world. What I've discovered is that making this connection allows for simplicity, peace, and wisdom.

Locating Mission

We know from psychology that the human brain likes categories. We interact with thousands of sensory inputs every day and need categories to make sense of it all. And yet the categories we use change how we experience a thing. Take anxiety for instance. If you study anxiety under the category of biology you may focus on physical symptoms, the sympathetic nervous system, and biological interventions. If you study anxiety under the category of relationship you may focus on attachment, current social stressors, and protective factors. If you study anxiety under mental health interventions, you may focus on cognitive restructuring and psychological techniques to reduce anxious thoughts. Clearly, the categories we use influence our experience and interpretation of a construct. Theologians are not immune to this, as they too tend to study concepts under umbrella categories. This is helpful, except for when it isn't. Some things fit into categories more easily than others. Mission is a nomadic topic that has been studied under many different umbrella themes. Given that categories shape how we understand a thing, this has influenced our Christian approach to mission.

Mission and soteriology. In the twentieth century it was common to study mission under the umbrella category of soteriology—the doctrine of salvation. From this vantage point, one of the most important things we Christians can do is go out into the world to save lost souls.

In middle school, having just learned Bill Bright's Four Spiritual Laws, I (Mark) recall sitting down with a peer after we played a baseball game and explaining to him how all of us are sinners, that Jesus has built a bridge through the sacrificial death of Jesus, and that he could have the gift of eternal life by saying a prayer and inviting Jesus into his heart. It took incredible courage for me to approach this friend and share with him, but it was all worth it when it worked! He said the prayer and became a Christian. I spoke of it freely in my youth group and probably would have gotten lots of high-fives except that we did low-fives back then.

Though I'm about to criticize myself for this individualistic view of mission, I should first say two good things about this story. First, I take Jesus to be quite serious when he offered words of Great Commission: "Go therefore and make disciples of all nations, baptizing them in the name of the Father and of the Son and of the Holy Spirit, and teaching them to obey everything that I have commanded you" (Mt 28:19-20). Jesus revealed God's heart for mission with these words and invited us to be participants in that mission. My clumsy, awkward conversation with my middle school friend came at least partly from a desire to obey Jesus, and I take that to be a good desire. Second, God really does save us. My understanding of God and humanity today doesn't fit as well with the Four Spiritual Laws as it did back in middle school, but I still hold firmly to the conclusion that Jesus invites us into the salvation we long for. Back then I thought only in terms of eternal life, which should not be minimized, but now I've come to think that we make the word *saved* too small when we only think of something that happens after we die. God knows I have needed a lot of saving in my life, and I am grateful for how God's faithful presence continues to save me from my selfish and wayward inclinations and from the ways I have been blind to the astonishing magnitude of God's love for all creation. Even as I write this story, I find myself pausing and praying for my middle school friend, that he has also known the saving presence of Jesus throughout these many years.

Now for the more critical look at mission coming from a desire to save my friend. Have you noticed that I haven't mentioned the name of my middle school friend? I don't remember it. In fact, I hardly remember any conversations with him after that day he invited Jesus into his heart. I had done my job by bringing another soul to heaven someday, and so I reveled in a sense of satisfaction about being a good Christian. My witnessing may have been at least as much about me as about him, and I feel sad and embarrassed about that today.

A decade or two later I started hearing about "friendship evangelism." This seems to be a huge improvement over the view that mission emanates from an individual trying to obey Jesus' command to "go make disciples." Friendship evangelism sees mission as rooted in human relationship. If I care about you, and we are in a relationship, then it is only natural to tell you about the things that are important to me, including my beliefs about God. Friendship evangelism has been robustly criticized in recent years because it can seem that the whole point of forming relationships is to win people to Jesus. In this case, it really is little more than the individualistic approach to evangelism that I learned in middle school.

These views of mission emanate from soteriology (the doctrine of salvation). We are trying to live out the Great Commission, to save lost souls, and to help them follow the ways and teachings of Jesus. I find the soteriological urge of mission tugs at me often in the context of counseling and psychotherapy.

I met Elena after she experienced a difficult breakup, when she came to psychotherapy to address symptoms of depression and anxiety. As we explored this in the first session, it became evident that she had ample experience with breakups, in part because of repeatedly choosing abusive and addicted men. Though she did not meet criteria for dependent personality disorder, she certainly had some traits of this. It was hard for Elena to be alone, so she often found the first man who would have her and then ended up in damaging relationships. Eventually the man would leave her for someone else, or she would decide she needed to escape the abuse, and she would add one more breakup to her relational resume.

I noticed two other things in the first few sessions with Elena. First, she wasn't quite sure what to do with me as a male therapist. She drew attention to her attire and appearance, compared the ease of speaking with me to the difficulty she had speaking with her previous boyfriend, and apologized for being a few pounds overweight. It was clear that she didn't know how to relate to me as a person who would never have any sort of romantic or sexual relationship with her. Second, I noticed a deep relational yearning in her for something more than she could find in her series of relationships with men. She longed for security, a relational home, a place of safety where she was known and loved. It occurred to me how much knowing Jesus could help her in her quest for love and meaning.

Within three sessions I understood the dilemma facing Elena and me, and it was essentially the Question. Her whole life was crying out for something deeper than what she had experienced—for faith, for meaning, for fellowship and connection, for abundant life in Jesus. But at the same time, she had dependent traits and was having difficulty knowing how to relate to me without resorting to old relational patterns. If I would have shared my Christian beliefs with her as I had with my middle school friend, she would have likely been receptive to my words, but what would that do for the dependency patterns and the psychological issues that I was agreeing to help her address? If I turned into just another persuasive male in her life, even for a good cause, then it might work counter to our treatment goals. We'll return to Elena's story later in the chapter.

Mission and ecclesiology. A second category that has been used to study mission is ecclesiology (the study of the church). Perhaps the clearest biblical example of this is seen in Acts 2 on the day of Pentecost. The Holy Spirit filled a gathering of people, Peter gave a fabulous sermon, and three thousand people were added to the church in a single day. Ever since we have hoped for the same in places of worship—that we would gather, experience the presence of God, hear good preaching, and grow in number.

For the past twenty-five years I have worked with clergy, both in my research and my clinical practice. The fabulous-sermon fantasy, coupled with imagining adding thousands of new members as a result, is never far from a pastor's consciousness. It would be impossible to communicate how deeply most Christian ministers feel the pressure of this ecclesiological view of mission. If their churches are not growing they feel personal shame and often face criticism from their denominational leaders. Coupled with the demographic reality that church attendance is declining throughout the country, this leaves many pastors feeling the weight of presumed incompetence, failure, and shame.

There are good reasons to locate mission within ecclesiology. First, we have just hinted at church sustainability and growth. One could look skeptically at this, as if we are just talking about a business model where growth is revered as the epitome of success, but that trivializes the point regarding the church. Church growth is not simply about meeting the budget, but is—or should be—more about making the words and heart of Jesus available to a hurting world. Whether locating mission in soteriology or ecclesiology, the Great Commission is the central organizing and motivating factor.

Second, mission could be deemed to be the primary work of the church. From this perspective, this commissioning of the church in Matthew 28 is also establishing the blueprint for how the church should operate. It is interesting to consider who was present when Jesus gave the words we now call the Great Commission. It was the eleven disciples who remained after Judas's suicide. Jesus was not simply talking to individual followers, but to those who would eventually establish the church that would become the largest religion in the world.

Third, just like a beautiful symphony is an event to behold, with different instruments making various sounds at just the right moments, so also locating mission with the church demonstrates how the various gifts of individuals fit together into beautiful community that can be attractive to the world. In saying this, we recognize that the church hasn't always been attractive to the world, but when it works well it can be exquisite in its beauty. Some with the gifts of hospitality and mercy organize shelters and food pantries and community gardens. Others with gifts of teaching offer words of instruction and insight. Those with prophetic inclinations offer warnings at critical moments. Taken in concert, the church can demonstrate beautiful mission to the world.

God as the Source of Mission

Like all human efforts, these approaches to mission are a mixed bag of altruism and egocentrism. Connecting mission to soteriology comes from good motives to help save lost souls. Those who form relationships with their neighbors in order to share the gospel are also trying to follow the ways of Jesus in reaching out to those who are missing the fullness life has to offer. Seeing mission as part of the church is also reasonable. Growing churches can be beautiful, as it was on the day of Pentecost, and reaching out to a hurting world in an organized way reflects the heart of Jesus.

Without wanting to discredit these views, we introduce another possible view of mission—one that was prominent in the early church, then mostly disappeared for many centuries, but has regained attention in the past seventy years. In this view the source of mission is located within the very *being* of a trinitarian God.

In the early church the word *mission* was used to talk about the Trinity: the sending of the Son by the Father and the mutual sending of the Holy Spirit by the Father and the Son. Within this frame the first mission does not follow the Great Commission; it precedes it. Mission is located within the activity of God. The sending of Jesus (by the Father) to a particular culture in order to embody and translate the divine message of creation, reconciliation, and redemption was the consummate mission. Jesus came and infused a particular culture with this gospel of hope and redemption. In this view the source of mission is not culture or ecclesiology or even soteriology but is rooted in the very being of God (Sanneh, 2004; Walls, 2002).

Rooting mission in God's trinitarian nature began with the early church and then reemerged following World War I as more missiologists began noticing theologians such as Karl Barth. Barth believed that mission originated from the character of God: first manifested in God's covenantal relationship with Israel; then through the life, death, and resurrection of Jesus; and finally in the sending of the Holy Spirit. Barth's theology was quite radical in nature by placing mission under the umbrella of trinitarian theology (as opposed to soteriology or ecclesiology) because if mission is core to the being of God, it tells us something about how God is oriented toward the world (Bosch, 1991). This is often referred to as the *missio Dei* (the mission of God/ the sending of God).

At first glance this may seem like a trivial distinction, but we suggest that it is critically important in understanding who we are as Christians and how we see and conduct ourselves in relation to God and God's world. And if this is so, then it also affects who and how we are in the counseling or psychotherapy office.

When I learned Bill Bright's Four Spiritual Laws and tested them out on my middle school friend, I viewed mission in ways that resembled a recruiting or rescue operation—going out into the world, finding lost souls, and bringing them safely back into the security place of the church where God is most fully experienced. Similarly, friendship evangelism, church-growth strategies, and much of the missionary movement in recent centuries have been focused on bringing people in. At first glance this seems to be the obvious conclusion in response to the Great Commission: "Go therefore and make disciples of all nations, baptizing them in the name of the Father and of the Son and of the Holy Spirit." But notice the quiet assumption in these views is that God primarily resides in the church. We go out and bring people home to where God lives.

The alternative view—and the prominent one among early Christians—is more outward facing. Mission emanates from God and points outward to the world. With this view of mission we are not recruiting for God, but God is moving forward into a world that God loves deeply. *The very character of God is missional.* With this perspective in mind, consider again the words and context of the Great Commission:

> And Jesus came and said to them, "All authority in heaven and on earth has been given to me. Go therefore and make disciples of all nations, baptizing them in the name of the Father and of the Son and of the Holy Spirit, and teaching them to obey everything that I have commanded you. And remember, I am with you always, to the end of the age." (Mt 28:18-20)

Here we see Jesus sent with authority into the world to live out God's mission and inviting his followers to be part of this outward-facing mission. We so often read this assuming the key phrase is "go and make disciples," but what if the key phrase is actually this: "remember I am with you always, to the end of the age." With the first reading we presume that mission involves going out into the world and bringing people back to the heart of God. With the second we see a triune God whose mission is to be present with us. This God invites us to participate in the mission of creation, reconciliation, and redemption.

Where we locate the study of mission may seem like arbitrary debate for theologians, but it actually holds significant implications. When studied under ecclesiology, mission is largely seen as a *thing* the church does in efforts of expanding the church. When studied under soteriology it is done largely for the purpose of salvation, typically to prevent people from experiencing the wrath of God in their afterlife. But when mission is located in the nature of God it shows us something of how God is oriented toward the world (Bosch, 1991).

With my patient Elena, I struggled knowing how much to introduce my views of God into our work together, knowing that her patterns of dependency would make her receptive to my words but might also keep her from seeing how much she relied on the opinions of men to guide her paths through life. I desperately wanted to say the words that might bring her into the fold, but this rescuing view of mission might actually compromise our psychological work together. As a licensed psychologist I had some important contractual and moral obligations to consider the psychological outcomes of our work. It was the reason she came to see me. Even so, it nagged at my conscience to think I might have something more important than psychology to offer Elena.

My resolve was further tested about two months into treatment when a former boyfriend contacted Elena and asked her to move back in with him. She had broken off the relationship several years earlier because he was a drug dealer who abused her. Of course, I knew it would be a terrible idea for Elena to get back together with him, but again the psychological treatment required me not to be another male telling her what to do. She needed to make this decision. We worked for several weeks in therapy to consider the pros and cons of getting back into this relationship, and she ultimately decided not to. She made this good decision on her own, without any direct advice from me.

Still, I felt like I was torn between my responsibility as a Christian and my responsibility as a psychologist. Would God agree with my priorities to stay congruent in my role as a mental health professional while this dear soul longed for some deeper meaning in life? But what if mission is about God's heart and God's actions in the world, and is larger than I imagine, and much, much bigger than me? What if God has a purpose and a view of all the moving pieces, so that I can remain consistent in my role as a psychologist without God pacing up in heaven saying, "Oh no, McMinn missed another opportunity."

A couple months later Elena came to a session and announced that her neighbor had invited her to church. After discussing her relationship with her neighbor and her feelings about church I simply said, "That sounds like a nice invitation." It was the only time in our treatment that I gave direct advice to Elena, and it was very muted at that. She likely didn't even recognize it as advice. Elena came the following week with a story of incredible spiritual transformation. She continued growing in faith over the coming weeks and developed a spiritual vitality and psychological strength that delighted us both. Our treatment ended well, with Elena experiencing a sort of hope she had never known.

Not every story ends this way, but it serves as a powerful reminder that mission is embedded in God's nature rather than our efforts, flowing from the presence of God through our neighbors and therapists and nature itself. We could not shut off the mission of God even if we wanted—it flows through life as a fierce river of love, a relentless torrent of grace. God was already there with Elena before I showed up as her therapist. We don't initiate God's work in the world, we simply pay attention, hold our patients prayerfully in the light of Christ, and respond to God's heart, to God's abiding presence with us. The self-revealing God, made known most clearly in Jesus, is with us always, "to the end of the age."

The *missio Dei* (or the missional nature of God) tells us that God is relationally oriented *toward us* and is *for us*. The incarnation is the most profound and mind-boggling illustration of God's missional and relational nature; God is not distant or removed from us as Greek dualism might suggest but chooses to come be with us. Rather than mission being a second-thought action—something Jesus thought up and commissioned after his resurrection—or program the church engages in for the purpose of salvation or church growth, mission is essential to God's being and is therefore part of our identity as the church. Mission is not so much a task as it is a way of being oriented to the world. As Bosch writes:

> *Missio Dei* has helped to articulate the conviction that neither the church nor any other human agent can ever be considered the author or bearer of mission. Mission is, primarily and ultimately, the work of the Triune God, Creator, Redeemer, and Sanctifier, for the sake of the world, a ministry in which the church is privileged to participate. Mission has its origin in the heart of God.

God is a fountain of sending love. This is the deepest source of mission. (Bosch, 1991, p. 392)

Bosch's words highlight two essential features of the *missio Dei*: that God is by nature missional—that is, God is at work mending and tending the universe—and that we the church are invited to participate in God's missional nature.

And so, we return to the Question: do we share our faith in counseling or psychotherapy? If the question is about using the Four Spiritual Laws or seeking to do the missionary work common in soteriological or ecclesiological views of mission, then no, we do not often see counseling as the place to share our beliefs about God. But if we see God as missional, turned toward humanity and all creation in love, facing outward to offer us glimpses of God's self-offering, gracious heart, then yes, all counseling is participating in God's missional nature. God the Father sends the Son, the Son and the Father send the Spirit, and we are invited to participate in this grand mystery that emanates from God and results in the work of the Spirit made visible

GOD'S MISSIONAL BEING

Remember those categories theologians use? These categories have often been used to divide God's function and being. For example, theologians will talk about the economic Trinity (God's activity in the world) and the immanent Trinity (God's being) as two separate things. When mission is talked about from this dualistic lens it's often been historically understood as a *function* of God. When our study of God starts with this dichotomy, it naturally follows to think similarly about the church (being vs. acts of the church) and our very selves (who we are vs. what we do). However, missional theology is careful to not make God's activities secondary to God's being; it takes seriously the sending forth of Godself in love *as essential to who God is*, not a mere function of God. We learn who God is through God's actions—and coming to be with us reveals something essential about who God is. The incarnation was much more than a functional trip for God; this was the giving and revealing of God's very self! In this sense Christ is both *what* is proclaimed as well as *how* it is proclaimed. Being and function are married in one single event, and the church is invited to participate.[a]

---

[a] For further reading on the immanent and economic trinity, see Karl Rahner's (1970) book *The Trinity.*

in human form. This is the missional invitation of God, that we participate in bearing witness to the very character of God that turns toward us and reaches out to wherever we may be. In this sense, all counseling attuned to the missional character of God, marked by the guidance and fruit of the Spirit, is sharing our faith. One might even argue that counseling that is not specifically attuned to God still reflects God's missional nature in the world through conveying common grace.

Implications for Counseling and Psychotherapy

If mission begins in God's nature and then flows outward to the church, to humanity, and to all creation, this has important implications for how we think of our work as counselors and psychotherapists. We offer a few implications here, again hoping that our ideas will help generate more new thoughts and implications through conversations in classrooms and conference rooms as readers discuss what it means for God to be missional.

God is already at work. God is always and already engaged in mission to the world. This is core to God's being—our work is to notice where God is already working and come alongside.

Earlier in the chapter we observed that we may have made the word *save* too small in our Christian circles. Jesus saves us in all sorts of ways—not just by offering eternal life. Similarly, we may have made the word *faith* too small by equating it with belief. Recently, Franciscan priest Richard Rohr has appreciatively described how the psychologist and author David Benner draws a distinction between faith and belief, noting that they are actually quite different (Rohr, 2017). Beliefs are constructs we accept to be true, but faith is trust. To have faith in God, then, is not so much about what doctrines we hold to be true, but to rest in mystery without trying to have answers to every question.

In this sense, Carl Rogers had faith in humanity. Rogers (1957) believed humans would naturally grow when given a nurturing environment. Similarly, as counselors and psychotherapists with faith in God, we can trust that God is already at work in our patients' lives, moving them toward wholeness. This is not an assumption that can be fully proven through Scripture or doctrine or any other rational means, but rather an ability to rest in the mystery, awe, and beauty of a loving God. Faith in a missional God takes some of the pressure off of us to "fix" our patients. Rather, we are invited to come alongside the redemptive, holy work that is already occurring.

This may seem a subtle distinction, but we argue otherwise. If we see it as our job to save our patients from their suffering, pain, questions, and uncertainties—either in this life or in an afterlife—we are taking God's mission on as ours. In contrast, we can, in faith, release this mission to God where it rightfully belongs because God is always turned toward the world.

When we read of the fruit of the Spirit in Galatians 5:22-23 (love, joy, peace, patience, kindness, generosity, faithfulness, gentleness, and self-control), we often focus on the fruit. But what if we turn this around and take the main point of this passage to be the Spirit rather than the fruit. Here we see a missional God, turned toward the world. The fruit of the Spirit point toward a missional God and show us what it looks like to live in service to God's mission, representing God to the world around us.

Jonathan came to me (Mark) for help because a judge told him to. His anger problem landed him in court, and the judge decided counseling would be a better option than jail on this first offense. At first it seemed he was attending because of the legal consequences if he failed to show up, but eventually Jonathan began settling into the process of counseling and looking honestly for the source of his anger. Along with his distress about a dysfunctional and abusive family of origin, he eventually surfaced some deep and important questions about God. As I ponder this, I am reminded that God is at work—in Jonathan's conviction, in the judge who sent him for help, in the movement from defensiveness during his first sessions to a more open exploration of himself in later sessions, and in his desire to probe questions of ultimate meaning and significance.

Integration Conversation Starters

1. If beliefs are constructs we hold to be true, and faith is trusting in the character of God despite the deep questions and uncertainties of life, how do you find yourself drawn to each? How might this affect your work with patients?
2. If God is missional, and always turned toward the world, what implications does this have for how you sit with your patients?

I-Thou versus I-it. It is not uncommon in the town where I (Megan Anna) live to see members of the Latter-day Saints (LDS) on their mission. When I see missionaries approaching I notice my body clench up as I brace for impact. My past experience tells me that while their intentions are good, the missionaries would like *to do something* to me: they would like to show me the truth and as a result have my beliefs and practices change. Over the course of several conversations, I have become better at attempting to engage them as people (rather than *things* or *its* to be avoided) before politely declining their message.

This model of mission is not unique to the LDS Church. As a teenager I went on evangelism trips in order to introduce people to Christian belief and practices. In this model of evangelism, we see ourselves as holding the truth, as if we are carrying a precious container to pass on to others so that they might also hold this container of truth. I might use tools like apologetics to convince you this is a container worth holding. My goal is for you to hold the same beliefs that I hold.

But if we locate mission under the umbrella of trinitarian theology (God's essential being), it becomes less about passing out containers of belief and more about how and who we are in the world. Our being bears witness to God's being. How we are oriented in relationship with ourselves and others is reflective of and bears witness to the relational character of God. Evangelism is about extending an invitation to others into this way of being in the world. Rather than calling for apologetics and argumentative practices, this places emphasis on internal processes such as sanctification and moral development as we grow in our ability to bear witness to God through how we are in the world (Guder, 2000).

To be missionally oriented toward our patients holds similar parallels. With the move toward *missio Dei* we move beyond thinking about psychotherapy as a program or method (something we do to our patients) to more about our way of being oriented toward the other in a way that bears witness to the nature of God.

Every experienced therapist knows there is some tension between learning therapeutic techniques to use in the office and actually being relationally present with our patients. Techniques have their place, of course, but whenever they compete with or detract from the relationship itself they seem ineffective or even destructive.

Jessica Benjamin (2004) explores the "doer/done-to" dynamic that unfolds in relationships where one person becomes subject and the other object. In a doer/done-to dynamic, one person (the subject) feels pulled to act upon or do something to the other (the object). Both people in this dynamic are struggling to see the other and both experience being pulled into the other person's power. This concept is juxtaposed with what Benjamin calls the "symbolic or interpersonal third" where mutual recognition can occur (Benjamin, 2004, p. 11). Here two subjects encounter one another, creating a shared space of mutual recognition (seeing the other, allowing space to be impacted by the other).

Benjamin's concept draws from and is similar to Martin Buber's (1958) philosophical work on I-Thou and I-it relationships. Buber's I-Thou speaks to the ability to honor another person's humanity as we recognize and see the sacredness in self and in the other, rather than relating to the other as an *it* or an object. When we fall into a doer/done-to dynamic we have fallen into an I-it dynamic where we relate to the other as an object. An I-Thou connection allows us to see the sacredness of the other. According to Buber, I-Thou encounters between humans can exist because of God's I-Thou encounter with humanity.

Perhaps what I find most captivating about these concepts is the fact that doer/done-to dominates so many of the social and cultural systems that influence our daily lives. And this sits in radical juxtaposition to the Christian gospel where we create space to be seen by and to see the other (mutual recognition). Christ came to meet us in the incarnation—to have contact with us, through flesh, through words, to be present with us. When we recast an understanding of mission from a thing we *do* toward a way of *being* oriented to the other, it shifts from an I-it relationship to an I-Thou relationship.

QUERIES FOR PATIENTS

Consider asking your patients questions such as:

1. It takes courage to reach out for help in times of depression. How is it feeling to be sitting here talking about this?

   Rather than offering a solution or treatment plan, the counselor is first trying to understand the relationship that is emerging in the office.

2. I see a sort of desperation on your face, like someone needs to take you seriously and that's just not happening. Am I getting this right?

   This calls for a relational connection even when the patient might not be thinking beyond the experience of misery. Consider this as you read the following case example.

Even after we understand this distinction between doer/done-to and mutual recognition, some patients may evoke in us a strong desire to revert back to the doer/done-to patterns. Early in my clinical work I (Megan Anna) experienced this pull with Jack, a patient whose history involved trauma and addiction. Much of his life had been shaped by doer/done-to dynamics. In the first session I noticed feeling disconnected from myself, inept, and clumsy. My normal questions ran flat. He seemed to be saying, "It's awful; just make it stop" and "I've tried everything; nothing works." Perhaps the low point of the session was when he asked: "I mean seriously, do you have a magic pill you can just give me?" He was in pain and wanted me to fix him. In response, I felt as if a tidal wave had overtaken me and I had been swept up into something larger than myself. After reflecting on this experience of being pulled into a doer/done-to dynamic, I thought about how he must be feeling as a new father: hopeless, powerless, cast into an inescapable role. He felt utterly done-to in the process of becoming a father, and together we colluded so that he could pass this experience to me. Pulled into this tidal wave I frantically began *doing to* him: providing psychoeducation and suggesting interventions that fell on ears not ready to hear them. Sadly (and understandably) Jack didn't return for a second session.

In this work we will get pulled into moments of doer/done-to dynamics. These dynamics can show up like an undertow—surprising us in a current that feels stronger than we can resist. What is most helpful here is not berating ourselves when this happens (or demeaning the patient by simply dismissing them as a "difficult patient") but being curious about why this has occurred and how it may relate to the patient's experience of life outside the therapy office.

Integration Conversation Starters

1. Reflect on a time when you've experienced this doer/done-to dynamic. This might involve being treated as an object by someone attempting to exert their will on you, or it could be a time when you were pulled into a doer dynamic, as in the clinical example I have just offered. What was that experience like for you?

2. Reflect on different clinical experiences you have had. Are there certain types of patients that pull a more "doing" mode from you? Which types of patients do you feel most comfortable "being" with?

AUTHOR DIALOG: WHAT ABOUT EVANGELISM?

Mark: Is there ever space for evangelism?

Megan Anna: The church has often split over categories of "social gospel" and "evangelism." Part of what draws me to missional theology is that it takes seriously both the need for evangelism and the need for social transformation. In fact, these are united: the missional nature of the church includes bearing witness to the mission of God. Proclamation is certainly a piece of this.

Still, evangelism considered within the context of God's mission feels different from many evangelistic experiences. It is an embodied and relational evangelism that avoids any hint of a doer/done-to dynamic and is more akin to Buber's I-Thou (1958). For example, Guder notes, "Evangelizing churches are churches that are being evangelized" (2000, p. 26). In other words, the church is forever converting. The church that is being evangelized—ever formed into the character of God—is the evangelizing church as it invites others into the community while proclaiming salvation. In this sense the church that participates in God's mission overflows to the world.

Mark: This is a lovely notion for the church. How would you apply these notions in the context of counseling or psychotherapy?

Megan Anna: I am drawn to the psychoanalytic idea of "co-created" space as being helpful here—the idea that our personhood is always a part of the process of therapy and we are co-creating relational experience with our patients. These co-created spaces have the power not to simply change our patients but also to influence and change us. Co-created relational moments are periods of profound connection characterized by authenticity, "feeling felt"—moments of being seen and present with one another. There is an element of immanence in these deep moments of connectedness (Vogel & Mitchum, 2017). These sacred moments have the ability to transform us as psychotherapists too. There is humility to the idea that we are an "ever-converting church," and there is humility to the idea that we are ever-transforming or converting therapists. I think these moments in therapy embody what it is to be missionally oriented toward the other and to understand ourselves as participating in God's mission—which is always bigger than us and is interested in our transformation and growth. To be missionally for the other means we are willing to be impacted by God's activity and mission in our life. In addition to being transformed in these moments we are also offering the other a profound experience of Christian presence, and we are often using selective words in these moments.

Perhaps as we bring word and deed (i.e., Christian presence) together through therapeutic spaces, this is embodied mission. As Bosch (1991) notes: "The deed without the word is dumb; the word without the deed is empty. Words interpret deeds and deeds validate words" (p. 420).

Questions of ultimate meaning. I (Mark) was part of a radio interview once with a man who had just published a book about the dangers of psychology. He raised a question that I have heard often as a critique of those who integrate psychology and Christianity: Might it be possible that by alleviating emotional pain, we are short-circuiting God's intended work in our patients' lives? Perhaps the turmoil they experience might be an impetus to seek Jesus, but instead they come to a psychologist where they learn how to feel better and then have no reason to seek a higher and more transcendent hope. When I frame this conversation in the classroom, I often just ask if we run the risk of making happier sinners and thereby rob our patients of the possibility of abundant and eternal life? It turns out these questions make for good conversations, whether on radio or in the classroom!

It is important to realize that any view of what it means to be saved is embedded in a particular historical context. Early church writers focused on the importance of the beginning of Jesus' life on earth, the incarnation—that God would become human in fulfillment of a grand and mysterious plan to demonstrate God's immense love. This was carried forward by the Eastern Orthodox Church, who see being saved as a process ultimately marked by experiencing union with God, becoming more like Jesus and thus more fully the humans we were created to be. By becoming human and taking on human flesh, Jesus became the second Adam, thus restoring human nature and inviting us to a higher way of being (Daley, 2006; see Rom 5:12-21, 1 Cor 15:22, 45).

The Western church, both Catholic and Protestant, took the doctrine of salvation in a different direction by focusing on the end of Jesus' earthly life. Substitutionary models of atonement (see chapter four) brought hope that Christ would save us so that our eternal lives might be lived in harmony with God. And three days later we see the power of resurrection, and thus the hope of our own resurrection and life eternal.

In the wake of the eighteenth-century Enlightenment, liberal Protestant theologies—and later contextual theologies—began to focus on the middle of Jesus' life, focusing on Jesus as an exemplar of moral character and advocate for social change. Here the focus was on the ministry of Jesus' life on earth, and salvation called us to challenge and change unjust social structures and live more virtuous lives (Bosch, 1991). This view is a present-oriented view of salvation (restoration to shalom, wholeness in the here and now).

Notice that these different views of salvation focus on various times in Jesus' life. The early church looked at the birth of Jesus. The Western church focused more on the death of Jesus. The exemplarist view of Jesus after Enlightenment focused mostly on his life—between his birth and his death. Is it possible that all three of these traditions belong in our conversations when it comes to how Jesus saves us—including all elements of Jesus' life: birth and incarnation, earthly life, death and resurrection?

Most of us face a temptation to overemphasize one aspect of Jesus while discounting other parts. I (Megan Anna) personally run the risk of underemphasizing the end of Jesus' life—the death and resurrection. But whenever I lose a part of the whole, I lose an important aspect of the saving power of Christ. If I focus exclusively on the beauty of the incarnation—God coming to live with us—I lose sight of the enormous sacrifice God made. I need to be in conversation with people who value this part of Jesus' story to help nudge me to remember God's gracious and sacrificial love.

How we view salvation, and specifically which parts of Jesus' life we focus on most naturally, can have implications for the counseling and psychotherapy work we do. Those who most naturally focus on the beginning of Jesus' life may tend to hold a good deal of hope for human progress through progressive maturity as we see in ourselves and our patients an ability to grow toward unity with God. They may also be naturally attuned to empathy; just as Jesus came to be with us in our broken world, so we are also called to be with our patients in their times of suffering (Heb 4:15). Their faith in the human condition may at times make them shy away from utilizing interventions and confrontation, which can be therapeutically helpful. At other times it may be challenging for these counselors and psychotherapists to distinguish their work from the work of spiritual direction.

Those who focus most naturally on the middle of Jesus' life and his earthly ministry may do a beautiful job of helping patients identify their values and the internal drives that motivate them. They may also be quite attuned to the social structures that perpetuate injustice and oppression. These counselors value virtue development, social change, and deconstructing cultural narratives, with Jesus serving as the exemplar of moral character. The challenge these counselors may face may be the possibility of avoiding conversations that look directly at personal agency and responsibility contributing to the problems at hand.

Those who focus on the end of Jesus' life will likely be most concerned about matters of sin, grace, forgiveness, and individual responsibility. Rather than just providing temporary relief for the struggles facing their patients, they look at a longer view of eternal wellness and hold that view to be of utmost importance. They may run the risk of engaging in sin-based or problem-saturated conversations with patients.

When we consider what it means for our patients to be saved, we ought to also consider our natural inclinations for how we view the life and work of Jesus. And when we see our inclinations, then we do well to look for conversation partners who are naturally drawn to other views of salvation. For example, when my patients talk about shame and "being bad," I notice a reflex to move them away from shameful talk by normalizing their behavior or reassuring them. This reflects my discomfort with addressing the end of Jesus' life. But then I am reminded that there is often therapeutic value in walking with my patients into their guilt, shame, and discomfort. If I am too quick to save them from their guilt, then I may also prevent them from experiencing the grace, forgiveness, and transformation they long for.

Integration Conversation Starters

1. What part of Jesus' story are you tempted to discount? Which parts are you most comfortable with? How do you see this playing out in your clinical work?

2. Take on an alternative or contrary thought to what you may be naturally inclined toward. For five minutes ponder the view of salvation that is most uncomfortable for you. What is meaningful about this view of Jesus? How does it help you see people and be with them more fully?

Implications for Christian Community

Though our primary focus in this book relates to counseling and psycho-therapy, it also seems important to reflect on how a missional understanding of God's nature might impact Christian communities. We are thinking of Christian community broadly, as what might occur in places of worship but also in Christ-centered training programs.

Ephesians moments. Jesus didn't exactly leave a rule book when he left. Beyond "go therefore and make disciples of all nations" (Mt 28:19), he didn't give much explicit instruction on how to be Christian. In fact, Jesus was Jewish through and through. He followed Torah, honored most Jewish rituals, and attended temple, even referring to the temple as his Father's house (Walls, 2002).

What we learn about being Christian tends to come after Jesus as the biblical authors interpreted Jesus' words and life. Much of what we see in Acts and the epistles is the working out of Christian beliefs in an increasingly diverse world. There was a monumental moment in the apostle Peter's life that reminds us of today's context and provides a model as we consider Christian community.

Despite the call to make disciples of all nations, the Christian movement initially stayed within Jewish culture (Walls, 2002). This all changed when Peter experienced a radical call to witness to the Gentiles (see Acts 10), which he first resisted but later embraced. Eventually Peter became a passionate spokesperson for Gentiles (Acts 15:7-21). Some Jewish Christians wanted to function as the guardians of Christianity, allowing Gentiles in as long as they followed the rules: observing Jewish culture, rituals, and ways of thinking. But Peter's call was even more radical than simply tolerating and inviting the Gentiles in; this was a call to let the gospel get messy with Gentile hands, freeing the gospel to be translated into a new cultural context.

Jesus did not come to earth within a vacuum; he took on a particular culture and ways of thinking when he came and translated the divine message to humanity. Peter's call was to continue the translation process to new frontiers. This is somewhat unique to Christianity among monotheistic religions. For example, in Islam, the Arabic language is integral for understanding Koran, law, and religion—the message must stay in the original linguistic-cultural form (Sanneh, 2004).[1] In Christianity, the gospel is most fully evident

---

[1]Sanneh (2004) refers to this as "mission by diffusion," where religion moves out from the original cultural base and is implanted into new societies through a process of cultural assimilation. This

in interaction *with* culture. It is alive, moving, being translated and made new, always relevant in new frontiers and cultures. At its core, Christianity embraces cultural diversity. This was built into the fabric of the church in the monumental decision not to require Gentiles to conform to Jewish rituals such as diet and circumcision (Walls, 2002).

If Peter's call to release the gospel to a culture considered heathen wasn't radical enough, it becomes even more radical in what missiologist Andrew Walls (2002, p. 72) has deemed the "Ephesian moment." Traditionally, the meal table divided the Jews and Gentiles due to the dramatically different cultural values and laws around food. In the same way, a natural progression would have been to have two distinct Christian cultures: one for Gentiles and one for Jews. And yet we see a call to a different way of being in the world in the letter to the church at Ephesus:

> For he is our peace; in his flesh he has made both groups into one and has broken down the dividing wall, that is, the hostility between us. He has abolished the law with its commandments and ordinances, that he might create in himself one new humanity in place of the two, thus making peace, and might reconcile both groups to God in one body through the cross, thus putting to death that hostility through it. So he came and proclaimed peace to you who were far off and peace to those who were near; for through him both of us have access in one Spirit to the Father. So then you are no longer strangers and aliens, but you are citizens with the saints and also members of the household of God, built upon the foundation of the apostles and prophets, with Christ Jesus himself as the cornerstone. In him the whole structure is joined together and grows into a holy temple in the Lord; in whom you also are built together spiritually into a dwelling place for God. (Eph 2:14-22)

Here the call is toward one Christian community, rather than creating parallel Christian communities. The one Christian community is made more whole when lived in relation to one another. Diversity and unity walk together. Diversity itself is essential to the fabric of the church's unity. We are not unified despite our diversity, we are made whole because of our diversity (Forman, 1957).

---

is juxtaposed with "mission as translation" which places a high value on the receiving culture and assumes that all cultures can host and be transformed by the truth of the gospel (p. 29).

The division being addressed here, in addition to being about ethnicity and culture, was also about lifestyle. These lifestyle differences were celebrated at the very place that historically marked their differences: the meal table. These followers of Jesus ate together often, because the meal table demonstrated their unity in Christ. As Walls (2002) reflects: "The shared table was the acid test. It stood for diverse humanity redeemed by Christ and sharing in him" (p. 78).

Ephesians teaches us that no one culture is guardian of the gospel. We release the gospel to be translated to new contexts, in faith that God is ultimately interested in the transformation of all cultures—each bringing something different to the table, and each open to learning from the other as we eat together. In Christianity, we don't simply tolerate or coexist with diversity, we need it. It makes us better, giving us a fuller picture of God. Diversity helps make us whole as it refines and increases our collective wisdom. Embracing diversity is essential to God's missional character and is woven into the fabric of the kingdom of God (Rev 7:9).

Unfortunately, this Ephesians moment was only briefly a lived reality. The destruction of the Jewish state in 70 CE, the disbanding of the Jewish church, and the success of Gentile Christianity made the church monocultural once again, albeit a Hellenistic (Gentile) version (Walls, 2002). While this monocultural expression of Christianity has persisted, with the significant expansion of Christianity through Latin America, Asia, and Africa, we find ourselves in another Ephesians moment.

Within the United States, Christianity is becoming increasingly divisive on lifestyle, political, and racial lines. In a 1960 interview Martin Luther King Jr. famously commented that "11:00 on Sunday morning is one of the most segregated hours, if not the most segregated hour, in Christian America" (Spivak, 1960). Dr. King wisely reflected that the integration of the church would not occur through legal means but would need to be initiated by the church itself. Since the time King was writing we have seen increased levels of integration in society thanks to legal measures, but the church has not done as well at initiating increased integration and community across ethnic lines.

Whether viewing this Ephesians moment through the lens of cultural diversity in the United States or international diversity, it shapes our understanding of Christian community. Walls (2002) warns us of two potential pitfalls. One temptation is to guard "standard" Christianity as it is experienced in one particular culture. This was the error of colonialism. The second is to see everyone's individual faith as valid for that individual, as if it doesn't impact others. This may well be the error of postmodernism. The first pitfall fails to celebrate diversity, the second fails to seek unity. Both of these pitfalls cause us to miss the Ephesians moment, which celebrates both unity and diversity. Christianity's unity is strengthened by diversity; it can be dangerous to translate and interpret Christ on our own. We are all better when we interpret and translate Christ in relationship to one another (Forman, 1957).

This belief that we are all made more unified and whole through embracing and making space for our diverse understanding and expressions of Christianity is an unapologetic belief that forms the bedrock of this project. At the same time, diversity will only be helpful if we are around the table together, conversing with one another. While we cannot all break bread with one another, it is our dream that the conversations sparked by this book will help all of us encounter more Ephesians moments.

Integration Conversation Starters

1. Walls describes two pitfalls: to either insist on uniformity for the sake of unity or to "tolerate" diversity through disengagement. The challenge is to have a diverse and unified community. Why might this be important? How can you see such a community being helpful? What gets in the way of holding unity and diversity together?

2. How do we embrace diversity of thought in the classroom? In therapy? With our colleagues? What strategies can be used in the classroom to avoid the second pitfall Walls describes? In other words, how can we remain in conversation despite our diversity?

Psychotherapists contributing to theology? This notion makes us somewhat uncomfortable, and we suspect it makes some readers uncomfortable too. Psychotherapists contributing to theology? Don't we need to know three languages and endure seven years of graduate school to do such a thing?

Largely influenced by Greek thought, Christian theology since Constantine has tended to be conducted "from above." A theology from above prioritizes principles and ideas, with application being secondary (Bosch, 1991). It tends to be interested in finding and starting with the abstract truths through the use of philosophy and reason. This view from above is often considered to transcend culture and history, and as such the task of modern theology has often been to decipher the objective, timeless truths of the Bible so that we can then apply them to our daily lives.

An alternative to theology from above is theology that uses concrete experience as the starting point for understanding God, this is often deemed a "theology from below." In recent years, with postmodernity and the growth of Christianity in the Global South, there is a rise of contextual theologies. While theology from above partners primarily with philosophy to accomplish its tasks, theology from below and contextual theology draw a great deal from social sciences (Billman & Migliore, 1999). This theology is a *doing* sort of theology, focusing as much on orthopraxy (right living) as orthodoxy (right belief).

Of course, both orthodoxy and orthopraxy are important, but we appreciate Barth's warning that theologians often function like "a lonely bird on a roof" (a reference to Psalm 102:7). In contrast, a theology from below is done from the trenches, with the suffering. Those of us who do psychotherapy recognize this posture because we sit with the suffering every week.

A view from above and a view from below can work together in a "hermeneutical circle" where there is a dialectical relationship between theory and praxis. Rather than thought and reason being placed on one side and action on the other, they are understood as more integrated and interdependent (this would be another example where being/essence and function are married rather than separated as has often been done in modernity). As liberation theologian Gustavo Gutierrez (1990) argued, both orthopraxis and orthodoxy get lost if they don't have the other. The best theologies hold both together.

I (Mark) have noted with dismay how difficult it is for doctoral students in Christian psychology programs to maintain and grow in faith during their training years (see Fisk et al., 2013, for research on this topic). As I have discussed this with scores of students, my tentative conclusion is that our Christian theologies do not give students adequate room to make sense of the suffering they encounter as they do their clinical work. A sense of tragedy settles over me whenever I realize that we are sending some of our brightest young Christians out into the world where they encounter deep suffering and struggle, while not equipping them with a theology that will hold them, allowing them to make meaning of what they experience.

We need theology that can speak to pain—theology that is contextual, birthed in the trenches. In writing this book, Megan Anna has given me hope by reminding me that cultures outside of the West (cultures less influenced by Enlightenment ideals) have been better at recognizing contextual theologies that address pain and suffering as part of their lived reality. In the Western world we tend to have difficulty with this (see chapter one on lament), though there certainly are exceptions, such as black, womanist, and Latinx, among other theologies. We are reminded of the powerful words of Ellen Charry (2001), a renowned theologian and former mentor of Megan Anna's, who wrote: "We theologians have abandoned the practitioners, and we should be ashamed. Perhaps it is not too late to begin repairing the damage" (p. 133).

Psychotherapists in conversation with religious leaders can help articulate a theology of hope and meaning in a world afire. We are in the trenches, and we have something important to bring to the conversation.

Integration Conversation Starters

1. How can you imagine psychotherapists partnering with and shaping theology?
2. What pitfalls and dangers do you see in a tradition that focuses too much on a theology from above? What pitfalls and dangers do you see if the pendulum were to swing too far toward a theology from below?

Toward a Missional Psychology

The first Bible verse that many of us memorize is John 3:16: "For God so loved the world that he gave his only Son, that everyone believes in him may not perish but may have eternal life." God loves this world, and so our theologies must actively engage it.

Missio Dei, the mission of God, reminds us that missiology is not some subset of a larger theology, but it is at the heart of all theology because God's heart is missional. God is always sending out, turned toward the world, loving and saving rather than condemning (see the next verse after the one we memorize first, John 3:17).

For those of us interested in psychology and theology, it seems reasonable to consider a question that the two of us have been pondering throughout this book project: What might a missional psychology look like? We suggest four core elements to a missional psychology while realizing that much more needs to be worked out in conversation with theologians and psychologists.

First, because God loves the world and is always turned toward the world, a missional psychology should be actively engaged in understanding and serving the world. This could never be a psychology that is limited to the ivory tower of academics but must be engaged in the lived reality of everyday life. Jennifer Ripley (2012) reflects on the history of the integration movement with its focus on cognition and calls for integrationists to "move beyond academic and cognitively addressing differences between psychology and Christianity and do something practical for the world" (p. 150). She casts a vision of what applied Christian psychology may entail: increased involvement in global mental health crises through increased international partnership and training, involvement in the health-care crises (such as what is being done with primary care psychology), and increased utilization of and presence at the intersection of technology, research, and education.

Second, a missional psychology is local insofar as it is lived out in a particular context and community. Just as the word of God is interpreted and lived out in particular faith communities, so also a missional psychology must be adaptable for particular needs and populations. One psychologist serves those who face severe and persistent mental illness. Another works with couples in crisis. A third sees those experiencing racial trauma and discrimination. A fourth works in a recovery and rehabilitation setting. A fifth works in a student counseling center. A sixth works in a physician's office doing primary integrated care. We could go on and on. In each case, the ways they understand and live out a missional psychology will be distinct and nuanced.

Third, a missional psychology feels more like hope than despair. We might look at the world and see incredible political divide, natural disasters, and human suffering everywhere we look. Psychotherapists might be especially prone to this view because we sit with pain day after day. Without denying or dismissing any of the world's suffering, a missional psychology sees hope in the midst of it all. God is present with us, leaning toward us, working in our midst. Our task then isn't so much just tolerating the suffering life brings us as it is learning to rest, with relentless faith, in the presence of a loving and mysterious God at all moments in life, including the ones that are most painful and difficult.

Fourth, a missional psychology should include human thriving as well as human suffering. The field of positive psychology (see McMinn, 2017, for more) reminds us that God attends to the world in order to offer us gifts of life abundant. Yes, our world suffers under the weight of oppression and sin of all sorts, but God's missional character is turned toward us in hope. God is turned toward us in grace. The fruit of the Spirit, which is about God's character more than ours, is to be enjoyed around tables all over this world God loves so deeply.

Further Reading

Donovan, V. J. (1978). *Christianity rediscovered.* Maryknoll, NY: Orbis Books.

Freire, P. (2018). *Pedagogy of the oppressed.* New York: Bloomsbury Publishing.

Guder, D. L. (2000). *The continuing conversion of the church.* Grand Rapids: Eerdmans.

Walls, A. F. (2002). *The cross-cultural process in Christian history: Studies in the transmission and appropriation of faith.* Maryknoll, NY: Orbis Books.

Watkins, M., & Shulman, H. (2008). *Toward psychologies of liberation.* New York: Palgrave Macmillan.

Further Watching/Listening

Sacks, J. (2017, April). *How we can face the future without fear, together* [Video file]. Retrieved from www.ted.com/talks/rabbi_lord_jonathan_sacks_how_we_can_face_the _future_without_fear_together?language=en

Tippett, K. (Host). (2004, November 18). "Don Saliers and Edward Foley—The meaning of communion: At the table" [Audio podcast]. *On being.* Retrieved from http://onbeing .org/programs/don-saliers-and-edward-foley-the-meaning-of-communion-at-the-table/

6

God with Us

WHERE IS GOD AMID THE DEEP
UNCERTAINTIES OF LIFE?

THE VERY WORD *integration* implies wholeness. With integration, we seek integrity, completeness, fulfillment. And so, it seems fitting in this final chapter to offer a big-picture glimpse of what we have attempted to accomplish throughout these various chapters on lament, Ecclesiastes, *imago Dei*, atonement, and *missio Dei*. The essence of this book and of how we understand faith in a complex and pluralistic age is to affirm the great mystery of Christianity: that God chooses to be with us. This happened most prominently in a dirty Bethlehem barn a couple millennia ago when Immanuel, "God with us," became the inflection point of our modern calendar systems. Christmas reveals the heart of a relational God who showed up in a dark and uncertain world, but God's presence is not fully defined by or contained in the incarnation. It's more that the incarnation reveals the abiding character of God, who has always been with us, and who still shows up. Every chapter of this book explores this remarkable theological proclamation—that we are not alone in our questions and suffering and uncertainties. God is with us. In the *hebel* of our fragile existence, in our confused and sometimes chaotic understanding of who God is, in our questions about how we are saved and what we are being saved from, in our deepest sorrows and struggles, in every corner of this beautiful damaged world, God is with us.

And if this is true, or even if it approximates what is true, then our primary work as counselors and psychotherapists is to relax into the peaceful posture of rest known only to those who are deeply loved. From this place of security, we sit with others and offer them glimpses of hope. This, it seems to us, is the fullness of integration—that God's presence in our world ultimately informs and transforms our presence with one another. Put simply, integration is love. As God loves and accepts us, we are to love and accept one another (see Rom 15:7). We may hesitate to use the word *love* in counseling or psychotherapy because love is so easily conflated with sex in our highly sexualized world, and sex never has a place in psychotherapy, but if we could distill our view of love down to its purest form then we would be back to the simplest truth of integration in the psychotherapy office—that we are deeply loved people, called to love one another.

Brooke, a thoughtful, intelligent, and passionate young woman, came to me (Megan Anna) during her senior year of college. She had a heart for the hurting world, with a marked tendency to overextend herself, and she struggled to offer the same compassion to herself that she so naturally extended to others. It soon became clear that driving much of her anxiety and depression was an inner dialog which she nicknamed her "master." Her master had a longstanding history, being forged in her early years in the throes of trauma and abandonment. In fact, it was hard for Brooke to see the master as simply a part of herself; it felt like *all of her.*

My work with Brooke was humbling and awe provoking in that I quickly realized I was just one piece of the work God was already up to in her life. Early in treatment, when we began to explore an issue or idea, Brooke would often leave sessions with uncertainty. Then she would return the next week to discuss how throughout the week she had gained insight through conversations with professors, listening to sermons, or private times of prayer. She described rich and beautiful connections that helped her make meaning of herself and the world. We'd get the ball rolling in therapy, but God would do so much more with it throughout the week.

During one session we were discussing the shameful voice that told her she needed to *be more.* Using a third-wave cognitive behavior therapy strategy, we talked about noticing and distancing from these thoughts. Initially she struggled with this, as the master would get stronger and work harder to get her caught up in an argument about her badness. Given this push and pull I wasn't sure about the intervention, but the next week Brooke returned beaming. As she was able to create distance from the thoughts, space opened up for her to hear the quiet voice of God, reminding her that she is loved.

The healing Brooke experienced delighted me. In addition to joining with the work God was already doing in her life, I also had the pleasure of bearing witness as this woman transformed from a place of shame and doubt toward one of self-acceptance. And here I pause to note that even the term *self-acceptance* seems more pallid and therapeutically sterile than what I intend to communicate. Brooke was able to touch what many of us long for—an acceptance of self where personal identity is anchored in God. This sort of

DOING INTEGRATION AND BEING INTEGRATED

For years, I (Mark) have had students in my classes or under my supervision yearning to know how to do this thing we call "integration." Shall we pray with our patients? Is it okay to refer to Scripture? Should we bring up church involvement? Is there ever a place for talking about theology in psychotherapy? Honestly, I think I have consistently frustrated these students with my lack of answers. Sometimes they look at me as if I know the answers to these questions but am simply choosing not to answer.

I don't blame my students for wanting to know how to *do* integration. I want to know also, but the truth is, I don't. At least I don't know in any generalized way that could take form in specific counseling strategies or methods. Counseling is as much art as science and requires incredible attentiveness to the patient and circumstances. Choosing to use an explicit spiritual intervention can be incredibly useful, incredibly harmful, or anywhere in between, depending on the situation and circumstances.

These days I am much more inclined to think of integration as a way of *being* in the office (and out of the office) than as something we do. To what extent am I aware of God's presence in the complex and challenging work we are doing? How am I being personally formed so that I can communicate God's love in relation to the other? Am I able to host conversations in the office that honor the dignity of the other, demonstrating sincere curiosity and humility? Am I attuned to the present moment, and willing to stay in the moment even when my mind is racing a million miles a minute toward the latest evidence-based intervention? Ultimately, these are all questions about being a loving presence with the hurting soul that is sitting with me. They are questions about recognizing and reflecting—however dimly—the loving presence of God in our broken world.

deep self-acceptance freed Brooke to freely gift her passion, creativity, and love outward to the world. There is no sophisticated model for integration at play here; what I needed to do with Brooke was simply to create a space of acceptance that allowed for God's presence while having ears to hear when she talked about her spiritual life. God was with us in the therapy room each week, and God continued to be with Brooke in the intervening times through her relationships, in church, in nature, and through prayer.

God was also with me through Brooke's presence. Seeing the transformation in her reminded me anew of the power of divine presence. Yes, it can be frustratingly ambiguous when we talk about what it means for God to be with us in the psychotherapy room, and I suspect there are no good ways to quantify this, but still it seems both powerful and evident in this work we are blessed to do.

God has persisted in being with and for us throughout time. We draw on the imagery of God the Creator, Redeemer, and Sustainer to provide a frame for taking a deeper diver into this conversation.

God the Creator

From the beginning we see a God who is for and with us. In chapter three (on *imago Dei*) we explored how the Hebrew creation account differs from the gods represented in other ancient Near Eastern accounts. God blessed creation from the beginning. Built into the fabric of the creation narrative is a God who desires to be with us. At times our Christian tradition has struggled to hold onto and retain this basic foundation and premise of God's blessing.

Brueggemann (1982) reflects how this original blessing (God who is for and with us) can at times be obscured behind a theology of sin. A theology of blessing is sometimes buried in traditions that tend to overemphasize the "deep gulf between the goodness of God and the unhealthiness of the world" (Brueggemann, 1982, p. 36). The starting point of creation is goodness as God blesses, creates, and calls creation "good." A theology of blessing speaks to the expansive, generative, life-giving power God infuses into ordinary life.

As one who has written a fair amount about sin (e.g., McMinn, 2008), I (Mark) have been challenging myself recently to ponder ways I might focus overly much on sin. My interest in sin emerged from a deep, abiding interest in grace, and I have argued that we cannot understand one without the other. But the deep gulf Brueggemann describes between a good God and a broken world has been evident in my writing and thinking about sin and grace over the years. One of the ways I am challenging myself is to pay more attention to the goodness of creation, noticing the splendor of cedars and oaks, watching seedlings grow into mature plants, and standing amazed at the process, listening to the birds sing, paying attention to the vistas in this gorgeous valley where I am blessed to live. Nature reminds me how much I belong to something bigger than myself. I recently read two books with the title "Original Blessing" (Fox, 1983; Shroyer, 2016). I liked one book quite a lot more than the other, but both challenged me to recall that the first truth of creation—the most original thing—is God's love and blessing rather than sin.

Genesis 1-11 plays out like a cosmic love tragedy, serving as a prophetic backdrop for which the rest of the biblical narrative unfolds. God, in immense love and abundance, creates and invites creation into relationship, and yet again and again humanity turns away from God. Brueggemann (1982) observes:

> The main theme of the text is this: God and God's creation are bound together in a distinctive and delicate way. This is the presupposition for everything that follows in the Bible. It is the deepest premise from which good news is possible. God and his creation are bound together by the powerful, gracious movement of God toward that creation. (pp. 23-24)

Similarly, if we read the New Testament assuming that sin is the most original part of the story, then God's grace seems to be offered as a corrective for our sin problem. But instead, we could read the New Testament through the lens of original blessing. Yes, we have a sin problem, but the foundational truth of all creation is first the truth of blessing and the deep, abiding love of God. Read in this light, grace is an enormous gift flowing out of God's abundance (Barclay, 2015), revealing the very character of God. Viewed in this way, grace is not relegated to the New Testament where a particular dispensation allows God to treat humanity differently than before, but it is always evident through the entire narrative of human history. God's movement toward creation is unrelenting. It is filled with self-offering grace and generosity.

In creation, throughout the prehistoric narratives of Genesis 1-11, throughout the years of slavery in Egypt, during forty years of wandering in the desert, God remained present. During Israel's sojourn in the wilderness God came as a pillar of fire leading the people at night; during the day God was a pillar of cloud. God's presence was relentless: "Neither the pillar of cloud by day nor the pillar of fire by night left its place in front of the people" (Ex 13:22). God persisted in being present, functioning as Israel's servant by carrying the torch ahead of Israel in the wilderness, providing for their needs (Moltmann, 1992). A God this passionately and enduringly bound to humanity suggests that God also suffers alongside us as we journey through deserts. As German theologian Jürgen Moltmann (1992) reflects: "He binds himself so closely to Israel that he becomes one heart and one soul with her, as if he were her 'twin brother.' So Israel's shame is God's shame too, Israel's exile is God's exile, Israel's sufferings are God's sufferings" (p. 49). This is a God in the trenches with Israel, suffering alongside, taking on their shame. And this sort of "being with" brings consolation and hope in the midst of deep anguish (Moltmann, 1992).

Persistence in the face of attachment injury. We crave connection and attunement amidst deep anguish; as relational beings, attachment buoys us in the face of suffering. Sue Johnson (2008), one of the founders of emotionally focused therapy, has contributed helpful language for understanding how human vulnerability and relational needs and patterns get played out through the lens of attachment. Johnson explores how we put out "attachment cues" when we need connection with a significant other. When these cues are missed or neglected this may move us into "attachment protest." For infants this looks like crying. For adults it may also look like crying; however, we tend to get more creative in our attachment protests the more life experiences we gather. When we protest and continue not to be heard this may result in an "attachment injury." Many other events can also result in attachment injuries: betrayal, perceived abandonment, relational misses, and disconnections. When our attachment cues and protests are continually met with misses and rejection this leaves a lasting impact. When someone's attachment cues are denied deep enough or often enough this will influence how they go about signaling for attachment. Johnson works with partners to identify when they have become stuck in a perpetual loop of attachment injury, helping patients to name their attachment vulnerabilities and needs and move toward connection. This is risky business, as it requires a partner to be vulnerable and honest about their desires and attachment needs—something that is hard to do when we are feeling injured and protective of ourselves. It takes vulnerability and risk to get out of the misconnection loop and into authenticity, intimacy, and connection.

One of the first couples I (Mark) saw in my early career was an unhappily married couple who couldn't figure out how to see and respond to one another's bids for attachment. Brent was inclined toward a domineering style, seeing himself as the spiritual and relational leader in the home and attempting to accomplish this with military precision. His bids for connection tended to be sexual, and often without the relational warmth that Jill longed for. Rather than seeing his desire for sex as a relational bid, she viewed it as an effort to be controlling and demanding, and so resisted. Over time, both felt isolated, misunderstood, and rejected. Things spun out of control when Jill found an attuned and caring male friend. They had a short-lived affair, which upped Brent's demands for relational closeness through sexual encounter. This, in turn, frustrated and alienated Jill. Though she felt repentant and ashamed of the affair, she could not find her way back to relational warmth toward Brent even as she complied with his frequent requests for sex. Because she lacked enthusiasm, Brent perceived even more relational rejection. After a year with all three of us working as hard as we could to improve their marriage, I recall a session where we all sat in tears and concluded the damage could not be repaired. I ran into Brent a year later and he told me that he and Jill were divorced, and recovering.

Perhaps this is part of why we are so drawn to and horrified by the love tragedy of the biblical narrative: God continually experiences attachment injury and yet God does not respond in the predictable way. God remains steady, despite the attachment injuries endured. God takes these on and continues to call and invite humans into relationship. God is singularly unique in this ability to persist despite attachment injuries. We as humans tend to not fare as well when our attachment cues are persistently neglected. Often when we've lost a sense of safety and trust our calls for attachment become more strained or pricklier, or they simply stop coming.

1. When you experience attachment injury or attachment misses, what do your attachment protests look like? How might this be activated when working with clients?

2. Though the theme of this chapter is God with us, we hold this as a theological truth that may not always be self-evident. After times of loss or trauma, sometimes we and our clients may experience attachment injuries with God, as if God is not with us at all. We may ask, "God, where were you? Why did you let this happen?" When people are experiencing an attachment injury with God, how do you sit with them in this?

Against all odds: Reflections on faith and cognitive dissonance. We live in a world where young girls and boys are sold like cattle into the sex industry (Panko & George, 2012), where 3.1 million children die of undernourishment every year (UNICEF, 2018), where suicide rates among teens have increased by 20 to 30% in the United States since 2007 (Center for Disease Control, 2017). With all the natural disasters, human disasters, and systemic sin, it's hard to navigate this world and avoid the question, "God, where are you?"

It's beautiful to read words about original blessing and God's commitment to the earth's well-being, but so often we sit with people in some of their darkest moments. What does this theology really do for us? Is it Pollyannaish of us to persist in belief in the goodness of God and the goodness of creation? Are we engaging in cosmic denial when we hold onto belief of a good God despite all of the contemporary data?

These are not new questions. Likely, these are similar to the questions the Israelites asked during the exile. Estranged from family members, facing early death and inhumane conditions, Israelites may have wondered where Yahweh was amidst their suffering and cries of protest. One way of learning how Israelites made sense of these questions is by looking to the first creation narrative, likely written during the Babylonian exile (Brueggemann, 1982). It's striking that this beautiful story of God's presence and commitment to creation was cultivated and written during a time of suffering, a time where people likely struggled and felt abandoned. Exacerbating their abandonment was the fact that they lived in a swirl of Babylonian theology asserting that their gods had defeated Israel's God. Amidst Israel's suffering they had the audacity to proclaim that God is still the "Lord of all of life" (Brueggemann, 1982, p. 25). This Judeo-Christian creation story is a bold theological assertion: despite the present circumstances, God is the creator of all life and chooses

AUTHOR DIALOG: HEBREW SCRIPTURES

Mark: Megan Anna, as we have worked on this book together, I notice how often you refer to the Hebrew Scriptures, or what we might commonly call the Old Testament. This has both surprised and delighted me, because it is so different than what most Christians talk about these days. I hear many more sermons about the New Testament than the Old. What inspires you to look so frequently to the Hebrew Scriptures as you ponder the integration of psychology and Christianity?

Megan Anna: Well, how many words do we have left until we exceed our word count? I could write many words on this, but I'll refrain and keep it to these two thoughts: it speaks into our mess, and it can be a voice inviting us back into our full humanness.

I fell in love with the gritty, messy, contextual nature of Hebrew Scripture while at seminary. In many ways it reminds me of our current context. As we live through a massive shift from a modern frame of reference toward a postmodern frame, our context is a bit messy and gritty. Additionally, our relationship to knowledge is shifting. Rather than starting from a top-down approach (starting with systematic theory or "objective reality"), we are increasingly engaging a bottom-up approach—starting with the messy, relational contexts from which we live. From these spaces emerge embodied and contextualized truths, meanings, questions, and life lessons. In many ways the Hebrew people were doing something similar. In this sense it is a "contextual theology." Personally, this resonates with me deeply.

Another reason I am drawn to Hebrew Scripture is the embodied nature of it—the mind and soul intermingle in a humanizing and refreshing way. I suspect that one of the reasons we're experiencing such a whiplash to modernity is because we're reacting to what it has done to us (for example, the modern concept of "buffered" self as explored in chapter three). We live in a disembodied culture, alienated from the rest of creation, each other, and ourselves, making it incredibly difficult to be a whole, integrated self. I think the Hebrew Scriptures offer wisdom that may be helpful as we find our way back to humanness.

to be bound to creation in grace. God watches over creation and is committed to its growth and well-being. From the pangs and despair of imprisonment, this narrative proclaims that God is still with us and has not abandoned us.

Leon Festinger (1962) developed cognitive dissonance theory to describe the common experience of being misaligned. When our beliefs, attitudes, and behaviors are in conflict we experience cognitive dissonance. As humans we innately strive for balance and consistency, and one way we do this is to reshape our beliefs and attitudes in order to fit our actions. This can be a rude awakening to those of us who wish to believe it works the other way around—that we shape our actions based on our values and beliefs (Hilberg, 2017). We work to bring our beliefs into alignment with our behavior in order to reduce the anxiety and tension caused by cognitive dissonance.

Recently my (Megan Anna's) five-year-old took up chess, so we frequently spend summer afternoons playing. He has a warm and wonderful attitude and is a good sport about losing, except that he really doesn't like losing his queen, the most powerful piece on the chessboard. When I capture his queen it is common for him to create a rule so that we can undo the last move and he can reclaim her. My son is practicing impressive skills at resolving the cognitive dissonance that comes up for him: he values following the rules and he also values keeping his queen in the game. When he creates a rule that justifies saving his queen, he is aligning his beliefs, attitudes, and desires in a way that allows him to continue to play with ease.

While cognitive dissonance theory has been around for some time, research looking at how this influences belief formation remains limited (Hilberg, 2017). Our minds don't like cognitive dissonance, so we will chew on a problem until we have landed on a conclusion to resolve the tension, even if it's a painful conclusion. Holding the goodness of God, God's commitment to be with us in suffering, in a world afire with pain is often a significant source of cognitive dissonance for people of faith. How can God be both loving and powerful while still allowing such pain and struggle in the world (see sidebar "Theodicies" in chapter one)? While surely there are many alluring ways to solve this dissonance, there are two that seem most common (see figure 2).

One possibility is that we can solve the dissonance by keeping faith in a good God and dismissing or ignoring suffering. This can be as simple as denying and avoiding interacting with suffering or it can also take the shape

Solution 1: Minimize or trivialize the pain

Solution 2: Move away from God

Solution 3: Embrace mystery, hold tension, be open to lament

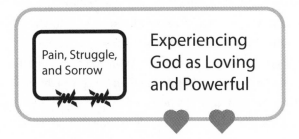

Figure 2. An implicit tension

of supposing a cause for the suffering (i.e., "she must have done something to deserve it," "the earthquake was God's punishment for their Muslim beliefs," and so on). Social psychologists call this the "just-world assumption"—that we resolve our tension with the suffering of the world by assuming others somehow get what they deserve (Lerner, 1980).

A second possibility is that we can deny that God is both loving and powerful, perhaps moving toward deconversion and abandoning faith. Most of us have probably seen the national polling data showing how prominent this has become.

But there is also a third alternative, which is to hold on to the dissonance. What if faith is more a mystery to behold than a logic problem to be solved? What if we can hold faith in God while still honestly lamenting the pain of the world? Over the last several years I have been intrigued by why some persist in faith despite the odds, despite the dissonance, and what makes the difference.

I find the writers and thinkers I am nourished by are those who have journeyed through complexity—those who sit in the tension of cognitive dissonance. Supreme Court Justice Wendell Holmes once remarked: "The only simplicity for which I would give a straw is that which is on the other side of the complex" (Howe, 1961, p. 109). I suspect a faith that can hold onto God's goodness amidst the muck is a faith that has journeyed through the complexity.

I met Jake, a political science major, during his junior year of college. He had a passionate and aching heart for the world and struggled to make sense of a good God amidst the "contemporary data" of a world afire with suffering and pain. Why was God not acting? Why was God silent? These are questions I often sit in with people on the cusp of deconversion; they are the tipping point for many. As I sat with Jake I wondered which direction this question would take him. Would he journey to the other side of complexity? Jake and I explored much in our work together: Where is God amid the suffering? What is the role of the church in being God's response to the suffering? Is there space for belief in a God who is boldly present amidst suffering and yet does not change it? How do we understand the God who did not allow the cup to pass from Jesus but who was with him until the bitter end on the cross? Jake cycled between hope and disbelief on an emotional roller coaster as he navigated his faith crises and identity under the weight of these questions. While it was temping to bring in my own personal perspectives of how I have come to understand God amidst suffering, I knew that telling Jake the answers I had come to on my own journey through complexity would not magically transport him to the other side of complexity. I became his companion, helping to identify the questions and tensions he was asking, being a safe place to explore his questions, and (when appropriate) pointing him toward the voices and witnesses of the others who had walked the path of complexity to sojourn with him.

The creation narrative, written in the crux of suffering, claims the simplicity on the other side of complexity. This is not a rose-colored-glasses, simplistic proclamation of faith, but a declaration and praise of God's goodness amidst the bewildering confusion and despair that come with pain and isolation. It provides us with a model of how to avoid the two pitfalls of the quandary: denying suffering or abandoning faith. But it does require us to hold some dissonance as we move toward believing that God is with us, holding us, in the midst of suffering. This is a simplicity of presence. Maybe God being with us is more important than cinching down an answer to the deep existential questions that are fueled with "contemporary data."

Intrapersonal Conversation Starters

1. If applicable, what allows you to persist in faith despite "contemporary data"?
2. When faced with suffering, do you notice yourself leaning toward one of the poles we have described: denying suffering or disbelief? If so, how might this impact your clinical work?

Jesus the Redeemer

Arguably the most dramatic embodiment of God with us is through the incarnation—the *logos* taking on human flesh (Jn 1:1). And yet the drama starts with the meekness of an infant's cry.

It's one thing to imagine God in the throne room of heaven and quite another to ponder the stench of a stable, the arduous work of a carpenter, the thirst that must have accompanied treks through the sun-scorched Palestinian landscape, the fatigue of dealing with crowds day after day, the anguish of Gethsemane, the blood-stained cross. God chose to come near through taking on the myriad of experiences that come with having a human body. I (Megan Anna) was slow in coming around to recognizing the importance of the embodied life Jesus lived on this earth for thirty-three years prior to his crucifixion. It was through the writings of Japanese novelist Shūsaku Endō that my appreciation for the significance of this embodied God took new life. Endō (1978) wrote about the power and beauty of a God who chose to come, experience embodiment, and suffer with us. In Endō's stories he often depicts the weakness, emancipation, and "ugliness" that Jesus took on as he chose to enter the pain of the world. In his novel *The Samurai* (1983), the samurai, the central character, who at first couldn't fathom why the priests worshiped a weak God dying on a cross, later came to write this about Jesus:

> I can believe in Him now because the life He lived in this world was more wretched than any other man's. Because he was ugly and emaciated. He knew all there was to know about the sorrows of the world. He could not close His eyes to the grief and agony of mankind. That is what made Him emaciated and ugly. (p. 220)

At first the samurai, with his cultural value of strength and honor, could not fathom bowing down to a weak and miserly God. It was in touching this God amidst his suffering and realizing the purpose of God choosing weakness that he came to belief.

Worshiping a God who chooses weakness is countercultural. Endō does a beautiful job depicting Jesus, who took on the human experience of suffering out of his commitment to be humanity's "eternal companion" (Endō, 1978, p. 80). Jesus suffered so that when we experience the throes and pangs of life, we need not be in it alone. In moments of darkest pain, we have an eternal companion.

Just as the embodied life of Jesus is a profound way God persists in being with us, so also the death and resurrection of Christ marks a significant moment. When Jesus died, the curtain in the temple is ripped. Prior to this, God met people at the temple. The ripping of this curtain represented the expansive presence of God now moving beyond the temple. Through Jesus' death the presence of God has now expanded and moves beyond: "No longer does God sit in his holy temple (Ps 11:4), whose destruction the ripped curtain epitomizes. God remains with us, crucified with us and for us" (Black, 2005, p. 52). This was the great democratization of God's presence—now opened up to the whole world.

I met Jessie just after she ended a tumultuous and traumatic marriage. She was experiencing guilt, shame, confusion, and anger—along with depression and a heightened sense of isolation. Though in the past she received significant comfort from God, now she felt blocked whenever she tried to connect with

God. Painful thoughts and memories would intrude and "get in the way." I wondered aloud if it was possible that God would be interested in these thoughts too—that perhaps these thoughts were not simply intrusions but actually some intuitive recognition that God is big enough to hold all of her. Jessie, having consistently spent a great deal of energy attempting to get rid of weakness *so that* she could go to God, looked at me with baffled but intrigued eyes. She returned to the next session in a much better mood. Once again, she experienced connection with God, describing how she invited God into the terror and pain. Rather than trying to get rid of her suffering and weakness so that she could get back to God, she started inviting God into the pain and vulnerability. Not only did this mean that once again she felt connected to God, it also meant that more of her was connected to God, even her confused and shameful parts. If God were only interested in connecting with "spiritualized" parts of us, I suspect God would not have chosen to take on humanness, experiencing it all. Precisely because God took on these human experiences, we can hold hope that God desires to connect with us in all our complexity and messiness.

Though I (Mark) resist metaphors that cast the therapist as Jesus, it seems important to notice the posture we take in the therapy office in relation to the way Jesus chose to enter the world. If we enter into counseling relationships with the goal of being all-powerful and all-knowing—the expert who comes to save the suffering—we will likely fail our patients and ourselves. But if we enter in humbly, as fellow pilgrims who understand complexity and suffering and pain, then we are more likely to make genuine, healing connections with those who seek our help. Some place deep in the human heart seems to yearn for another to listen, to care, to understand, to be with us. This is the transformative essence of the Christian story, that God loves us so immensely that Jesus would come to be with us.

In one of the most beautiful passages of the New Testament—and one of the very first christological arguments about the divine nature of Jesus—the apostle Paul describes the humility incarnate so poignantly:

> If then there is any encouragement in Christ, any consolation from love, any
> sharing in the Spirit, any compassion and sympathy, make my joy complete: be
> of the same mind, having the same love, being in full accord and of one mind.
> Do nothing from selfish ambition or conceit, but in humility regard others as

better than yourselves. Let each of you look not to your own interests, but to
the interests of others. Let the same mind be in you that was in Christ Jesus,

who, though he was in the form of God,
did not regard equality with God
as something to be exploited,
but emptied himself,
taking the form of a slave,
being born in human likeness.
And being found in human form,
he humbled himself
and became obedient to the point of death—
even death on a cross. (Phil 2:1-8)

Jesus is with us in our confusion and struggle and squalor. This is the great
self-emptying, seen in Jesus who has every right to assert authority and
superiority over the rest of us. But instead, Jesus humbles himself, even as
we who have no right to assert superiority over one another squabble about
who is greatest. This is the humble Jesus who comes to be with us and then
invites us to accept one another even as he has accepted us (Rom 15:7).

Integration Conversation Starters

1. We rightly see God as powerful and mighty, but with the incarnation we see a
   God who comes in vulnerability and weakness. Theologians refer to the keno-
   sis (self-emptying) revealed in Jesus. How does this view of God change the
   way you think about yourself in the world? Might it change the way you sit with
   patients?

2. Have you seen patients who feel a need to shield God from their true feelings
   and thoughts, as with the example of Jessie? How have you tended to respond?
   What sort of therapeutic responses might help your patients be more wholly
   themselves in God's presence?

The Sustaining Spirit

Jesus provides us with helpful imagery in describing the Spirit: advocate,
guide, helper, counselor (e.g., Jn 14:26, 16:7). Even with this helpful imagery,
describing the precise characteristics and personhood of the Spirit can

be challenging. Candles are so often used in Christian worship, and sometimes it seems that the flickering flame—moving and warming and brightening—does a better job explaining the Spirit than words (see sidebar "The Spirit as Flickering Flame"). Still, in the pages of a book we are limited to words and the pictures they create, so we explore three images here: the Spirit as sustainer, companion, and intercessor in suffering, the Spirit as midwife to new life, and the creative, expansive energy of God's Spirit.

THE SPIRIT AS FLICKERING FLAME

Over many years of being involved in the integration of psychology and Christianity, I (Mark) have been surprised how little we discuss the work of the Holy Spirit. There are exceptions, such as Siang-Yang Tan's fine work on this topic (e.g., Tan & Gregg, 1997), but for the most part we have written and discussed two persons of the Holy Trinity.

As I've pondered this lack, I have begun to feel some compassion and understanding toward all of us doing this work. The language of integration has been the written and spoken word. We write books and articles, talk together at conferences, teach our classes with our required textbooks and written paper assignments. This has been a cognitive, intellectual endeavor for the most part, and pneumatology (the study of the Holy Spirit) is not as easily contained in words and intellectual concepts as other theologies may be.

And so we offer the picture of a flickering flame, knowing that candles are used in worship through many traditions and times. The mesmerizing movement of a candle flame—moving with the wind, never being quite predictable enough for mathematic description—provides a subtle reminder that the Spirit is alive and active in every part of our lives, including our professional work.

I once had a colleague who would bring a candle into the classroom each time he taught, perhaps without consulting our institution's fire safety protocols. It seemed an unusual practice to me years ago even apart from the fire risk, but now I am drawn to this as a practical way of remembering that God's presence can never be reduced to our ideas, words, theologies, and theories. This is an active presence, an experiential, moment-by-moment presence. God's Spirit is moving with us, lighting our way.

The Spirit as sustainer, companion, and intercessor in suffering. The Spirit of God is present amidst suffering. This sounds like a sterile theological assertion, but it is also a deep personal comfort. Whatever our struggle, our loss or quandary, whatever challenges we face that resist solutions, God's Spirit is present with us, sustaining us and bringing us comfort. This has not only been true since the time of Jesus on earth, but throughout all human history.

Beginning in the Hebrew Scripture we see this in the portable tabernacle constructed during Israel's long sojourn in the wilderness. The tabernacle demonstrated God remaining present in the middle of difficult circumstances while speaking to the "descent and indwelling of God in space and time" (Moltmann, 1992, p. 47). This dwelling of God, referred to in Hebrew as *Shekinah*, holds Israel's joy and pain, and comes to take on particular meaning in the presence of suffering. The *Shekinah* traveled with the Israelites into exile and remained present during their deepest anguish. Back then, as is still true now, God's indwelling Spirit is present in suffering.

The Holy Spirit being present in suffering continues into the New Testament, accompanying Jesus into the terror of suffering and death: "Christ, who through the eternal Spirit offered himself without blemish to God" (Heb 9:14). Here we see the mystery of the Trinity: three in one. Jesus and the Holy Spirit are one, and yet distinct. In their distinction the Spirit ministers to Jesus: "The Spirit does not suffer in the same way, for he is Jesus' strength in suffering. . . . On Golgotha, the Spirit suffers the suffering death of the Son, without dying with him" (Moltmann as quoted by Rennebohm & Thoburn, 2017, p. 133).

Beyond being present with and providing strength during suffering, the Spirit also provides communication when words fail us: "Likewise the Spirit helps us in our weakness; for we do not know how to pray as we ought, but that very Spirit intercedes with sighs too deep for words" (Rom 8:26). The Spirit is present with us, sustaining us and communicating on our behalf because—as every experienced psychotherapist understands—words are often not enough.

Within the Hebrew tradition, the idea of *Shekinah* has continued to mean that whenever people gather to study Torah they invoke the presence of God. The *Shekinah* is made manifest as we create sacred relational spaces, characterized by Buber's I-Thou encounter (Rennebohm & Thoburn, 2017). Though the psychotherapy relationship isn't typically for purposes of studying Torah or the Bible, it is certainly a place where I-Thou encounters occur, where two souls commune and work both with words and with realities that are too big for words. It seems a reasonable assertion to say that as we step into relationship with our patients the Spirit who sustains, strengthens, and communicates amidst suffering is there with us.

So often throughout my career I (Mark) have been asked about praying aloud with patients as part of psychotherapy. This is a complicated question that I have attempted to address elsewhere (McMinn, 2011), though imperfectly. But one thing that remains crystal clear in my mind is that silent prayer is a beautiful part of the work we do in our counseling offices. I sometimes tell my students that my favorite prayer is a brief, one-word utterance: "Help!" And the thing is, God does help. Time after time I have sensed the sustaining, encouraging presence of God's Spirit as I recognize the limits of my own abilities and call out to God for sustenance and direction. God with us is not at all a sterile theological concept to me, but a lived reality experienced year after year, session after session, while sitting with people in anguish and suffering.

It's sometimes surprising for new counselors and psychotherapists to realize how lonely the work can be. We sit with people in conversation all day long, so how could this possibly be socially isolating? But soon we realize how lopsided these conversations are as we settle into the reality that we are ones who listen and know the other while professional boundaries prevent us from being known by our patients. Yes, we may have colleagues in the office, but each of us closes our door hour after hour to engage in sacred and healing and yes, lopsided, conversations with those who need our help. So while we may be in the vicinity of colleagues, we are rarely interacting with them. And sometimes when we head home in the evenings to the ones we love, we are so relationally exhausted from the day that we choose to read a book or watch television rather than engaging in the mutually satisfying relationships that we most long for. Thankfully, over time we come to recognize the reality of this loneliness and find ways to counteract it. We learn to put the book down in the evening and engage with our friends and partners over meaningful conversation. We prioritize staff meetings or lunches with colleagues in the office. And we come to recognize God's spirit as a steady, compassionate companion, not only for our patients but for ourselves as we sit hour after hour holding our patients' heavy and wounded stories, sometimes feeling as if the weight of the world were on our shoulders.

Integration Conversation Starters

1. When and how have you noticed the sustaining presence of God's Spirit when doing counseling or psychotherapy?
2. In what ways, if any, does it resonate to think of psychotherapy as lonely work? How do you find God's Spirit to bring hope and comfort when you encounter this loneliness?

The Spirit as midwife to new life. The Holy Spirit does more than be present amidst suffering and provide us strength. The Spirit also acts as midwife to redemption, ushering in new life. In the great trinitarian mystery, we even see the Spirit in a midwife role in relation to Jesus: "The Spirit's companionate presence accompanies Jesus onto the cross and into death, and then is there to usher in new life through the resurrection" (Rennebohm & Thoburn, 2017, p. 133). The Spirit ushers us to the other side of suffering, inviting us into abundant life, while clothing us with "power from on high" (Lk 24:49). The Spirit moves creation toward new life, inviting us into an "ongoing process of becoming" (Rennebohm & Thoburn, 2017, p. 132).

Those of us who are licensed clinical professionals typically work out a deal with our patients and their health insurance carriers to identify and treat a set of symptoms, to get our patients back to "normal" so they can carry on with the social and occupational requirements of life. We consider this healing, but fairly often we encounter some greater, more astonishing reality that counseling is not just about removing unwanted symptoms or restoring a person to normal. Sometimes, many times perhaps, it is about offering our patients a glimpse into a better life, a connected and relational life where they dare to dream and hope and imagine new possibilities. We witness this over and over in our careers, and with any luck it never stops taking our breath away. The power of relational transformation is simply stunning. And for those of us who consider our work integrative, each of these opportunities allows us to bear witness to the redemptive work of God's Spirit, who is bringing forth new life from the pangs of suffering.

Integration Conversation Starters

1. How have you experienced the power of new life as you sit with suffering souls?

2. When experiencing this sort of transformation, some counselors are inclined to take personal credit ("I'm a good therapist"), others are inclined to give God's Spirit credit for the change ("This was so much bigger than me; God deserves the credit"). Can you imagine an integrative way to explain these good outcomes—one that both validates the counselor's work and skill while also acknowledging the active midwifery role of God's Spirit?

The creative, expansive energy of God's Spirit. Moltmann (1992) brings depth to the conversation of the character of the Holy Spirit by connecting the Holy Spirit described in the New Testament to the Spirit of God described in the Hebrew Scriptures. *Ruach* is a word used 380 times in the Hebrew Scriptures to describe the Spirit of God. *Ruach* means "something living and moving over something that is rigid or dead" (typically translated "breath," "wind," or "spirit"). Twenty-seven times *ruach* is applied to Yahweh, roughly translating to something like "the moving, alive, expansive presence of Yahweh is here" (Moltmann, 1992). This is a creative, expansive energy. God's presence does not close places; rather, it opens up spaces.

As I (Megan Anna) read Moltmann's (1992) reflections on Yahweh's *ruach*, I experienced expansion taking place within. I found myself pouring over the following passage, aware it spoke a deep truth that I did not yet fully comprehend. I felt a deep connection to a rich, potentially painful, and transformative truth. I found myself returning to these words over and over, allowing them to wash over me with pain and pleasure:

> In the elemental experiences of life, love and death we are touched by perceptions of a sensory kind. . . . They mold us, and become our companions. They are events in the past, which never become "past," but are continually present to us. We repress them, we work on them, we puzzle over them and interpret them, for we have to live with them. Our biographies are molded by experiences like this. . . . Even today I can still feel shaken by the terror of early experiences of death, even if I am no longer consciously aware of them, and even though "the activity of my reason" tells me that these experiences are forty-seven years old, and go back to the fire-storm that raged through Hamburg

in 1943. But for all that, these experiences are present with me still. I can feel myself back into them, and they still plunge me into the same terror as they did then. . . . We can never say about an experience of this kind "I had it" as if it were finished and done with, something past and gone. We are continually still involved in experiencing confronting events like these. . . . For primary experience is something that "happens to us," something that overpowers us without our intending it, unexpectedly and suddenly. . . . The person who experiences is changed in the process of experiencing. So although in German one talks about "making" an experience, it is not I who "make" the experience. It is the experience that "makes" something of me. (Moltmann, 1992, pp. 20-23)

In modern philosophy and theology (and perhaps in modern psychology) experiences are often squeezed into the realm of reason. We use words to remember and describe an experience, and in so doing we cheapen it. This is reflective of the Western tendency to place the center of human identity within the realm of consciousness, reason, and will, and to diminish the importance of bodily perceptions and sensations (Moltmann, 1992).

Counselors should know better. We work every day with people whose struggles are not just in the mind but are deeply embodied. In *The Body Keeps the Score,* Van der Kolk (2014) demonstrates how the body remembers trauma on a neurological level. Our life experiences are not just cognitive memories that we have and move past; they mold and shape us, and we continue to carry them with us in our bodies. These events from the past become organically integrated into our entire bodies, impacting our brains, hearts, immune systems, and body composition even as they inform the existential questions that shape how we navigate life.

Still, even those of us who are counselors and psychotherapists sometimes struggle with our lived, experiential, embodied ways of knowing. When sharing the above Moltmann text with my therapist and exploring my tendency to keep experiences at arm's length by relegating them to my intellect, I mentioned how I found myself deeply drawn to this passage due to my desire to open myself more fully, allowing experiences to mold me. My therapist reflected, "There is part of you that wants to go under the knife of experience." I suspect that on one level we are all always "under the knife of the experience," but how fully we surrender ourselves to such a thing is another matter. Are we welcoming the molding and formation that comes through lived, embodied experiences or pushing away and closing ourselves from this possibility?

Maybe one reason it is so difficult to willingly "go under the knife" is related to the idea of *hebel*, explored in chapter two. Experiential living requires an ability to live in the moment, releasing illusions of control and embracing all its wildness and uncontrollability. It means we hold the one- and five-year plans loosely; we loosen our tight grip on control and predictability. This mission would be utterly terrifying if it weren't for the hope of Yahweh's *ruach*.

Integration Conversation Starters

1. How willing are you to "go under the knife of experience" (i.e., to be impacted by the people you meet, the interactions you have, the moments of terror, the moments of hope)?

2. How do you assess your patients' relationship to experience? When they talk about experience, are they keeping it locked in the realm of rationalism and will? Are they inviting the work of the Spirit to be with and transform them?

3. How open are you to inviting God's Spirit into the therapy room to be with you and your patients as you mutually go "under the knife of experience"? How is this related to the task of spiritual formation?

God's Spirit is present with us in our experiences—the joyous ones and the terrifying ones—and then invites us to be spiritually formed in response. This is not a haphazard, willy-nilly forming, but one that calls us forward toward life abundant, toward vitality and redemption. "*Ruach* creates space. It sets in motion. It leads out of narrow places into wide vistas, thus conferring life" (Moltmann, 1992, p. 43). *Ruach* invites us to experience the expansive space of God's freedom, and within this space we are invited to become more fully alive.

God meets us in our little experiences and creates wide vistas that are life giving and transformational. Furthermore, within the kabbalistic Jewish tradition, *Makom*—a secret name for God—means "wide space" (Moltmann, 1992, p. 43). God not only creates wide, expansive places, God *is* wide space. God widens the narrow. If I did not believe that God's Spirit meets me in the narrow passages of personal experience, I would struggle to willfully choose to "go under the knife of experience" and open myself to be changed and molded by life events. It is confidence in the ever-present *ruach* of God, who is committed to suffering with, being with, and opening up wide vistas, that provides me with confidence to take the leap and meet myself and my patients in our narrow edges of experience. Yahweh's persistent presence with us is ever opening up spaces and creating new life. God's Spirit provides Christian therapists an anchoring comfort and confidence as we enter the enclosed and sometimes terrifying spaces of human experience.

Further Reading

Fujimura, M. (2016). *Silence and beauty: Hidden faith born of suffering.* Downers Grove, IL: InterVarsity Press.

Moltmann, J. (1992). *The Spirit of life: A universal affirmation.* Minneapolis: Fortress Press.

Further Listening

Mackie, T., & Collins, J. (2017, February 23). "The Holy Spirit part 1: The Spirit of the OT vs. the Spirit of Christianity" [Audio podcast]. *The Bible Project.* Retrieved from http://thebibleproject.com/podcast/holy-spirit-part-1/

Mackie, T., & Collins, J. (2017, March 3). "The Holy Spirit part 2: God's Ruakh" [Audio podcast]. *The Bible Project.* Retrieved from http://thebibleproject.simplecast.com/episodes/7a491f36-7a491f36

Mackie, T., & Collins, J. (2017, March 10). "The Holy Spirit part 3: Holy Spirit in the New Testament" [Audio podcast]. *The Bible Project.* Retrieved from http://thebibleproject.simplecast.com/episodes/220a40c1-220a40c1

FINAL CONVERSATION

God in the World

We have offered a number of conversation suggestions for those reading this book as part of a class or other study group.

Final conversation: Describe a time when you have been keenly aware of God's presence in the midst of your work as a counselor or a psychotherapist. What was that experience like for you? How did it impact the counseling work you were doing at the time?

Epilogue

When two people relate to each other authentically and humanly,
God is the electricity that surges between them.

Martin Buber

THIS BOOK IS UNAPOLOGETICALLY DIALOGICAL. It emerged from
our own dialog—a father and daughter curious about life's big questions—and
soon the vision grew as we recognized the relevance of these conversations
in the classroom and the counseling room. It seems fitting at the end of this
project to pause and reflect on some things we are learning about dialog.

Dialog is not just about talking. There's plenty of talking going on in our
increasingly polarized world, and not nearly so much listening. I suppose
any parent and child go through seasons where we talk more than we listen,
but one of the sweet discoveries of this project is that we are at a point in life
where we listen well to one another, and cherish the words we hear and the
person behind the words. It's fairly easy for a daughter and father—both
grown and sharing similar professional interests—to value one another as
we dialog, and more difficult when sitting with a patient with a personality
disorder or in a group of people angry about ideological or political differences. Still, we hope the example of dialog we share in these pages may help
us all aspire to true listening and real conversation in the places where this
is difficult.

We also are learning to imagine dialog in its historical and conceptual
diversity. The two of us are separated by twenty-six years, which is a substantial gap and one we hope contributes to the book, but some of the ideas
we discuss here are separated by thousands of years. Dialog is enriched if we
can go back and ponder old ideas even as we consider the newest things we
are learning and thinking. One of the great joys of writing this book has been

to engage the dialogical method through bringing together theological and psychological concepts that span centuries, methodologies, and cultures.

It has been exhilarating to invite others into our dialog, which reflects how much we are learning to value hospitality in scholarly conversation. This book was refined in the context of dialog with students, colleagues, and an expert publishing team. John Ruskin, a nineteenth-century artist and social critic, suggested that people are shaped by *how* they create more than *what* they create. It's not so much about the product as about the toil that goes into the product. We are grateful for the opportunity to write this book, as the dialogs going into its creation have shaped us.

Perhaps the theme that strikes us most is the relational nature of the work we do and the conversations we host. Whether teaching, doing clinical work, relating to God, or writing a book, our profession calls us to relationship. Thus, to say that the content and process of this book are dialogical is ultimately to say it is about relationship. Martin Buber understood dialog as much more than a technique. Dialog is a posture toward the other, a turning toward and opening of oneself to the other (Friedman, 2002). As such, writing this book has involved continually bringing ourselves back into a posture of being oriented to the other—back into a posture of willingness to learn from the other. It has been humbling to recognize how easy it is to step outside of this posture.

In this work we are called to do as counselors and psychotherapists, we continually and imperfectly attempt to bring ourselves back to a posture of *being* with one another more than *doing* for or to the other. As we learn to do this we open ourselves to the possibility of transformative dialog, leading to greater encounter with the *ruach* of God (the expansive, creative God who opens up space).

One of the very best things about writing this book is anticipating the dialog yet to come as we share these words with students and colleagues in the years to come. We are grateful to you, our reader, for engaging with us in this process.

References

Abi-Habib, R., & Luyten, P. (2013). The role of dependency and self-criticism in the relationship between anger and depression. *Personality and Individual Differences, 55,* 921-25.

Ainsworth, M. D. S., Blehar, M. C., Waters, E., & Wall, S. N. (2015). *Patterns of attachment: A psychological study of the strange situation.* New York: Psychology Press.

Akunna, G. I. (2015). An African Igbo perspective on mourning dances and their application to dance/movement therapy. *American Journal of Dance Therapy, 37,* 39-59.

Alavi, S. Z., Amin, F., & Savoji, A. P. (2013). Relationship between pathological guilt and God image with depression in cancer patients. *Procedia—Social and Behavioral Sciences, 84,* 919-24.

Aponte, H. J., & Kissil, K. (2014). "If I can grapple with this I can truly be of use in the therapy room": Using the therapist's own emotional struggles to facilitate effective therapy. *Journal of Marital and Family Therapy, 40,* 152-64.

Aslan, R. (November 16, 2017). *God: A human history.* Presentation given as part of the Literary Arts lecture series. Portland, OR.

Augustine. (1986). *The confessions of St. Augustine.* (H. M. Helms, Trans.). Brewster, MA: Paraclete.

Augustyn, B. D., Hall, T. W., Wang, D. C., & Hill, P. C. (2017). Relational spirituality: An attachment-based model of spiritual development and psychological well-being. *Psychology of Religion and Spirituality, 9,* 197.

Aulén, G. (2003). *Christus victor: An historical study of the three main types of the idea of atonement* (A. G. Hebert, Trans.). Eugene, OR: Wipf and Stock Publishers.

Bailey, K. L., Jones, B. D., Hall, T. W., Wang, D. C., McMartin, J., & Fujikawa, A. M. (2016). Spirituality at a crossroads: A grounded theory of Christian emerging adults. *Psychology of Religion and Spirituality, 8,* 99.

Baloyi, L., & Makobe-Rabothata, M. (2014). The African conception of death: A cultural implication. In L. T. B. Jackson, D. Meiring, F. J. R. Van de Vijver, E. S. Idemoudia, & W. K. Gabrenya Jr. (Eds.), *Toward sustainable development through nurturing diversity: Proceedings from the 21st International Congress of the International Association for Cross-Cultural Psychology.* Retrieved from http://scholarworks.gvsu.edu/iaccp _papers/119/

Baltes, P. B., Staudinger, U. M., Maercker, A., & Smith, J. (1995). People nominated as wise: A comparative study of wisdom-related knowledge. *Psychology and Aging, 10,* 155-66.

Barclay, J. M. G. (2015). *Paul and the gift.* Grand Rapids: Eerdmans.

Bass, D. B. (2018). *Grateful: The transformative power of giving thanks*. San Francisco: HarperOne.

Batto, B. (2013). *In the beginning: Essays on creation motifs in the ancient Near East and the Bible*. Winona Lake, IN: Eisenbrauns.

Bediako, K. (1994). Understanding African theology in the 20th century. *Themelios, 20*, 14-20. Retrieved from http://s3.amazonaws.com/tgc-documents/journal-issues/20.1_Bediako.pdf

Beilby, J., & Eddy, P. (Eds). (2006). *The nature of the atonement: Four views*. Downers Grove, IL: InterVarsity Press.

Benjamin, J. (2004). The analytic third: Beyond doer and done-to. *Psychoanalytic Quarterly, 72*, 5-46.

Billings, J. T. (2015). *Rejoicing in lament: Wrestling with incurable cancer & life in Christ*. Grand Rapids: Brazos Press.

Billman, K. D., & Migliore, D. L. (1999). *Rachel's cry: Prayer of lament and rebirth of hope*. Cleveland, OH: United Church Press.

Black, C. C. (2005). The persistence of the wounds. In S. Brown & P. Miller (Eds.), *Lament: Reclaiming practices in pulpit, pew, and public square* (pp. 47-58). Louisville, KY: Westminster John Knox.

Blair, C. E. (1997). Understanding adult learners: Challenges for theological education. *Theological Education, 34*, 11-24.

Bosch, D. J. (1991). *Transforming mission: Paradigm shifts in theology of mission* (Vol. 16). Maryknoll, NY: Orbis Books.

Bourgeault, C. (2004). *Centering prayer and inner awakening*. New York: Cowley Publications.

Bowlby, J. (2008). *Attachment*. New York: Basic Books.

Bowler, K. (2018a). *Everything happens for a reason: And other lies I've loved*. New York: Random House.

Bowler, K. (2018b, December). *Kate Bowler: "Everything happens for a reason"—and other lies I've loved* [Video file]. Retrieved from www.ted.com/talks/kate_bowler_everything_happens_for_a_reason_and_other_lies_i_ve_loved

Boyd, G. A. (2010). *Present perfect: Finding God in the now*. Grand Rapids: Zondervan.

Bretherton, I. (1985). Attachment theory: Retrospect and prospect. *Monographs of the Society for Research in Child Development, 50*, 3-35.

Brock, R. N. (1988). *Journeys by heart: A Christology of erotic power*. Chestnut Ridge, NY: Crossroad.

Brock, R. N., & Parker, R. A. (2001). *Proverbs of ashes: Violence, redemptive suffering, and the search for what saves us*. Boston: Beacon Press.

Brown, B. (2010). *The gifts of imperfection: Let go of who you think you're supposed to be and embrace who you are*. Center City, MN: Hazelden Publishing.

Brown, W. P. (2001). Whatever your hands find to do: Qoheleth's work ethic. *Intepretation, 55*, 271-84.

Brown, W. P. (2011). *Interpretation: A Bible Commentary for Teaching and Preaching—Ecclesiastes*. Louisville, KY: Westminster John Knox.

Brueggemann, W. (1982). *Interpretation: A Bible Commentary for Teaching and Preaching—Genesis*. Atlanta: John Knox Press.

Brueggemann, W. (1986). The costly loss of lament. *Journal for the Study of the Old Testament, 11,* 57-71.

Brueggemann, W. (1995). The formfulness of grief. In P. D. Miller (Ed.), *The Psalms and the life of faith* (pp. 84-97). Minneapolis: Fortress Press.

Brueggemann, W. (2002). *Reverberations of faith: A theological handbook of Old Testament themes* (1st ed.). Louisville, KY: Westminster John Knox.

Brueggemann, W. (2017). *Sabbath as resistance: Saying no to the culture of now.* Louisville, KY: Westminster John Knox.

Buber, M. (1957). *Pointing the way: Collected essays.* New York: Harper & Row.

Buber, M. (1958). *I and Thou* (2nd ed.). New York: Charles Scribner's Sons.

Calvin, J. (2008). *Institutes of the Christian religion* (H. Beveridge, Trans.). Peabody, MA: Hendrickson.

Capps, D. (2005). Nervous laughter: Lament, death anxiety, and humor. In S. A. Brown & P. D. Miller (Eds.), *Lament: Reclaiming practices in pulpit, pew, and public square* (pp. 70-79). Louisville, KY: Westminster John Knox.

Carter, J. D., & Narramore, B. (1979). *The integration of psychology and theology: An introduction.* Grand Rapids: Zondervan.

Center for Disease Control. (2017). Morbidity and mortality weekly report. Retrieved from www.cdc.gov/mmwr/volumes/66/wr/mm6630a6.htm

Charles, Marilyn, informal lecture, George Fox University, Newburg, OR, November 2017.

Charry, E. T. (2001). Theology after psychology. In M. R. McMinn & T. R. Phillips (Eds.), *Care for the soul* (pp. 118-34). Downers Grove, IL: InterVarsity Press.

Christodoulou, N. G., & Christodoulou, G. N. (2013). Financial crises: Impact on mental health and suggested responses. *Psychotherapy and Psychosomatics, 82,* 279-84.

Clifford, R. J. (1994). *Creation accounts in the ancient Near East and the Bible.* Waddell, AZ: Catholic Biblical Association of America.

Coan, J. A. (2010). Adult attachment and the brain. *Journal of Social and Personal Relationships, 27,* 210-17.

Coan, J. A., Schaefer, H. S., & Davidson, R. J. (2006). Lending a hand: Social regulation of the neural response to threat. *Psychological Science, 17,* 1032-39.

Cone, J. H. (1997). *God of the oppressed* (Rev. ed.). Maryknoll, NY: Orbis Books.

Crisp, O. (2020). *Approaching the atonement: The reconciling work of Christ.* Downers Grove, IL: InterVarsity Press.

Daley, B. (2006). *Gregory of Nazianzus* (The Early Church Fathers). New York: Routledge.

Dalley, S. (1989). *Myths from Mesopotamia: Creation, the flood, Gilgamesh, and others.* New York: Oxford University Press.

Davis, E. B., Moriarty, G. L., & Mauch, J. C. (2013). God images and God concepts: Definitions, development, and dynamics. *Psychology of Religion and Spirituality, 5,* 51-60.

Davis, E. F. (2009). *Scripture, culture, and agriculture: An agrarian reading of the Bible.* New York: Cambridge University Press.

Descartes, R. (2016). *Discourse on method and meditations of first philosophy* (E. S. Haldane, Trans.). Digitreads.com Publishing.

Duhigg, C. (2014). *The power of habit: Why we do what we do in life and business.* New York: Random House.

Emerson, M. O., & Smith, C. (2001). *Divided by faith: Evangelical religion and the problem of race in America.* New York: Oxford University Press.

Emmons, R. A. (2013). *Gratitude works! A 21-day program for creating emotional prosperity.* San Francisco: Jossey-Bass.

Emmons, R. A., & McCullough, M. E. (2003). Counting blessings versus burdens: Experimental studies of gratitude and subjective well-being. *Journal of Personality and Social Psychology, 84,* 377-89.

Emmons, R. A., & Stern, R. (2013). Gratitude as psychotherapeutic intervention. *Journal of Clinical Psychology: In Session, 69,* 846-55.

Endō, S. (1978). *A life of Jesus.* (R. Schuchert, Trans.) New York: Paulist Press.

Endō, S. (1983). *The Samurai.* (V. Gessel, Trans.) Great Britain: Penguin Books.

Exline, J. J., Kaplan, K. J., & Grubbs, J. B. (2012). Anger, exit, and assertion: Do people see protest toward God as morally acceptable? *Psychology of Religion and Spirituality, 4,* 264-277.

Exline, J. J., & Martin, A. (2005). Anger toward God: A new frontier in forgiveness research. In E. L. Worthington (Ed.), *Handbook of Forgiveness* (pp. 73-88). New York: Routledge.

Exline, J. J., Pargament, K. I., Grubbs, J. B., & Yali, A. M. (2014). The Religious and Spiritual Struggles Scale: Development and initial validation. *Psychology of Religion and Spirituality, 6,* 208-22.

Festinger, L. (1962). *A theory of cognitive dissonance.* Stanford, CA: Stanford University Press.

Fisk, L. K., Flores, M. H., McMinn, M. R., Aten, J. D., Hill, P. C., Tisdale, T. C., Reimer, K. S., Maclin, V., Seegobin, W., & Gathercoal, K. (2013). Spiritual formation among doctoral students in explicitly Christian programs. *Journal of Psychology and Christianity, 32,* 279-90.

Ford, D.F., & Higton, M. (Eds.). (2002). *Jesus.* Oxford: Oxford University Press.

Forman, C. W. (1957). *A faith for the nations.* Philadelphia: Westminster Press.

Foster, R. (1998). *Streams of living water: Celebrating the great traditions of the Christian faith.* San Francisco, CA: HarperSanFrancisco.

Fox, M. (1983). *Original blessing.* Santa Fe, NM: Bear & Company.

Fox, M. V. (1999). *A time to tear down and a time to build up.* Grand Rapids: Eerdmans.

Francis, L. J., Gibson, H. M., & Robbins, M. (2001). God images and self-worth among adolescents in Scotland. *Mental Health, Religion & Culture, 4*(2), 103-8.

Friedman, M. (2002). Martin Buber and dialogical psychotherapy. *Journal of Humanistic Psychology, 42*(4), 7-36.

Gallup. (2018). "Religion." Retrieved from http://news.gallup.com/poll/1690/religion.aspx

Geller, S. M., & Porges, S. W. (2014). Therapeutic presence: Neurophysiological mechanisms mediating feeling safe in therapeutic relationships. *Journal of Psychotherapy Integration, 24,* 178-92.

Gibson, D. (2017). *Living life backward: How Ecclesiastes teaches us to live in light of the end.* Wheaton, IL: Crossway.

Gillespie, M. A. (2008). *The theological origins of modernity.* Chicago: University of Chicago Press.

Gilligan, C., & Snider, N. (2017). The loss of pleasure, or why we are still talking about Oedipus. *Contemporary Psychoanalysis, 53,* 173-95.

Gingrich, F., & Smith, B. (2014). Culture and ethnicity in Christianity/psychology integration: Review and future directions. *Journal of Psychology and Christianity, 33,* 139-55.

Gonzalez, J. L. (1985). *The story of Christianity, Vol. 2: The reformation to the present day.* San Francisco: HarperSanFrancisco.

Gottlieb, L. (2019). *Maybe you should talk to someone: A therapist, her therapist, and our lives revealed.* New York: Houghton Mifflin Harcourt.

Green, J. B. (2006). Kaleidoscopic view. In J. Beilby & P. Eddy (Eds.), *The nature of the atonement: Four views* (pp. 157-85). Downers Grove, IL: InterVarsity Press.

Green, J. B., & Baker, M. D. (2011). *Recovering the scandal of the cross: Atonement in New Testament and contemporary contexts* (2nd ed.). Downers Grove, IL: InterVarsity Press.

Guder, D. L. (2000). *The continuing conversion of the church.* Grand Rapids: Eerdmans.

Gunton, C. E. (2003). *The actuality of atonement: A study of metaphor, rationality and the Christian tradition.* London: T&T Clark.

Gutierrez, G. (1990). *The truth shall make you free: Confrontations.* Maryknoll, NY: Orbis Books.

Hall, M. E. L. (2016). Suffering in God's presence: The role of lament in transformation. *Journal of Spiritual Formation & Soul Care, 9,* 219-32.

Hall, T. W. (2007). Psychoanalysis, attachment, and spirituality part II: The spiritual stories we live by. *Journal of Psychology and Theology, 35,* 29-42.

Hardy, E. R. (Ed.). (1954). *Christology of the later fathers* (Vol. 3). Louisville, KY: Westminster John Knox.

Hayes, S. C., Strosahl, K. D., & Wilson, K. G. (2012). *Acceptance and commitment therapy: The process and practice of mindful change* (2nd ed.). New York: Guilford.

Heschel, A. (1951). *The Sabbath, its meaning for modern man.* New York: Farrar, Straus and Young.

Hick, J. (2010). *Evil and the God of love.* New York: Palgrave Macmillan.

Hilberg, N. (2017). Cognitive dissonance and "the will to believe." *Fudan Journal of the Humanities and Social Sciences, 10*(1), 87-102.

Hoekema, A. A. (1994). *Created in God's image.* Grand Rapids: Eerdmans.

Hoffman, M. T. (2011). *Toward mutual recognition: Relational psychoanalysis and the Christian narrative.* New York: Routledge.

Hofmann, W., Gschwendner, T., & Schmitt, M. (2005). On implicit–explicit consistency: The moderating role of individual differences in awareness and adjustment. *European Journal of Personality, 19,* 25-49.

Holladay, W. L. J. (1990). *Jeremiah: A fresh reading.* Cleveland: Pilgrim Press.

Hood, R. W., Hill, P. C., & Spilka, B. (2018). *The psychology of religion: An empirical approach* (5th ed.). New York: Guilford Press.

Hooper, N., Erdogan, A., Keen, G., Lawton, K., & McHugh, L. (2015). Perspective taking reduces the fundamental attribution error. *Journal of Contextual Behavioral Science, 4,* 69-72.

Howe, M. D. (Ed.). (1961). *Holmes-Pollock letters: The correspondence of Mr. Justice Holmes and Sir Frederick Pollock, 1874-1932* (2nd Ed.). Cambridge, MA: Belknap Press.

Hua, Z. (2013). *Exploring intercultural communication: Language in action.* New York: Routledge.

Hughes, R. (1993). *Culture of complaint: The fraying of America.* New York: Oxford University Press.

Humphreys, K. (2018, March 23) Americans take more pain pills—but not because they're in more pain. *The Washington Post.* Retrieved from www.washingtonpost.com/news /wonk/wp/2018/03/23/americans-take-more-pain-pills-but-not-because-theyre-in -more-pain/?utm_term=.5606110fe3e8

James, W. (1887, February). The laws of habit. *The Popular Science Monthly,* 433-51.

Jayawickreme, E., & Blackie, L. E. (2014). Post-traumatic growth as positive personality change: Evidence, controversies, and future directions. *European Journal of Personality, 28,* 312-31.

Jenkins, P. (2008). *The new faces of Christianity.* New York: Oxford University Press.

Johnson, E. L. (2007). *Foundations for soul care: A Christian psychology proposal.* Downers Grove, IL: InterVarsity Press.

Johnson, E. L. (Ed.). (2010). *Psychology and Christianity: Five views* (2nd ed.). Downers Grove, IL: InterVarsity Press.

Johnson, E. L. (2017). *God and soul care: The therapeutic resources of the Christian faith.* Downers Grove, IL: InterVarsity Press.

Johnson, S. (2008). *Hold me tight: Seven conversations for a lifetime of love.* New York: Little, Brown and Company.

Johnson, W. S. (2005). *Jesus' cry, God's cry, and ours.* In S. A. Brown & P. D. Miller (Eds.), *Lament: Reclaiming practices in pulpit, pew, and public square* (pp. 80-94). Louisville, KY: Westminster John Knox.

Kalu, O. U. (Ed.). (2005). *African Christianity.* Trenton, NJ: African World Press.

Kapic, K. M. (2017). *Embodied hope: A theological meditation on pain and suffering.* Downers Grove, IL: InterVarsity Press.

Kelley, M. M. (2010). *Grief: Contemporary theory and the practice of ministry.* Minneapolis: Fortress Press.

King, M. L., Jr. (1960). Interview on "Meet the Press." Transcribed "Meet the Press" [Video file]. Retrieved from www.youtube.com/watch? v=1q881g1L_d8

Knabb, J. J. (2016). *Faith-based ACT for Christian clients: An integrative treatment approach.* New York: Routledge.

Knowles, M. S., Holton, E. F., III., & Swanson, R. A. (2012). *The adult learner* (7th ed.). New York: Routledge.

Koenig, H. G. (2018). *Religion and mental health: Research and clinical applications.* London: Academic Press.

Koenig, H. G., King, D. E., & Carson, V. B. (2012). *Handbook of religion and health* (2nd ed.). New York: Oxford University Press.

Kübler-Ross, E. (1969). *On death and dying.* New York: Macmillan.

Lambert, M. J. (1992). Implications of outcome research for psychotherapy integration. In J. C. Norcross & M. R. Goldfried (Eds.), *Handbook of psychotherapy integration* (pp. 94-129). New York: Basic Books.

Lerner, M. J. (1980). *The belief in a just world: A fundamental delusion.* New York: Plenum Press.

Letterman, D. (Host). (2017). Barack Obama [Television series episode]. In D. Letterman (Host), *My Guest Needs No Introduction.* New York: Netflix. Retrieved from www.netflix.com

Limburg, J. (2006). *Encountering Ecclesiastes: A book for our time.* Grand Rapids: Eerdmans.

Lipka, M. (2015, May 13). A closer look at America's rapidly growing religious 'nones.' *Pew Research Center.* Retrieved from www.pewresearch.org/fact-tank/2015/05/13/a-closer-look-at-americas-rapidly-growing-religious-nones/

Lipka, M. (2016, August 24). Why America's 'nones' left religion behind. *Pew Research Center.* Retrieved on from www.pewresearch.org/fact-tank/2016/08/24/why-americas-nones-left-religion-behind/

Longman, T. (1998). *New International Commentary on the Old Testament: The book of Ecclesiastes.* Grand Rapids: Eerdmans.

Lum, W. (2002). The use of self of the therapist. *Contemporary Family Therapy, 24,* 181-97.

Maimela, S. S. (1986). The atonement in the context of liberation theology. *International Review of Mission, 75*(299), 261-69.

Marshall, I. H. (2000). Jesus in the drama of salvation: Toward a biblical doctrine of redemption (Review). *The Journal of Theological Studies, 51,* 589-93.

Maslach, C. (1982). *Burnout: The cost of caring.* Englewood Cliffs, NJ: Prentice-Hall.

May, R. (1983). *The discovery of being.* New York: Norton.

Mbiti, J. S. (1990). *African religions and philosophy* (2nd ed.). Portsmouth, NH: Heinemann.

McAdams, D. P. (1993). *The stories we live by: Personal myths and the making of the self.* New York: Guilford.

McInerney, M., Mellor, J. M., & Nicholas, J. H. (2013). Recession depression: Mental health effects of the 2008 stock market crash. *Journal of Health Economics, 32,* 1090-104.

McKee, Tim. (2015, October). The geography of sorrow: Francis Weller on navigating our losses. *The Sun Magazine.* Retrieved from www.thesunmagazine.org/issues/478/the-geography-of-sorrow

McMinn, M. R. (2008). *Sin and grace in Christian counseling: An integrative paradigm.* Downers Grove, IL: InterVarsity Press.

McMinn, M. R. (2011). *Psychology, theology, and spirituality in Christian counseling* (Rev. ed.). Wheaton, IL: Tyndale.

McMinn, M. R. (2017). *The science of virtue: Why positive psychology matters to the church.* Grand Rapids: Brazos Press.

Middleton, J. R. (2005). *The liberating image: The* imago Dei *in Genesis 1.* Grand Rapids: Brazos.

Miller, A. (2008). *The drama of the gifted child: The search for the true self* (Rev. ed.). New York: Basic Books.

Miller, D. (2003). *Blue like jazz: Nonreligious thoughts on Christian spirituality.* Nashville: Thomas Nelson.

Mitchell, K. R., & Anderson, H. E. (1983). *All our losses, all our griefs: Resources for pastoral care.* Louisville, KY: Westminster John Knox.

Moltmann, J. (1992). *The Spirit of life: A universal affirmation.* Minneapolis: Fortress Press.

Moriarty, G. L., & Hoffman, L. (Eds.). (2007). *God image handbook for spiritual counseling and psychotherapy: Research, theory, and practice.* Binghamton, NY: The Haworth Pastoral Press.

Nasimiyu-Wasike, A. J. (1991). Christology and an African woman's experience. In R. Schreiter (Ed.), *Faces of Jesus in Africa* (pp. 70-81). Maryknoll, NY: Orbis Books.

Network for Grateful Living, A., & Gnarly Bay (Producers). (2017). *A grateful day with Brother David Steindl-Rast* [Video]. Available from http://gratefulness.org/grateful-day/

Nieuwsma, J. A., Walser, R. D., & Hayes, S. C. (Eds.) (2016). *ACT for clergy and pastoral counselors: Using acceptance and commitment therapy to bridge psychological and spiritual care.* Oakland, CA: Context Press/New Harbinger Publications.

Niles, A. N., & O'Donovan, A. (2019). Comparing anxiety and depression to obesity and smoking as predictors of major medical illnesses and somatic symptoms. *Health Psychology, 38,* 172-81.

Noffke, J. L., & Hall, T. W. (2007). Chapter 4. Attachment Psychotherapy and God Image. *Journal of Spirituality in Mental Health, 9,* 57-78.

Nouwen, H. J. M. (1990). *Here and now: Living in the Spirit.* New York: Crossroad Publishing.

O'Connor, K. M. (2002). *Lamentations and the tears of the world.* Maryknoll, NY: Orbis Books.

Padilla, R. (1983). Christology and mission in the two thirds world. In V. Samuel & C. Sugden (Eds.), *Sharing Jesus in the Two Thirds World* (pp. 12-32). Grand Rapids: Eerdmans.

Panko, T. R., & George, B. P. (2012). Child sex tourism: Exploring the issues. *Criminal Justice Studies, 25,* 67-81.

Peck, M. S. (1978). *The road less traveled: A new psychology of love, traditional values, and spiritual growth.* New York: Simon and Schuster.

Peters, T. (2018). The *imago Dei* as the end of evolution. In S. P. Rosenberg, M. Burdett, M. Lloyd, & B. van den Toren (Eds.), *Finding ourselves after Darwin: Conversations on the image of God, original sin, and the problem of evil* (pp. 92-106). Grand Rapids: Baker Academic.

Peterson, L. (2019). Commemorative preface. In E. H. Peterson, *A long obedience in the same direction: Discipleship in an instant society.* Downers Grove, IL: InterVarsity Press.

Pew Research Center. (2011). Faith in Flux. Retrieved from www.pewforum.org/2009/04/27/faith-in-flux/

Pew Research Center (2014). *Political polarization.* Retrieved from: https://www.pewresearch.org/topics/political-polarization/

Plantinga, A. (1989). *God, freedom, and evil.* Grand Rapids: Eerdmans.

Post, S. G. (2005). Altruism, happiness, and health: It's good to be good. *International Journal of Behavioral Medicine, 12,* 66-77.

Rahner, K. (1970). *The Trinity.* Tunbridge Wells, Kent: Burns & Oates.

Reichenbach, B. R. (2006). Healing response. In J. Beilby & P. R. Eddy (Eds.), *The nature of the atonement: Four views* (pp. 196-201). Downers Grove, IL: InterVarsity Press.

Rennebohm, S., & Thoburn, J. (2017). Psychotherapy and the Spirit-in-process: An integration of process theology, pneumatology, and systems psychology. *Journal of Psychology & Christianity, 36,* 131-38.

Ripley, J. S. (2012). Integration of psychology and Christianity: 2022. *Journal of Psychology and Theology, 40*, 150-54.

Rogers, C. R. (1957). The necessary and sufficient conditions of therapeutic personality change. *Journal of Consulting Psychology, 21*, 95-103.

Rohr, R. (July 16, 2017). Faith and belief: A system of beliefs or a way of life? Retrieved on September 14, 2019 from https://cac.org/system-beliefs-way-life-2017-07-16/

Sacks, J. (2011). *The great partnership: Science, religion, and the search for meaning.* New York: Schocken Books.

Sandage, S. J., & Brown, J. K. (2018). *Relational integration of psychology and Christian theology: Theory, research, and practice.* New York: Routledge.

Sanders, J. (2007). *The God who risks: A theology of divine providence* (2nd ed.). Downers Grove, IL: InterVarsity Press.

Sanneh, L. (2004). *Translating the message: The missionary impact on culture.* Maryknoll, NY: Orbis Books.

Satir, V., Banmen, J., Gerber, J., & Gomori, M. (1991). *The Satir model: Family therapy and beyond.* Palo Alto, CA: Science and Behavior Books.

Schore, A. N. (2014). The right brain is dominant in psychotherapy. *Psychotherapy, 51*, 388.

Schreiner, T. (2006). Penal substitution view. In J. Beilby & P. Eddy (Eds.), *The nature of the atonement: Four views* (pp. 67-98). Downers Grove, IL: InterVarsity Press.

Schwager, R. (1999). *Jesus in the drama of salvation: Toward a biblical doctrine of redemption.* Chestnut Ridge, NY: Crossroad Publication.

Schwartz, C., Meisenhelder, J. B., Ma, Y., & Reed, G. (2003). Altruistic social interest behaviors are associated with better mental health. *Psychosomatic Medicine, 65*, 778-85.

Seow, C. (1997). *Ecclesiastes: A new translation with introduction and commentary.* New York: Doubleday.

Seow, C-L. (2001). Theology when everything is out of control. *Interpretation: A Journal of Bible and Theology, 55*, 237-49.

Sharp, C. J. (2010). *Wrestling the Word: The Hebrew Scriptures and the Christian believer.* Louisville, KY: Westminster John Knox.

Sharp, C. J. (2014, December 28). Commentary on Jeremiah 31:15-17 [web log post]. Retrieved from www.workingpreacher.org/preaching.aspx?commentary_id=2301

Shroyer, D. (2016). *Original blessing: Putting sin in its rightful place.* Minneapolis: Fortress Press.

Shults, F. L. (2003). *Reforming theological anthropology: After the philosophical turn to relationality.* Grand Rapids: Eerdmans.

Siegel, D. (2014, February). The self is not defined by the boundaries of our skin. *Psychology Today.* Retrieved from www.psychologytoday.com/us/blog/inspire-rewire/201402/the-self-is-not-defined-the-boundaries-our-skin

Siegel, D. J., & Bryson, T. P. (2012). *The whole-brain child: 12 revolutionary strategies to nurture your child's developing mind.* New York: Bantam.

Siegel, D. J., & Hartzell, M. (2014). *Parenting from the inside out.* New York: TarcherPerigee.

Simkins, R. A. (2014). The embodied world: Creation metaphors in the ancient Near East. *Biblical Theological Bulletin, 44*(1), 40-53.

Simpson, J., & Beckes, L. (2018). Attachment theory. In Britannica Online Academic Edition, Encyclopædia Britannica, Inc. Retrieved from: https://www.britannica.com /science/attachment-theory

Sisemore, T. A. (2014). Acceptance and commitment therapy: A Christian translation. *Christian Psychology: A Transdisciplinary Journal, 8,* 5-15.

Slattery, J. M., & Park, C. L. (2011). Meaning making and spiritually oriented interventions. In J. D. Aten, M. R. McMinn, & E. L. Worthington, Jr. (Eds.), *Spiritually oriented interventions for counseling and psychotherapy* (pp. 15-40). Washington, DC: American Psychological Association.

Smith, D. (1919). *The atonement in the light of history and the modern spirit.* New York: Hodder and Stoughton.

Snell, D. C. (Ed.). (2008). A companion to the ancient Near East. New York: John Wiley and Sons.

Snow, K. N., McMinn, M. R., Bufford, R. K., & Brendlinger, I. A. (2011). Resolving anger toward God: Lament as an avenue toward attachment. *Journal of Psychology and Theology, 39,* 130-42.

Sorenson, R. L. (1996). The tenth leper. *Journal of Psychology and Theology, 24,* 197-211.

Sorenson, R. L., Derflinger, K. R., Bufford, R. K., & McMinn, M. R. (2004). National collaborative research on how students learn integration: Final report. *Journal of Psychology and Christianity, 23,* 355-65.

Spivak, K. (Producer) (1960). Meet the Press [Television Broadcast]. Washington D.C: National Broadcasting Company. Transcription retrieved from: https://kinginstitute .stanford.edu/king-papers/documents/interview-meet-press

Stark, M. (2019, March). *The Transformative Power of Optimal Stress.* Post-conference workshop presented at the Christian Association of Psychological Studies annual conference, Dallas, TX.

Stoltzfus, K. (2012). Penal substitution, Christus Victor, and the implications of atonement theology for the integration of Christian faith and social work practice. *Social Work and Christianity, 39,* 310-26.

Strausberg, A. (2017, October 17). Where is God in the flood? *HuffPost.* Retrieved from www.huffpost.com/entry/where-is-god-in-the-flood_b_59e4aac6e4b09e31db975ac2

Strawn, B. D., Bland, E. D., & Flores, P. S. (2018). Learning clinical integration: A case study approach. *Journal of Psychology and Theology, 46,* 85-97.

Strelan, P., Acton, C., & Patrick, K. (2009). Disappointment with God and well-being: The mediating influence of relationship quality and dispositional forgiveness. *Counseling and Values, 53,* 202-13.

Sussman, M. B. (2007). *A curious calling: Unconscious motivations for practicing psychotherapy* (2nd ed.). Lanham, MD: Jason Aronson.

Tan, S-Y., & Gregg, D. H. (1997). *The disciplines of the Holy Spirit: How to connect to the Spirit's power and presence.* Grand Rapids: Zondervan.

Taylor, C. (2007). *A secular age.* Cambridge, MA: Harvard University Press.

Tedeschi, R. G., & Calhoun, L. G. (1995). *Trauma and transformation: Growing in the aftermath of suffering.* Thousand Oaks, CA: Sage.

Tedeschi, R. G., & Calhoun, L. G. (2004). Posttraumatic growth: Conceptual foundations and empirical evidence. *Psychological Inquiry, 15,* 1-18.

Tippett, K. (2016). *Becoming wise: An inquiry into the mystery and the art of living.* New York: Penguin Books.

Tippett, K. [kristatippett]. (2018a, September 28). Heartsick at the "right" & the "left." Politics has become the thinnest of veneers over human brokenness. The vast majority of us don't want to live this way. It is left to each of us, where we live, to start having the conversations we want to be hearing & grow this culture up [Tweet]. Retrieved from https://twitter.com/kristatippett/status/1045657173492191238

Tippett, K. (Host). (2018b, October 8). Can conversation make any difference in a time like this? [Audio podcast]. *On Being.* Retrieved from http://onbeing.org/programs /living-the-questions-5/

Tolbert, M. A. (2003). The gospel according to Mark. In W. J. Harrelson (Ed.)., *The new interpreter's study Bible: New Revised Standard Version with the Apocrypha* (pp. 1801-45). Nashville: Abingdon Press.

UNICEF. (2018). Malnutrition rates remain alarming: stunting is declining too slowly while wasting still impacts the lives of far too many young children. Retrieved from http://data.unicef.org/topic/nutrition/malnutrition/#

University of Massachusetts, Boston. [UMass Boston]. (2009, November 30). *Still face experiment: Dr. Edward Tronick* [Video file]. Retrieved from www.youtube.com/watch ?v=apzXGEbZht0

Van der Kolk, B. (2014). *The body keeps the score.* New York: Viking.

Vanhoozer, K. J., & Treier, D. J. (2015). *Theology and the mirror of Scripture: A mere evangelical account.* Downers Grove, IL: InterVarsity Press.

Vogel, M. J., McMinn, M. R., Peterson, M. A., & Gathercoal, K. A. (2013). Examining religion and spirituality as diversity training: A multidimensional study of doctoral training in the American Psychological Association. *Professional Psychology: Research and Practice, 44,* 158-67.

Vogel, M. J. & Mitchum, A. (2017, March). *Rethinking the self object: Holy Spirit, boundaries, and virtues.* Paper presented at Christian Association for Psychological Studies, Chicago, IL.

Waheed, N. (2013). *Salt.* Seattle, WA: CreateSpace Independent Publishing Platform.

Walls, A. F. (2002). *The cross-cultural process in Christian history: Studies in the transmission and appropriation of faith.* Maryknoll, NY: Orbis Books.

Weaver, J. D. (2001). *The nonviolent atonement.* Grand Rapids: Eerdmans.

White, G. B. (2015, June 12). Millennials in search of a different kind of career. *The Atlantic.* Retrieved from www.theatlantic.com/business/archive/2015/06/millennials-job-search -career-boomers/395663/

Whyte, D. (2015). *Consolations.* Langley, WA: Many Rivers Press.

Williams, D. S. (2013). *Sisters in the wilderness: The challenge of womanist God-talk.* Maryknoll, NY: Orbis Books.

Williams, J. G. (2007). *The Bible, violence, and the sacred: Liberation from the myth of sanctioned violence.* Eugene, OR: Wipf and Stock Publishers.

Wiman, C. (2010). Hive of nerves: To be alive spiritually is to feel the ultimate anxiety of existence within the trivial anxieties of everyday life. *The American Scholar, 79,* 62-71.

Wink, W. (1992). *Engaging the powers: Discernment and resistance in a world of domination.* Minneapolis: Fortress Press.

Wirzba, N. (2011). *Food and faith: A theology of eating.* New York: Cambridge University Press.

Wisdom 2.0. (2017). *A truly connected life: Dan Siegel, Wisdom 2.0 2017* [Video file]. Retrieved from www.youtube.com/watch?v=zF8nBDKxAQI

Wolterstorff, N. (1987). *Lament for a son.* Grand Rapids: Eerdmans.

Wood, B. T., Worthington, E. L., Jr., Exline, J. J., Yali, A. M., Aten, J. D., & McMinn, M. R. (2010). Development, refinement, and psychometric properties of the Attitudes toward God Scale (ATGS-9). *Psychology of Religion and Spirituality, 2,* 148-67.

Worden, J. W. (2009). *Grief counseling and grief therapy: A handbook for the mental health practitioner.* New York: Springer.

Wright, N. T. (2018, November 27). Qs on sacrifice, crucifixion and atonement [Audio podcast]. *Ask NT Wright Anything.* Retrieved from www.premierchristianradio.com /Shows/Weekday/Ask-NT-Wright-Anything/Podcast/2-Qs-on-sacrifice-crucifixion -and-atonement

Index